Guiding Young Children's Behavior:

Helpful Ideas for Parents & Teachers from 28 Early Childhood Experts

edited by
Betty Farber, M.Ed.

Preschool Publications, Inc.
Cutchogue, New York, U.S.A.

Guiding Young Children's Behavior:
Helpful Ideas for Parents & Teachers
from 28 Early Childhood Experts
Edited by: Betty Farber, M.Ed.
(Material adapted from articles that appeared in
Parent and preschooler Newsletter issues prior to 1997.)

Cover Design: Lester Feldman
Book Illustrations: Susan Eaddy
Book Design: Arthur Farber

© 1999 Betty Farber   Second printing May 2000.
printed in the United States of America   ISBN 1-881425-06-1

For information about quantity purchases contact: Betty Farber, President, Preschool Publications, Inc. P.O. Box 1167, Cutchogue, NY 11935-0888, U.S.A. Voice: (U.S.A.) 1.800.726.1708 • International 631.765.5450 • Fax: 631.765.4927 E-mail: preschoolpub@hamptons.com • www.preschoolpublications.com

Library of Congress Cataloging-in-Publication Data
Guiding young children's behavior : helpful ideas for parents &
    teachers from 28 early childhood experts / edited by Betty Farber.
        p.   cm.
    Includes bibliographical references.
    ISBN 1-881425-06-1
        1. Child rearing. 2. Parenting. 3. Preschool children—Conduct
of life. 4. Life skills—Study and teaching (Preschool)
5. Preschool children—Health and hygiene. 6. Moral education
(Preschool)   I. Farber, Betty.
HQ774.5.G85   1998
649' . 1—dc21   98-38173
                                                 CIP

Other Books about Young Children Published by Preschool Publications, Inc.:
The Parents' & Teachers' Guide to Helping Young Children Learn
Creative Ideas from 35 Experts

My Self My Family My Friends
26 Experts Explore Young Children's Self-esteem

CONTENTS

SECTION FOUR
COPING WITH STRESS IN SPECIAL SITUATIONS

SECTION FIVE
COPING WITH STRESS IN EVERYDAY SITUATIONS

SECTION SIX
KEEPING YOUR CHILD HEALTHY

SECTION SEVEN
EXERCISE AND FITNESS FOR YOUNG CHILDREN

SECTION EIGHT
YOUNG CHILDREN'S SAFETY

SECTION NINE
FINDING THE POSITIVES

Foreword

Guiding a child's behavior, as I found when my first born became a toddler, is no easy feat. It takes the skill of a scientist, the artistry of a painter, and the patience — well certainly more than I seem to have.

I have met thousands of parents through my workshops and have found that most parents blame themselves when their children misbehave. When it comes to having solutions for difficult and embarrassing behavior we sometimes feel as out of control as our children. I know that what I wanted was a guidebook that I could thumb through and get the right answers fast. *This is the book I would have liked to have.*

This collection of articles from the successful *Parent and preschooler Newsletter*, is designed to offer parents and teachers some guidelines, or rules of thumb, to help navigate the tricky waters between a child's intent and his behavior.

The well-identified sections cover the basic how-tos for managing and understanding children's behavior, as well as the difficult situations we face together. For example, in Neala Schwartzberg's chapter we confront the forgetfulness of children — while Paulette Bochnig Sharkey is helpful to children who have to say good-bye to friends when they move away.

This book reflects the best information in the field of child development and its chapters clearly state the basic dos and don'ts of parenting. The material is easy to follow and will help parents and teachers feel less confused and overwhelmed by children's behavior. But, what is most evident in the book's word, structure, and illustrations, is the wisdom and generosity the editor feels as she shares this information with the reader.

This is the second volume dealing with early childhood development that Betty Farber has edited. Once again she has provided the reader with smart and sensible tips and ideas. This book, like a favorite cookbook, should be close at hand at all times. Use it frequently for it, too, has some failproof recipes for you.

Sandra R. Wolkoff, CSW
Director, Training & Consultation,
North Shore Child & Family Guidance Center,
Roslyn Heights, New York

Section One
Guiding Young Children's Behavior

Section One
Guiding Young
Children's Behavior

Introduction

This conversation was overheard between a mother and her four-year-old child:
"Johnny, you *must* come here at once."
"Mommy, when you say *must*, I feel *won't* all over."

How do you set limits, teach self-control, and provide effective rules for young children while encouraging their independence and self-esteem? The authors of the chapters in this section offer practical ideas and specific strategies.

Although there are ways to discipline youngsters that are *never* acceptable (such as punishments that harm children physically or emotionally) there are methods of guiding behavior that *work*, and that are appropriate to use with young children.

While adults cannot be there to guide each child every minute, preschoolers can learn to cooperate, to problem solve, and to express anger without hurting others.

As one author states, "It is the task of parents and teachers to guide the young child to want to use acceptable behaviors." The eventual goal is to have children develop their own, inner self-control.

SECTION ONE
GUIDING YOUNG CHILDREN'S BEHAVIOR

Chapter 1
Dealing
with
Discipline

Betty Farber

*"There were Two little Bears
who lived in a Wood,
And one of them was Bad and the
other was Good."*

"There were Two little Bears who lived in a Wood,
And one of them was Bad and the other was Good.
Good Bear learnt his Twice Times One—
But Bad Bear left all his buttons undone."
(from "Twice Times" by A.A. Milne, <u>Now We Are Six.</u> E.P. Dutton, 1927)

Individual differences
Unlike the little bears in the poem, children should not be labeled as "Bad" or "Good." Instead, they are individuals who grow at different rates, and have different interests, strengths, and weaknesses.

As individuals, children also vary in their responses to discipline: Tommy's lower lip starts to quiver when Daddy raises his voice, while Jacob simply ignores a loud scolding. Katy has to be told, "No!" only once, while Mary needs more reminders. Since children are individuals, there is no "recipe" for setting limits. You need to find the strategies that work with *each* child.

Discipline that leads to self-control
The words *discipline* and *punishment* have been used interchangeably but *discipline* can have a more positive meaning. The first definition of *discipline* in Webster's dictionary is, "Training that develops self-control..." Discipline then, is *training*, — teaching your preschooler how you want him to behave — teaching your child what is *not* acceptable and directing him toward what *is* acceptable. Children may not know what the limits are or may want to test the boundaries. Parents are there to guide and direct their behavior.

Guidance can take the form of setting realistic expectations for your youngster, talking with him about problems that occur, and placing limits on his behavior when necessary. This kind of guidance is essential not only to help your child to grow to be a self-disciplined person, but also to help him feel safe and cared for. It sends the message to your youngster that you won't let him do what is unsafe or inappropriate. It is the message: "I'm going to take care of you." This message gives young children a sense of security.

As you guide your child, you want her to behave in ways that allow her to be safe and to get along with others. And your ultimate goal is to help her become self-disciplined. You want her to learn to behave as well when you are not there as when you are right beside her. This goal will take many years to realize. One way you can start moving your child toward self-discipline is to offer her the opportunity to make simple choices that affect her needs: what kind of juice she wants — or which story she wants you to read. This helps her to have confidence in her abilities and gives her a feeling of independence. This kind of guidance is a positive method of dealing with discipline. The goals of this kind of discipline are to help children feel secure, gain a feeling of self-esteem, and grow toward self-control.

Chapter 2
Guiding Young Children's Behavior: Techniques that Work

James Windell

*When Michelle's mother and father
realized that she did not
adapt easily to transitions,
they began to try to find techniques
that eased changes in her life.*

For Michelle, age four, change was a problem. Once established in any routine, whether it was reading, taking a bath, watching her favorite video, or settling in with a new baby-sitter, she clearly didn't like to be disturbed by a change in direction. When her mother and father realized that she did not adapt easily to transitions, they began to try to find techniques that eased changes in her life.

Before bedtime, her mother would announce: "In fifteen minutes all the sleepy children will be putting on their pajamas for bed." Thereafter, there would be regular announcements: "The children are getting so tired that they will be happy to put their pajamas on soon." And finally: "It's almost time for that big moment when the TV is turned off and sleepy children go to put on their nice, warm PJs." While Michelle would wrinkle up her nose at these messages or pretend she didn't hear them, they served to alert her to a change in routine. By the time zero hour had arrived, Michelle usually went to her room with a minimum of fuss.

Many situations with preschool children can he handled in simple and effective fashion by using the techniques described in this chapter. Little problems and challenges can be headed off so that they do not develop into bigger difficulties that are out of proportion to the actual event. Strategies that result in preventing temper outbursts, avoiding arguments fueled by fatigue, or eliminating power struggles with toddlers, are more effective than punishment and scolding.

They are helpful for the child and the parent. The child is spared some of the irritating and frustrating scoldings that are so much a part of the preschooler's life, such as: "No," "Stop touching that," and "Don't hit." And parents who use these techniques find alternative ways to manage children, bring about compliance, achieve an end, or short-circuit a struggle.

The Family Environment
Children thrive in family environments which are characterized by love, warmth, and affection. In order to create such an environment, parents need to provide generous amounts of praise, attention, and encouragement. It is best to avoid a punitive and critical atmosphere in which the child is often on the receiving end of scoldings, criticism, and punishment.

The use of the techniques in this chapter go well beyond creating a loving and warm atmosphere. It also lets children know you are willing and able to protect them from injury and harm, and that the house is truly a comfortable one for them — rather than one that contains numerous pitfalls and ways for children to get into trouble. Children can sense when the environment is one in which they can have fun and, at the same time, are protected.

Parents who use these techniques show that they have a good under-standing of early childhood development. They understand that children are beginners in life who are trying to master their own impulses, and learn the many new rules to which they are exposed. They realize that children are frequently going to forget rules, be overwhelmed by their impulses, and suffer setbacks. They understand that children must overcome the conflict between becoming independent and trying to please their parents. Parents who can be tolerant, understanding, and patient will find that many of these techniques are useful for guiding behavior with love and affection.

Parents need to have realistic expectations
Expect children to make mistakes, to forget rules, to test limits, and to need protection from themselves as well as the world around them. You can expect that children will fall down, disobey, and test your patience. As learners in life, children need the help and support of truly caring and loving parents who go out of their way to make the world a safe place in which to operate.

Some of the techniques for guiding behavior, described on pages 9-11, can change a *No* environment to one that is positive, calm, and, hopefully, more fun.

Specific Strategies to Use with Young Children

One snowy January day, twenty-two-month-old Brock was brought into the house by his mother, Mary. Brock had been having a good time playing outside in the snow for the first time in his young life. He, of course, had no concern about the frigid temperature or the length of time he had already frolicked in the snow. His mother did, though, and knew it was time to come inside. Brock responded by standing in the hall screaming and refusing to allow his mother to touch him or remove his coat, boots, or leggings. Mary sized up the situation quickly and walked over to the living room window and just looked outside while she waited for his temper outburst to subside.

After a couple of minutes, she began to comment about the squirrels who seemed to be playing tag with each other — darting back and forth over the snow and between two trees. "You want to look at the funny squirrels, Brock?" she asked quietly but with animation in her voice. Brock couldn't resist something so obviously interesting. As Mary described the action of the squirrels, she gently removed his winter apparel. Brock didn't seem to notice.

Technique #1: Distraction

What Mary did was very simple. She used *distraction* as a way to deal with a child who was throwing a temper tantrum. To try to stop the tantrum, she could have issued a warning or resorted to a threat. The use of *distraction*, however, avoided a battle of the wills with the risk of prolonging the tantrum and causing more unnecessary tears for Brock and guilt for Mary.

Technique #2: Offering substitutes

Besides *distraction,* parents can use the technique of *offering substitutes.* This is a technique that works very well with young children and allows mothers and fathers a chance to do something other than say, "No," or "Don't."

When Mandy is playing with the knobs on the TV which have fascinated her today, her father can say, "I'm going to read a story to some lucky girl in this room. Does Mandy know who that girl might be?" This gives Mandy an alternative that is attractive while also engaging in an activity (reading) that is approved and desired by the family.

Technique #3: Making a game of discipline

Making a game of discipline is another strategy that attempts to enlist the cooperation and participation of children. It's usually valuable when a task or challenge is not very appealing to children.

When children have to put toys away, eat an icky-tasting food, prepare for bedtime, or end a fun time in the bathtub, it is time to *make a game of discipline.*
• Make it a contest: "Let's see who can be first in getting ready for bed. Get on your mark, get set — go!"
• Set up a competition: "I think I can pick up more toys than you can!"
• Engage in fantasy play: "Let's pretend that there is this giant alligator that nibbles on children's toes. Children who put their socks and shoes on very quickly can save their toes."
These games can be fun ways for children to end up doing what they are supposed to without parental exasperation.

Technique #4: *Limiting access to objects or activities.*

With this approach, the parent removes toys or games that may cause frustration because they are too advanced for a youngster to handle — *before the child starts to play with them.* They can then be reintroduced later when they are suitable for the child's level of development.

A related technique is *childproofing your home* by removing seductive objects or temptations. By rearranging or storing away items that can be broken, the house or play area is made safe for children. This is a wise strategy as the alternative may result in too many "NOs," or be dangerous to children.

Technique #5: *Creatively using rhyming rules*
Children in the preschool years may have difficulty remembering some of your rules for behavior. To assist their memory, come up with rules that have a catchy rhyme. For instance: *A fight's not right,* or *End of the day, time to put your toys away,* or *Time for bed, to rest your head.* Children often remember rhyming rules for years.

Technique #6: *Giving leeway to make mistakes*
This technique is an important one because it reminds parents to maintain realistic expectations for children. By giving children the leeway to make mistakes, you allow them to try new behaviors knowing full well their efforts will be imperfect. By giving children this extra margin for error, you exempt them from punishment, scolding, or criticism. Children feel more secure when parents understand and accept their sometimes clumsy efforts. When you give leeway, you are encouraging healthy growth and development.

These techniques for guiding behavior make you, in the long run, a more effective parent.

Chapter 3
Problem-solving
Approaches
to Discipline

Judy David and Ellen Galinsky

*It is helpful to know
that the young child's
struggle for autonomy
is a normal aspect
of development.*

You've just folded the clean clothes, put them in the laundry basket and taken them upstairs As you start to put things away in the bureau, your three-year-old begins to toss the clothes out of the basket onto the floor. You say, "No," and that's his cue to throw them out even faster.

Struggle for Autonomy

During the preschool years, children are learning to become independent and establish a sense of control over their bodies and their lives. As many parents wistfully note, gone are the days of infancy when feeding, soothing, and playing were the primary tasks. Now parents are faced with a young child who wants to be independent and strong, who often declares his or her autonomy in no uncertain terms: "No." "It's mine." "You can't make me." Even when we do our best, our efforts may meet with resistance and rebellion from our child.

It is helpful to know that the young child's struggle for autonomy is a normal aspect of development. In fact, oppositional behavior is a positive milestone in development because it represents growth in mastery and a sense of independence. The preschooler's noncompliance is her way of saying, "I'm my own person," an important step toward feeling competent and good about oneself.

"Authority Stage" for Parents

Yet, just as children are passing through a stage in development, so are their parents. The issue for the parents of a preschooler parallels that of their child — establishing control and figuring out whether to say "Yes," or "No." For parents, this is the "Authority Stage" because the major task is determining the kind of authority you want to be. Related to this is figuring out what discipline strategies will work to get your child to do or not to do something in the short term, and to teach your child values in the long term.

Effective Discipline

The kind of discipline used by parents makes a difference. In one study, parents who used a reasoning approach (the "do it because there is a good reason approach") had children who were more self-reliant, self-controlled, explorative, and content than the children of parents who used the authoritarian ("do it because I'm the parent") or permissive ("do whatever you want") techniques. Tactics, such as hitting, criticizing, threatening ("I'm bigger than you are") tend to accomplish the opposite of what parents want.

Helping children understand the effect of their behavior on another person has been found to promote consideration. With this technique, you point out the direct consequences of the behavior for someone else, ("When

you throw the clothes on the floor, I have to pick them up and refold them")
or explaining another's feelings ("I'm so busy today, it makes me very
upset when I have to fold the laundry all over again").

Parents who control their children's impulses in a respectful way will
eventually engender cooperation as well as teach their child what to do.

Making Your Child a Partner

The cause of many conflicts between parent and child is the child's
demand for greater independence. When we teach our children
problem-solving skills, we are addressing the cause and giving them a
chance to exercise their independence. Even offering choices does not
enable the child to avoid or resolve problems in the future, because you
are presenting the choices and doing the thinking for the child. With the
problem-solving approach, the parent sets the limits but helps the child
think of ways to comply or use other approaches to getting what he needs
or wants.

Here is how one of us, Ellen Galinsky, used this approach with her
four-year-old son: *I explained that there were times I needed him to cooperate
quickly but the things I was saying were not working very well. I asked, "What
ideas do you have? What words could I say that would work better?" I was not
giving him control over limits — he had to stop when I said stop — but I was
giving him the opportunity to tell me how to do it more effectively. He said I
should say the word, "Warning." So I tried it. If he refused to come inside for
dinner, I would say, "This is a warning," and that would stop him. The next step
was to encourage him to think about what he wanted and how to get it another
way: "What else could you do to tell me you want to play longer?" He replied, "I
could say, 'I need 5 more minutes.' "*

As busy parents, we are often tempted to be efficient and solve our
children's problems for them. But when we teach them how to solve
their own problems, we are supporting their drive for autonomy. We are
building their confidence and coping skills. We are helping them learn to
take responsibility for themselves — a valuable lesson for preschoolers.

Generating Ideas to Solve Problems

There are many everyday situations where problem solving can be used. Children and adults grow and change by confronting and dealing with difficulties rather than avoiding them. The most important aspect to problem solving is being able to generate new ideas and try them out.

Problem: My children fight and argue with each other. I usually end up separating them. What other discipline techniques work with siblings?

A parent of a three-year-old daughter and a seven-year-old son found that problem-solving techniques worked to stop her children from fighting in the car. Pulling over to the side of the road didn't help much (and sometimes was not possible), lecturing didn't help, and getting upset didn't help. Before they were to get into the car, the mother would announce the rule, "No fighting in the car. It's too dangerous when I'm driving." Then she would give them a chance to problem solve: "Do you have any thoughts about how you could stop fighting?" Her son suggested a car "kit" so he would not be bored. Her daughter agreed this was a good plan, and they each collected toys in small shopping bags to take when they rode in the car.

It would be reassuring to think that once the children have come up with an idea then the problem has been taken care of once and for all. But problem solving is a process. One solution might work for a while and then we have to begin the process again: "The car kits are not keeping you from fighting in the car anymore. There can be no fighting while I'm driving. Who has another idea?" The three-year-old suggested they put a pillow in between them and each have a tape recorder to listen to. This new suggestion was agreed upon and it worked for some time.

Problem: My son Is frightened of things that seem silly to me. What can I do to make him less fearful?

One of the hardest dilemmas for parents is knowing when to push children and when not to. Do you make them secure by taking care of them or do you make them strong by giving them a nudge? One way to deal with this is to involve children in helping to solve their problems.

When four-year-old Russell went to the beach, he was frightened of the sand crabs. He refused to set foot on the sand and wanted to be carried. His mother explained. "At first, I was furious with him. I had these wonderful fantasies of him playing in the water and digging in the sand." His behavior didn't live up to her expectations, and that led to her fury.

"Then," she continued, "I decided to see his fear as a challenge. I didn't pick him up but realized that I could help him figure out how to deal with something that was hard for him. I asked him what he could do to help himself. He suggested a path of towels to step on. So I put one towel in front of another and, like a little king, he marched across the beach to where we were sitting. He didn't stay on his towel for long—in a few minutes he was fingering the sand and soon he was chasing the waves."

Children's fears, as irrational as they may seem to us, are real to them. Young children live in a magical world where distinctions between reality and fantasy are easily blurred. Their fears need to be treated with concern and respect. Russell's mother helped him take an appropriate developmental step in facing his problem and resolving it. Here are some solutions that other children have devised to ease their fears:

• a fish tank with a light in the bedroom for a child afraid of the dark
• a sword made of cardboard and aluminum foil in case a dragon comes
• an empty spray can of "monster" spray to get rid of monsters
• a happy face taped to the toilet

The fact of doing something in the face of fear builds children's self-confidence and coping abilities.

Problem: Sometimes there are issues that involve the whole family. How can we discuss them and deal with them?

The setting for teaching problem-solving skills can vary—the parent and child alone or a family meeting. The child must not be so upset or angry that she cannot listen. If there is an important family matter to resolve, children do not have a choice about participating.

In family meetings it is best to have routines that are understood and agreed upon. Here is one family's approach:

1. The adult states the problem to be addressed: "Dinner time is too hectic and there is too much fighting going on."

2. The adult asks for others' feelings about the subject. No accusations are allowed. Each person says what "I" feel and no one may interrupt. Some families use an egg timer to designate three minutes each.

3. A range of solutions is generated without criticism or comment. Young children like to see their ideas written down, even if they cannot read. This also reinforces the message that the problem was not "his fault" but existed apart from personalities.

4. The pros and cons of each solution are discussed and written down.

5. A solution is mutually agreed upon.

6. Generally, a trial period of a few days is determined and plans are made to talk at a future date about how the solution is working and to revise it, if necessary.

Discussions like this foster understanding and empathy. Children become less egocentric as they examine different points of view. They learn that people can cooperate to solve problems together. When we teach our children how to problem solve, we are helping them learn lifelong skills.

Discipline: Dos and Don'ts

Betty Farber

Dos

With your toddlers (1 to 2 years old):

Do say "No" only when necessary. Use, "No" for dangerous or hurtful things.

Do use distraction to keep your toddler from misbehaving. ("Here. You can hold your teddy bear while I put on your hat.")

Do childproof your home. Put breakables out of reach. Cover electric outlets.

Do emphasize the *positive* instead of the *negative*. Say, "Talk softly," instead of "Don't yell," and, "Please walk, " instead of, "Don't run."

Do set aside some special things to do for those particularly difficult times of the day. Provide items that are soothing and totally absorbing like a shoe box half full of salt or sand, with containers to pour the sand back and forth; or a basin with water and empty plastic squeeze bottles.

With your preschoolers (3 to 6):

Do let your child help you with simple chores, such as folding the wash or setting the table with safe, nonbreakable objects.

Do include your preschooler in planning family celebrations, such as birthdays and holiday festivities.

Do give your child choices whenever possible. This gives her a feeling of independence and self-esteem. A child who feels good about herself is more likely to behave well.

Do define clearly what you want your youngster to do, so that there is no misunderstanding. (For example: "You may ride your bicycle to the end of this block, and then you must turn around and come back.")

Do praise your child's efforts in trying to dress himself or in putting his toys away. Praise can be verbal ("Your room looks so neat!") or nonverbal (a smile of approval, a loving hug).

Do give your child attention when she behaves well rather than just when she misbehaves**.**

Do encourage children to use words when they're angry, rather than to use physical actions. (Example: "Don't take my toy. That makes me mad!")

Do talk to your preschooler seriously and reasonably if a rule is broken, explaining why the rule was set up. If the rule continues to be broken, use discipline that relates to the misbehavior. (Example: "You may not ride your bicycle any more today, because you forgot the rule about riding only to the end of the block.")

Do be consistent and follow through on your promises.

Do take time to listen to what your preschooler has to say. Children, like adults, are more likely to share their feelings when they believe someone is listening.

Don'ts

Don't use physical force on your baby. Hitting small children can be mentally as well as physically damaging.

Don't tell your preschooler to hit another child in reprisal. This stirs up feelings of fear and insecurity. Your child might become fearful of what she might do to others and afraid also for her own safety.

Don't threaten your child with abandonment or withdrawal of your love.

Don't scare him with threats that a policeman will lock him up.

Don't take lightly her threat that she will run away. (Tell her that you love her and would miss her.)

Don't use language you do not mean. (Such as, "I'll break your neck.") Your child may take it literally.

Don't treat one child preferentially over another one.

Don't use shame or sarcasm as a punishment. These may damage your child's sense of self-esteem.

Don't ignore behavior like hitting or biting. Your child may think, "Mom didn't say, 'No' so it's all right."

Don't be wishy-washy in telling your youngster about your expectations. A firm, loving approach works best.

A Common Problem — and Suggested Solutions

Betty Farber

The Problem

A mother and her son go to the park every day from ten to noon. He becomes very involved in playing with the other children. When it is time to leave, Larry invariably puts up a fuss, running away from her or crying. She doesn't want to make him miserable, but she has many tasks to do at home. She has to set a limit on her preschooler's time at the playground, or *she* would be miserable because *her* needs wouldn't be met. What can she do to improve the situation?

Children who are deeply involved in play experiences have difficulty in shifting gears and going on to another activity. This may cause conflicts when you, as a parent, must keep to a schedule. But parents have needs and rights too. Once this mother decided that two hours was the extent of the time her son could spend at the playground, she had to look at ways to set limits with her preschooler.

Some Suggested Solutions
Here are some different strategies for Larry's mother to try:
1. Prepare your child in advance for the time limitation. Discuss the situation with your son before you leave the house. Tell him that it is upsetting to have him run away and that you expect him to accompany you home without fuss. Show him your watch and tell him that when the hands are both on the twelve it will be time to leave. Give him a signal in the park five minutes before you are ready to leave, to prepare him for going.

2. **Accept your son's feelings about having to leave.** You could say, "I know you're disappointed because you'd like to stay and play, but (firmly) it's time to go home now."

3. **Distract him with something pleasant to look forward to at home.** Think of something to tempt him away. "We have a surprise for lunch. The frozen juice bars are ready for dessert!"

4. **Stand firm and self assured.** "I won't run after you. I'll wait here for you to come with me." If all of these strategies don't work at first, stand firmly in the face of tears, and be confident of your own judgment. Know that you are the kind of parent who says, "Yes" whenever you can, but that sometimes you have to say, "No."

Chapter 4
Setting
Limits

Nancy Samalin

*Try making the message positive
by saying, "As soon as
you've finished with your bath,
we can read a story."*

It's tough to be a parent!
No matter how much we want our children to be happy and cooperative, the need to set limits is a constant source of friction. Why? Because, instead of thanking us when we try to teach children <u>what is</u> and <u>what is not</u> acceptable, they are unhappy.

Children Don't <u>Like</u> Limits
I have never met a child who, when told she can't have what she wants, smiles sweetly and says, "Thanks, Mommy, for helping me to learn inner discipline." The children I know either sulk, whine, and cry, or become angry, resentful, and argumentative. They say things like: "You're mean!" "You're not my friend!" "Why can't I? Granny lets me." Or even — "I hate you!"

Parents Need to Set Limits
It's impossible to be a parent without having to be a "party-pooper." That's the least fun part of the job, albeit a necessary part. Remember, we are the ones who have to censor TV, make them go to bed when they want to stay up and play, refuse to buy them the toys or candies they insist they need, urge them to brush their teeth, make them put away their toys, and remove them from a friend's house just when they're having the most fun. The list is endless. What's a parent to do?

Suggestions to Help with Limit-setting
Here are some ways to decrease the number of power struggles, be firm and loving at the same time, and set limits without putting children down in the process.

1. Accept the fact that, as a parent, it is essential that you set limits.

2. Distinguish between what a child <u>wants</u> and what he <u>needs</u>. Children's <u>wants</u> are a bottomless pit: every toy advertised on TV, never having to clean up, brush their teeth, get dressed for preschool, etc. Their <u>needs</u> are very few: love and appreciation, food, shelter, structure, and the comfort of a familiar routine.

3. Accept the fact that when you do set limits, your children won't like it — and it's OK and normal for them not to. However, don't let that interfere with your doing it if you believe the limit is fair.

4. Choose your priorities (or — pick your battles). Save your big guns for the nonnegotiable issues. Try to say, "Yes" unless it is necessary to say, "No" — then stick to it.

5. Limit your use of the words, "No" and "Don't". If a young child hears what she **cannot** do all day long, she's sure to tune you out. (That is known as becoming "parent-deaf"!) Some toddlers only seem to hear the words that follow "Don't," as in "Don't run," "Don't touch that," "Don't hit." Tell them instead what they **can** do. They <u>can</u> pat the baby gently. They <u>can</u> run *outdoors*.

6. Don't expect youngsters to comply the instant you give an order. Allow a few seconds to process your words.

7. To avoid power struggles and engage a young child's cooperation, turn a command into a game or fantasy rather than barking orders. For example, instead of, "Pick up these toys this instant," say, "I'll bet you can't pick up those blocks before I count to ten."

8. Avoid threats. Many children see them as challenges to be tested. Others may get defiant or more resistant. Threats often begin with the word "If." Instead of saying, "If you don't take a bath now, you'll be punished," try making the message positive by saying, "As soon as you're finished with your bath, we can read a story."

9. Reinforce cooperative behavior. Whenever your child complies with your limit or cooperates, even if reluctantly, let him know you're pleased with him. Be sure to acknowledge his efforts. Children want our approval and need to know when we are pleased. Such statements as, "Thank you, Joey. I liked the way you played with the baby," or, "I noticed how quickly you cleaned up the puzzle pieces. I appreciate it," will go a long way towards encouraging cooperation.

10. Give children choices where appropriate. Distinguish between setting appropriate limits and trying to control areas of kids' lives where they need to have a say or where their autonomy is at stake, such as eating, toileting, clothing preferences, etc. (See the examples on the following pages.)

11. Give yourself a break. Remember that, being human, you can't always be consistent. There will be days and moments when nothing seems to work, especially when you're tired or under stress. Hang in there. Remember, a toddler's first declaration of independence is his use of the word "No."

Some Typical Dialogs Related to Limit Setting

One way to set limits and diminish power struggles is to decide what is really worth making an issue over, and to discriminate between what is and isn't negotiable. If we take a firm stand in areas on which clear limits need to be set, we can be flexible and give children choices in areas that are less important. This will enable them to feel they have some control over their lives.

1) Let's take eating. Here's a typical dialog I hear repeated almost daily in my workshops with parents:

Mom: Janie, eat your string beans.
Janie: I'm not hungry.
Mom: Come on Janie, let's not start. Just have a few bites.
Janie: I hate string beans. Why do I have to eat them?
Mom: They're good for you. Just have a few bites.
Janie: (Using her fork to spread the beans all over the plate) I'm full.
Mom: Young lady, I'm sick of these scenes. No wonder you're so skinny. You are going to sit here 'til you eat at least some of it — or no dessert.
Janie sulks. Mom gets furious, frustrated by this endless scenario.

Is this battle necessary?
Is something terrible going to happen if Janie doesn't eat her string beans? Trying to get Janie to finish her food by telling her she's skinny is bound to backfire — and it's an assault on her self-esteem. Telling her that beans are

good for her will certainly not make her more eager to eat something she obviously doesn't want. And do we really want children to use food to please us or get us angry? I doubt it. Nor does it make sense to reward children with dessert for eating something they didn't want. It's not as though they did something virtuous that deserved special merit. When parents allow children choices and take their eating preferences seriously, they are treating their youngsters with respect.

What could Mom say instead?

Perhaps Mom could respond to Janie's statement: "I'm not hungry," by saying, "Janie, only YOU know how your stomach feels. You can decide when you've had enough." One less daily battle... pleasant meal times... more autonomy for Janie!

2) One of the most difficult situations is when you are in a hurry (usually in the morning) and your child doesn't respond to your time schedule. If you want to make sure to get your youngsters to dawdle, just try to rush them. A strategy that usually works is to encourage their cooperation, rather than to nag them until they blow up!

Mom: Please get your clothes out and get dressed. It's nearly time for nursery school.
Lisa: (Whining) I don't know howww.
Mom: You are already four years old. You could do it when you were three.
Lisa: (No response.)
Mom: (Getting frustrated, changes her attitude, trying to encourage Lisa instead of making her more defiant.) Lisa, the carpool will be here any minute. I have to finish preparing your lunch. I'll never make it without your help.
Lisa walks into her room and reappears soon after, dressed and grinning.
Mom: What a help you were. Now we'll both be on time. Thank you honey.

3) Jay is going to a fancy birthday party and is wearing sweatpants and old sneakers.

Mom: Jay, why don't you put on your good pants for Rob's party?
Jay: No, it's the weekend and I can wear whatever I want.
Mom: That's true, and it's okay with me. But you might be uncomfortable because everybody will be dressed up. But you decide.
Jay: Okay. Maybe I'll change.
When he gets home, Jay says: Mom, you were right. Everyone was dressed up. Even Ben had on his good shoes and not dirty sneakers!

All the above dialogs are based on true incidents.

Chapter 5
Effective Rules
for Young Children

Pegine Echevarria

*Rules are as necessary
to running a family
as the rules of the road
are to driving a car.*

Three-year-old Jason is hitting his eighteen-month-old brother. His mother says, "You shouldn't hit your brother — you're bigger than he is." As a punishment she gives Jason a swat and a ten minute time out. A little later on he does it all over again. His mother doesn't know what to do. *(Rule: Don't hit.)*

Two-year-old Nancy wants the free candy on the counter in the video store. Her mother tells her, "No! It's almost lunch time." But Nancy keeps reaching for it. Finally, she makes a wild grab for the candy and it goes flying across the counter. An embarrassed mother makes a hurried exit as the child begins to scream. *(Rule: No sweets before a meal.)*

Five-year-old Kevin goes to the mall with his father. The boy asks his father for a dollar to play video games. Dad gives him the dollar and says "This is all you get." After he spends the money Kevin asks for more. When his father says, "No." Kevin starts to kick the machine. *(Rule: When there's an agreement about limits, it should be accepted.)*

Parenting and rules
Experiences like these are shared by parents everywhere. To avoid such confrontations, parents should have consistent, reliable rules that every family member can live with.

Rules are as necessary to a family as the rules of the road are to driving a car. Driving rules help us remain safe and secure through all kinds of conditions: rain, sleet, snow, emergencies, etc. Just as everyone who drives is expected to follow the rules of the road, everyone in the family is expected to follow the rules of the family.

Effective rules have the following characteristics:
• They are considerate of your child's self-esteem
• They are consistent, repetitive, and follow a routine
• They take into account your child's age and development
• They can be explained and understood
• They are flexible according to the environment
• They can include input from children as well as parents
• They teach

Effective rules are considerate of your child's self-esteem
What your child thinks of himself is important to consider when you establish a rule. Ask yourself, "How will this rule affect my child's feeling of self worth?" For example, in the incident described above it is important to have a rule that says that Jason can't hurt his younger brother. But it is also important for Jason to feel that he is getting his fair share of his parent's attention.

Andrea is five years old and her brother Kenneth is seven. When Kenneth comes home from school he needs quiet so that he can do his homework. However, Andrea wants to talk and play. Because she would not be quiet and let her brother do his homework, her parents were getting frustrated and made the rule: *Andrea must keep quiet while Kenneth does his work.* However, the rule was hurting Andrea's self-esteem because she felt that her needs were not as important as Kenneth's. After thinking it over, the rule was changed to: *Andrea will read a book with Mommy and then play by herself until Kenneth finishes his homework.* This rule was effective because both Andrea and Kenneth had their needs met.

Effective rules are consistent and repetitive
Rules should be consistent for all. When Jason's mother hit him (see above) for hitting someone smaller than himself she was being inconsistent. If Jason is bigger than his brother — Jason's mother is bigger than Jason. The rule is *don't hit.*

Repetition and routines teach rules. If your child is required to make his bed, daily repetition of the act of making up the bed will reinforce the rule. After a time it becomes a norm (a rule that is accepted as part of life). When dinner is over, Judy, a working mother, doesn't want to be the only person left in the kitchen cleaning up. Taking Judy's needs into consideration, the rule is *Everyone helps to clear the table after dinner.* For Julie, 3 years old, and Allen, 5 years old, the rule has become a part of their daily routine.

Effective rules take into account your child's age and development
A two-year-old's needs and abilities are very different from those of a four-year-old. In addition, even children within the same age group differ from each other.

In the above example, two-year-old Nancy wanted the candy on the counter. Her mother said, "No, It's almost lunch time." The rule was *No sweets before a meal.* Nancy was developmentally not ready to understand the concept of time. She is in the process of developing her self-assertiveness, beginning to learn about limits and choices. Her mother's expectations for her, at that moment, were incompatible with the child's stage of development.

On the other hand, the rule for five-year-old Kevin was appropriate for his age. The rule is *When there's an agreement about limits, it should be accepted.* At his age he has experienced, learned, and incorporated the concept of choices and limits. Kevin's reaction to his father saying, "No" is an indication that he needs structure and consistent limits in order to continue to develop self-control.

Effective rules can be explained and understood

"Why do I have to?" "Because I said so," is the typical response but not the best choice. Going back to the comparison with driving a car — understanding why we have to stop at a red light makes it much easier to accept the rule. If you don't stop you can cause an accident.

Explaining rules can be a frustrating experience for many parents, especially if the child continually asks, "Why???" However, if the rules can be explained with valid reasons for their use, it is easier to follow them. For instance, our next door neighbor is a 2 1/2-year-old girl named Alex. She loves coming to our house to play with our cats. I carefully explained to her that Stimpy, the gold cat, loves to be held and petted, but Rebecca, the colorful cat, will scratch and hurt her if she is held. At our house we tell all the children "Don't pet Rebecca." Alex, who is always holding Stimpy, understands the rule very well and tells everyone, *"Stimpy, yes — Rebecca, NO!"*

Effective rules are flexible according to the environment

The behavior expected in a restaurant is different from what is tolerated in the playground. The environment plays a key role in rule development. Talitha takes her son, four-year-old Andrew, to a play group three times a week. During free play he promptly runs to the jump on the trampoline, which he loves. Immediately, upon returning home, Andrew runs into his mother's room, climbs on her bed and begins jumping. Talitha stops Andrew from jumping and explains the rule: *Jumping is allowed on the trampoline at play group, but we do not jump on beds.*

Effective rules can include input from children

Because the rule has to be important to the people who are going to abide by it, young children can help create workable rules. In our house, for example, the members of the family felt that they could enter our five-year-old daughter's room anytime they wished. She didn't like this and proposed the rule that anyone wanting to enter must knock on her door three times. It was important for her own sense of power and privacy that everyone follow her rule. It had meaning for her. In different situations, each child has helped develop other family rules.

Effective rules teach

Parents need to ask themselves the following questions regarding rules for their children: *What do I want them to learn? Why do I want them to learn this?* and *What is the best way to teach them?*

Rules teach children many things: how to care, share, negotiate, and be safe, to mention a few. For example, Amy and Fran, two three-year-old friends, are playing with dolls. Amy grabs the doll Fran is playing with and Fran bursts into tears. Amy's mother tells her daughter, "That made Fran sad. If you want the doll that Fran has, why don't you ask her if you could trade dolls for a while." Amy's mom is teaching her to care, share, and negotiate.

Rules are the guideposts that keep our children going in the right direction. They are there to protect, support and guide their way, much in the same way that the rules of the road guide our travels. Rules don't determine the destiny of the journey — they just help us get there in one piece. Rules are there to help our children both in the present and the future.

Chapter 6
What Does It Mean
to Say, "No"
to a Child?

Nancy Balaban

*What does saying, "No"
mean to a child,
and what does saying, "No"
mean to parents?*

Six-month-old Cicely was sitting on the floor, chewing on the corner of a gift bag that had just contained a cuddly new teddy bear from grandpa. Now cast aside, teddy was lying unattended behind Cicely. It was the shiny paper bag that engrossed her.

"NO! NO!" commanded her father, David, from across the room when he noticed her chewing the paper bag. Cicely looked up briefly and continued chewing. "Does she understand what you mean?" queried grandpa. "I guess not," said David. He walked over and handed Cicely the new teddy bear in exchange for the bag.

David's "No" wasn't mean or bossy—he was simply setting up a beginning rule-to-live-by between himself and David. It was his own father's question that caused David to reflect on Cicely's six-month-old developmental limits. **What does a parental "No" mean to a child and what does saying "No" mean to parents? These are two very different but related questions.**

What does saying "No" mean to a child?

First, let's look at the child. Even a very young baby like Cicely, who has little understanding about causes, feels the parental displeasure in a "No."

As children grow to **toddlerhood**, they struggle mightily to control their impulses for the sake of pleasing their parents. But the going is rough. If a toddler could talk, she might say, "I'd certainly like to stop pulling these books from the shelf because my mom is saying 'No' and I want her to love me—but I can't stop because it's so much fun." Noncompliance with the parent's "No" is evidence not only of a toddler's lack of inner control but also an assertion of the child's "self."

By the time children become **three** they have a better grip on themselves. It's not <u>as</u> hard to stop doing something pleasurable and it's not <u>as</u> crucial to declare their personhood through a thunderous "No!" as it was when they were two. But three-year-olds don't have perfect control either. So gentle parental reminders are often needed.

At **four**, the scene shifts, and although four-year-olds have increased self-control, they have a brand new agenda. It's called, "You're not the boss of me!" No wonder the age is named "the adolescence of early childhood"! Standoffs between a no-saying adult and a no-saying preschooler are to be expected.

It's clear that saying "No" produces a complex brew—the child's stage of development is mixed with the parents' beliefs about what is right and what is wrong. Since parents evolve these values based on their individual preferences, their family background, and their life experiences, it's no surprise that saying "No" has many meanings.

What does saying "No" mean to parents?

"No" conveys prohibition ("No climbing on the bookshelf"). It conveys assertion of adult authority ("I said no more cookies"), or protection ("NO! Come away from the street!"). Sometimes "No" is a rejection ("No, you can't sit on my lap right now"). The tone of voice used and the incidents provoking the "No" are highly individual. Leaving toys out can be a serious violation of one parent's rules and of no consequence whatever to another.

Saying "No" makes some parents feel like Simon Legree, so they might try to avoid saying it. Others find that saying "No" makes them feel in control and they use it freely. Many find a path somewhere between these two extremes, using an explanation along with the "No." ("No climbing on the bookshelf because it might fall and hurt you.")

The goal, notwithstanding, is *to help children begin to develop their own, inner "No" and eventually move away from their dependence on their parents' "No."* When a preschooler stops herself from crayoning on the living room wall or pulling the cat's tail, we rejoice in a job well done. We feel gratified that another parental "No" has been incorporated into the child's evolving moral self.

Guidelines for Saying, "No"

Children react to "No" differently depending on their stage of development. For example, the toddler who methodically removes all her clothes each time the parent prepares to take her for an outing may be testing adult tolerance. It is a challenge to handle such a situation so that it doesn't grow into a major, daily contest of wills. Since the toddler may be looking for a way to get a rise out of the parent, the secret here would be to take the wind out of her toddler sails by <u>not</u> reacting. Picking her up, redressing her calmly, even while she screams and lurches, gives her the message that going out dressed is <u>not</u> negotiable. With consistent adult non-reaction, over time, most toddlers would begin to give up the undressing.

Not unusual for older preschoolers, on the other hand, is their frequent intolerance and jealousy of the attention their parents give to telephone conversations. "Wait until I finish," does not always soothe the suddenly demanding child.

Here are some guidelines that may help you think about the how, when, and why of saying no.

• Tailor your expectations to the abilities of your child.
Preschoolers need to know the reasons for "Nos." Make sure the reasons are short and to the point. Long, complex explanations often end up with the child doing or having what he wanted in the first place. "I'm going to answer the phone and I want you to wait a few minutes. When I'm done I'll get you what you need." After the call, "You did a good job of waiting. Now let's get the juice you want."

Toddlers, on the other hand, cannot wait as easily as the three or four-year-old, so it's prudent to make phone calls short or return the call later.

• Decide what your priorities are and set rules accordingly.
It's important to know the sorts of things that bother you the most. If you have some breakable items that you cherish, it's easier to put them out of reach on a high shelf than repeatedly to say "No" to a toddler. If you are bothered by toys scattered hither and yon through the house, it is more effective to join your child in a "pick up" using a small basket, than issue commands about no toys lying about.

• Be firm; be kind.
Think about your tone of voice. Is it a tone that would impel you, if you were the child, to comply, or one that would impel you to rebel or cower? It's important to convey to your son or daughter that you mean what you say and that what you are requesting or denying makes sense—to you as well as to your child.

• Be consistent.
If you believe that the "No" you are saying is reasonable, stick to it; don't backtrack. On the other hand, if you realize that your "No" is unreasonable, say so. "I just realized that it's really okay for you to climb to the top of that jungle gym and I was mistaken to say 'No.' Go ahead and I'll be right here to help if you need it."

• Set clear limits.
Children think differently from adults and do not always see the "whole picture" as we do. Children need to know specifically what's allowed. "You can go as far as the corner," or "Wait near the big tree," or "Stay at the top of the stairs." *Remember that children feel safe when they know exactly what they can and cannot do.*

Realize that saying reasonable "Nos" will help your child develop as a moral, caring, and fun-to-be-with person.

Chapter 7
Alternatives
to "Don't!"

Harriet Heath

The problem with
saying, "Don't"
is that the command
gives children no direction.

• Jeffrey, who is almost five, has just mastered the ability to swing at great speed any object that happens to be in his hands: lunch boxes, objects tied to strings, caps. For his two-year-old sibling, Christopher, the activity is downright dangerous. He wanders into the circumference of the swing and gets banged by whatever is at the end of the arm.

"Don't swing your lunch box!"

• Mother looking out the kitchen window sees four-year-old Katy busily picking tulips.

"Don't pick the tulips!"

• Eighteen-month-old Martin drags a folding chair over to the counter and climbs up.

"Don't stand on the chair!"

• Baby Cynthia wiggles over to another infant and starts grabbing her hair.

"Don't grab!"

So many "Don'ts." How many does a child hear in a day? And children need to learn them all.

What kind of children do parents want?

Hearing the "Don'ts," one wonders what kind of children do parents want? Passive ones who are quiet, not moving and devoid of curiosity? Where do our curious children fit in who live life joyfully and are eagerly searching to understand how their world works? How will they keep their love of life and learn what they can do, if all we give them are "Don'ts"?

The problem with saying "Don't" is that the command gives children no direction. It does not tell them what they can do. It does not inform them about what the problem is in what they are doing. It does not help them figure alternatives. The assumption seems to be that if children learn <u>what not to do</u> they will automatically know <u>what to do</u>. That is not the way children learn. "Don't" simply says to stop. This is necessary when the action is life-threatening, but it is deadening to their curiosity and enthusiasm when constantly used.

Alternatives to "Don't"

Jeffrey's mother could say, "What fun it is to swing the lunch box! Do you feel the pull as you twirl so fast? Where could you do that so you won't hit your little brother? And Jeffrey might answer, "I can go outside and swing my lunch box." "I could swing socks instead of my lunch box." "I can draw a circle and stay in it as I swing." "You can take Christopher into the kitchen while I swing."

Or the mother seeing her tulips disappearing from her garden might start with a <u>don't</u> but could also add: "They are beautiful waving in the breeze. We can wave as they do." And together they could wave with the tulips. "We can smell them..." "What else could we do?" Katy might say, "I could draw them and color them with all the colors in my crayon box ... or make paper ones." And "Next year we could plant thousands; then we can pick all we want to." Mother can add, "If we leave them in the garden they will bloom a long, long time. Shall we mark on the calendar when they bloomed and see how long they last? We can put the ones you've picked in a vase and see which lasts the longer, the ones in the vase or the ones in the garden." And Katy might have another solution, "I can pick lots of dandelions instead. Daddy is always pulling them up."

Dad, observing Martin climbing up on the folding chair near where he is making brownies could say, "Oh, you want to see. What a good idea to get something to stand on. But that folding chair might tip on you. Let's get the step stool."

Cynthia's mother could explain, "This is Sally. She has hair just like yours," as she hurriedly gets down on the floor with the two infants and strokes both Sally's and Cynthia's hair. "It hurts to have your hair pulled. She feels sad when her hair is pulled just like you do. Stroke it like this." As the mother talks she takes Cynthia's hand and helps her stroke Sally's hair.

The limitations are there:
"Don't swing where others can be hurt."
"Don't pick the tulips."
"Don't climb on tipsy chairs."
"Don't pull hair."
The emphasis and direction are different. The children's joy and curiosity are recognized, encouraged and shared. The children learn the reasons why they are expected to change their behavior. They therefore can base their future behavior on lessons learned at this time. The children are also given alternative ways of acting. In the process of having their behavior redirected, the children are learning life skills such as becoming aware of the effects of one's behaviors on others, and recognizing there is more than one way of doing something. Some math and science lessons creep in too.

While the "Don'ts" are quicker and more expedient, the questions are: *What do we want our children to learn?* and *How best can we guide them to becoming thoughtful, considerate people?*

Changing Behavior Without Using "Don't"

Three questions help refocus the don'ts:
- What are alternative behaviors for my child?
- What is my child's intent?
- What do I want my child to learn?

What are alternative behaviors for my child?

Thinking up alternative behaviors is a challenge. It makes parenting a creative endeavor. A mother came into a parent group one evening saying with surprise in her voice, "It's tough. I can't think up alternatives. The kids often come up with more ideas than I can."

"Brainstorming" is a way of thinking that stimulates the search for alternatives. The challenge is to come up with as many ideas as quickly as possible. All ideas are accepted. The more the better. Judging is suspended. Deciding which to implement comes later. Brainstorming is a very useful parenting skill and absolutely vital when attempting to refocus "Don'ts."

While parents often have to brainstorm on the spot and alone, brainstorming with others is usually more productive. The ideas of one person help stimulate the creative thinking of another. When possible, brainstorm with your parenting partner, a friend, another parent and, eventually, with your children.

Like the rest of us, children have to learn how to brainstorm. It can be done in stages.

Young children of a year or two learn there is more than one way of doing something. Dad in the vignette above showed his toddler an alternative, and safer, piece of furniture on which to stand. With this age child, the adult shows the way. As children become three and four they themselves can think of other ways to obtain the results they want. Four-year-old Katy added to her mother's suggestions as to what she could do with the tulips. When five-year-old Jeffrey was swinging his lunch box, the parent set the expectation that he could think of a way of having fun within the boundaries of safety.

Thinking of alternative behaviors is not easy. Most of us were not encouraged to do so. Much of the advice given to parents about setting limits is **in** the form of "Don't." Thinking of alternatives can be a challenge and even become a game. It certainly makes life more interesting. Once aware of alternatives, the decision becomes which alternative to choose. Two questions guide our choice: 1) What is my child's intent? 2) What do I want my child to learn?

What is my child's intent?

What a child is trying to do can guide the process of deciding which alternatives would work best. If Martin's intent in climbing on a chair was to see what his father was doing, then alternatives will be selected to accomplish this purpose. If Jeffrey's intent was to experience the feeling of swinging something on the end of a string, then the chosen alternative will let him continue swinging something safely.

The danger in seeking to identify the child's motivation is that we adults tend to read in our biases. Katy's mother told the parent group, "Knowing how much I enjoyed seeing the tulips in the yard, I just knew Katy was picking them to get back at me. But when I asked her why she did it," the mother continued, "Katy explained to me she thought they'd look beautiful in the vase like the flowers I'd brought home from the store last week." The child's reasons were different from those of the parent.

Nowhere is this danger of misinterpreting children's behavior greater than when siblings are involved. It would have been so easy for Jeffrey's mother to assume he wanted to hurt his brother. Objective observation, however, showed Jeffrey's mother that her son was focused on the swinging lunch box. He was oblivious to two-year-old Christopher. And most fives, developmentally, when totally involved, do not have the control to pull themselves back from the excitement of the moment to think about what might be the consequences of their action.

The child's behavior and developmental level give clues as to the child's intent, helping parents guard against reading their own interpretations into the situation. Young children's intent can usually be inferred from their behavior. Martin climbing up on the folding chair near his Dad explained without words exactly what he was trying to accomplish, that is, to see what his Dad was doing. The constant enthusiastic swinging of anything in their hands alerts parents of the five-year-olds that their children's intent is to test how it feels to swing something. For them it may be an early science lesson about centrifugal force.

Knowing what is typical behavior of children at specific stages of development can also help parents decipher what their child's intent is. Baby Cynthia, exploring another baby, is going about it with the same uncoordinated grabbing approach she exhibits when handling anything that catches her interest and is within her grasp. Recognizing this developmental pattern of grabbing when exploring keeps parents from assuming that Cynthia is trying to hurt the other baby (an adult interpretation). Instead, it suggests to parents that their responsibility is to help Cynthia explore the other infant more cautiously.

Knowing what children of a certain age are interested in also may guide in the decision-making process. Martin's behavior is typical of eighteen month olds who tend to want to see everything that is going on around them.

Recognizing intent by observing behavior and by using information about their child's developmental level helps the parent know when to suggest alternatives, when to encourage their children to think of them, and which alternatives to choose that will help their children accomplish what they are attempting.

What do I want my child to learn?
The choices the parents made are based on their values.
• *Suggesting alternatives* helps children to know that there is more than one solution to a situation.
  • *Choosing alternatives that allowed the children to continue exploring* demonstrates the importance parents place on curiosity.
•*Seeking to protect other children* demonstrates the importance of children caring for others.
•*Verbalizing potentially dangerous situations* assumes the importance of keeping children safe.

Thus the parent of the child swinging his lunch box brought to his attention the possible harmful affects as well as the fun of swinging. The adult with the crawling baby showed her how to get to know the other infant in a gentle way. The Dad recognized his son's desire to see what was going on but found a safer means. The mother whose child was picking tulips taught her child how to value nature by helping her learn other ways of enjoying the flowers.

Each incident is only one of innumerable occasions that will occur, giving parents the opportunity to guide their children toward long term goals as they grow from infancy to adulthood. Instead of focusing on the "Don'ts" parents can focus on what the child can do. This provides mothers and fathers with a method of guiding their children that allows them to implement their values. Furthermore, it gives children direction as to what is acceptable action.

Chapter 8
When Preschoolers
Use "Bad" Language

Bette Simons

*It is a shock to
mothers and fathers
when their child comes out
with words they only
expected to hear in
an "R" rated movie.*

Three-year-old Joseph is in tears as he tells his preschool teacher, "Kevin said my picture looks like doo doo."

When preschoolers start using language, teachers and parents can relish the growing assertiveness of a child who can now "use words" to express feelings. Not so long ago, if someone hurt his feelings, Joseph might just cry. Now he also uses language in order to deal with the situation.

While Kevin also used language to express his feelings, that language was hurtful to Joseph. When Joseph complains about Kevin's remark, the teacher doesn't say, "Kevin, you must not use bad words." She knows that Kevin's words show that he is learning the impact he can have by talking. Her task is to protect both Joseph's feelings and Kevin's language development.

Actually Kevin's words would be considered a mild form of bad language. Preschool teachers report hearing swear words and all sorts of "bad" language every day in their groups.

The importance of learning to "use words"
"He tooked it away from me," says Robert, a tearful three-year-old. The preschool teacher may beam with pride because Robert had almost no speech when he first entered school and now the social situation is getting him to talk. He is learning to interact with other children and with teachers. He is using language to get along in the world. He is encouraged to "use words," to express his needs and his feelings. If, on the one hand, he is told by teachers and parents to "use his words," and on the other hand, is warned "not to use 'bad' words," he is apt to get confused.

How children learn "bad" language
It's a shock to mothers and fathers when their child comes out with words they only expected to hear in an "R" rated movie. If your child comes home from preschool with colorful swear words, it does no good to ask yourself, "Where does my child learn these things?" The ability to use language is inborn, but the vocabulary children use is learned from the people around them. Sometimes children get the colorful language from their peers, from older children, from television, or overhearing adult conversation.

The importance of "keeping your cool"
Swearing offends many parents when they hear a little child use the words, because they refer to genital organs, sexual intercourse, or body wastes. The words may be sacrilegious or racially offensive —and do not reflect the family values you wish your child to have.

Chances are your child's first swear words are very mild compared to the possibilities that exist. How do you deal with this behavior? One problem is that, if parents tell children they must not use "bad" words, children discover they have something stronger than crying to express how mad they can get. The swearing can get worse when young children realize these words have the power to get a strong reaction out of the adults around them.

If you can think of your child as experimenting with language, it's easier to keep your cool and say something like, "I want to be called mommy, not _____. Your face shows me you are *really* angry." Be more ready to listen than to scold. One sure way to encourage language development is to be a better listener.

Experienced preschool teachers try to ignore swear words, unless they are used to hurt someone's feelings. They will repeat the words in order to take the wind out of the child's sails. "No, his name is not _____, his name is Joey," is something teachers and parents have to be ready to say. The more fuss made about certain words the more power the child feels they have.

Preschool teachers' priorities

Preschool teachers spend a good part of their days teaching children not to hit, bite, grab or push. If a child pushes another they say, "Tell him you don't like that." If a child calls other children names to hurt their feelings, teachers are likely to step in and see that the child is referred to by his or her own name. Teachers have the job of protecting bodies and feelings, but if they are going to monitor swear words they may find themselves doing nothing else. No one wants teachers to spend all their time walking around the playground deciding if "poo poo head" is really a bad word. There are more important things to notice, like the praying mantis someone found, and creative things to do, like buying another pretend cake from the children in the sandbox. Activities like these encourage language learning; scolding children for swearing inhibits it.

At home, parents can do the same thing—be good listeners. Your preschoolers are struggling to learn the language, and learning to express themselves. It's best to ignore the words and address the emotions.

What's a Parent to Do?

Encourage appropriate language.
When anyone has strong feelings, they need language to express them. When parents react to their own frustration by voicing their feeling in descriptive words, they give children good language models. They need to be careful as to which words they use because they can expect children to follow their lead.

Here are some possible words and phrases that might be used in your family to express anger: "Doggone!" "Shoot!" "Jiminy Christmas!" "Gosh darn!" "Drat" "Oh nuts!"

Excitement is easier. These days children are using the word "Carabunga" that they got from the Ninja Turtles, and "Good form!" is a compliment from the movie *Hook.* Then there's always "Superkalafragilistic-expealidosous." Moms who say, "Stupendous!" "Remarkable," or "Awesome," expose children to the idea that there are lots of words to express ideas. Focusing on showing children the possibilities of using language is positive, whereas censoring language cuts off communication.

Teach your child the meaning of the words they use.
When appropriate, preschoolers should be taught the meaning of the words they say. This means there is lots of teaching for a parent to do.

1. Names and uses of body parts.
Children need to know the names of all parts of their bodies and to have a good self-image. You may want to take some books out of the library that explain the workings of the human body in simple words and pictures, such as *What Am I Made Of?* by David Bennett (Aladdin Books edition, 1991). When children learn about birth and conception from their parents, their impression of these events is positive. This subject is not likely to be titillating when parents explain what the words really mean.

2. Racial and ethnic slurs.
Children learn from their parents attitudes about other races. If questioned by their preschoolers, parents can explain racial slurs by saying, "Sometimes, just to be mean, people use a hurtful word for a person's race or the country where he or his parents came from. We don't do that in our family. Here are the real names you should use." When you teach your child not to have biases, he or she will not want to hurt someone and will understand that these words are used to be insulting.

3. Religious slurs.
When parents teach their children to be respectful of other people's religious beliefs, this respect will be with them throughout their lives.

4. Body wastes.
The preschooler likes to make fun of urine and feces so much, that some preschools call the language <u>bathroom</u> <u>talk</u>. Parents, who get tired of how tickled children get talking about body waste, can tell them to go to the bathroom to talk bathroom talk. It's still best not to let children think they have gotten the best of you with words. Giggling children often stop and listen very quietly if a teacher explains what a bladder is or how food goes through the digestive system. Following it all the way to the sewage treatment plant is awesome.

A child who is healthily adjusted is part of his peer group. Preschoolers can be told that there may be words that are acceptable when they are playing with their friends. However, they shouldn't be used in the house, or around adults.

Let children have outlets for language.

Especially around four, children enjoy outrageous language. If a child loves creating colorful new language or bringing home swear words that are tiresome to the adult, consider hanging a puppet by a garbage pail, and saying, "This is the place for garbage talk." Or, do what the schools do and say, "Bathroom talk belongs in the bathroom."

Enjoy language with your child:

You can astound your child with words, just as well as he or she can astound you. Try something like, "It's remarkable how you think up things in your cranium." But you may get sent to the garbage puppet if you get too outrageous with your words.

Chapter 9
Dealing with
Unacceptable Behaviors

Bette Simons

---

*Unacceptable behaviors
are the ones that are
likely to harm children
physically or emotionally.*

No child is perfect, but teachers and parents know that there are some behaviors that are unacceptable. They are the ones that are likely to harm children physically or emotionally.

Two-year-olds can have terrible temper tantrums and sometimes bite other children. Threes can hit hard, push, and even scratch. Fours can hit even harder and send a former friend into tears with a choice name you are sure no one in your family ever used before. Fives can look like they are playing happily when closer examination reveals a group that has been organized by a child who gets loyalty by bullying.

The earliest and most troublesome unacceptable behavior in the preschool is biting. It can sweep through a preschool like the measles. It stays in the two's room the longest, but even an angry four-year-old might leave those painful punctures in the shape of a leaf on some sweet arm. The victims howl; parents can be furious and demand immediate action. Preschool teachers groan inwardly. They know there is no instant cure.

Children who can't use their words well, often discover effective ways to show anger, get attention, or possess another child's toy. A child may have come upon the act of biting in babyhood days when parents played, "I'm going to eat you up..." Innocently using this social gesture, a playmate might be tasted with startling results. Just as a jack-in-the-box pops up with a push on a button, a preschooler may get intrigued with an act that gets a child to cry and teachers to scurry.

"Look at Timmy's face!" the experienced teacher says to the biter. "That hurt him! We don't hurt our friends. And I don't want anyone to hurt you either!" She lets the children know that she is there to protect everyone — both physically and emotionally. *Children make bad mistakes, but they are not bad people.*

Very young children vary in how they respond to adults' reactions to their biting. Oftentimes preschoolers are not mature enough to empathize with others. They cannot put themselves in the other person's place. This will take time. All the fuss made over the biting is as intriguing as the thrill they get when they zip down the playground slide. The reaction to this behavior is so interesting that young children want to do it over and over.

Nowadays parents may need instant reassurance that there are no known cases of the HIV virus being contracted through a bite. Health authorities consider a bite "casual contact" and casual contact is not dangerous, though a parent may consider it a heinous crime — until their child does it.

It's true that children learn from watching others. After seeing the uproar that comes with a bite, a child might use the same behavior when someone won't yield a tricycle on demand.

Because children learn from watching others, it is especially unfortunate if adults use the same unacceptable behaviors to control little children. Understandably, parents want to put a fast stop to biting. But the statement, "I bit him back and he never did it again," worries those who know that teaching children through physical pain can cause them to store resentment that can flare up in worse ways, later in life. Such methods do not teach cooperative living.

Information hot lines that serve parents are getting more questions about biting than they did previously. One hot line worker says children are angry because they don't want to be separated from their parents so much. When young children are left in a place where there is competition for space and toys, their anxiety grows and they sometimes lose control. They show their needs as best as they can, with a powerful part of their bodies — the teeth.

Eventually, most children will graduate to expressing anger by hitting other children. Some of this is to be expected, but many children will hit very hard very often. When this happens, adults need to ask if the underlying cause has been addressed. In addition, they need to remind the child to, "Use your words! Tell her how you feel about that!"

As children get older and use their words, parents may be more shocked than pleased when the words the children use would not be spoken in polite society. Earlier, teachers urged parents to understand that biting and hitting, although unacceptable behaviors, are usual for youngsters who are learning to control their impulses. Now these teachers work to help parents understand that using words is a great progression for the development of socialization and language as well.

Even though children in groups are experiencing negative ways to socialize, they are learning positive ones at the same time. It is the task of parents and teachers to guide the young child to want to use acceptable behaviors.

Creating
Acceptable Behaviors

Unacceptable behaviors can keep a child from having positive experiences, endanger others and take the teacher's attention away from curriculum plans.

When any child calls attention to himself or herself more than most through unacceptable behaviors, it's an occasion for the preschool to bring it to the parent's attention.

"But I never let him watch Power Rangers," an exasperated parent may say. It's true. Though most early childhood teachers wish parents would control the violent TV and videos available, some parents who do, still have children who seem constantly angry enough to be harming others a good part of the time. Whether the child is chronically uncomfortable with allergies, or jealous of a sibling, or feeling denied sufficient time with a parent, unacceptable behaviors must be unlearned.

Biting: The two year old who persists with biting, may be saying as best as he can, that he is angry about something that is happening either at home or in school — or both.

When very young children bite, it's best for adults to fuss over the bitten child and wash the wound with soap and water quickly. Hug the biter as well as the bitten child and treat the matter as a bad accident, so no negative power is handed to the child who used his teeth so effectively.

Older two's who are making a habit of biting need to hear from adults a firm reprimand: "NO BITING!" They must be removed from the area immediately. Teachers and parents can talk about biting apples, carrots, and toast, but not our friends.

If children don't feel well physically, biting can just be a way of saying, "I've had it; take care of me." Staying home from preschool with an extra dose of good parenting can help.

If biting persists with children close to four, it can be a display of intense anger. It's a child's cry for help with something in life that should be investigated. A counselor can help both the family and the school. If language is delayed and it's too frustrating to "use your words," a speech/language teacher can help.

Scratching, hitting, and kicking: When there is no attempt to determine the underlying cause of unacceptable behaviors, it is common to find that when biting stops, something else starts.

Preschools have materials that children can use to express anger about issues for which there is no cure. For example: parents must work, and children must be cared for in preschool. But preschoolers can scratch through the chocolate pudding on the finger painting paper. Children can beat the play dough with a mallet. They must learn that they may not squeeze the guinea pig, but they may squeeze the goop and poke holes in the clay. Small cardboard boxes can be kicked. Other safe items for hitting or kicking could be bean bags or an inflated Bozo.

Hitting is inevitable among children in groups. But children who hit with things like shovels must be stopped immediately and the implements removed. Later on, the adult can give the object back to the child, saying, "How will you use this now?" Giving the child many chances to do the right thing is as important as firmly stopping the wrong thing.

Startling words: The child that says, "That was a dumb thing to do!" when another child knocks over a carefully constructed block building, is using words to get along in the world. On the other hand, calling a child "Dumbie" or a worse name, requires adult intervention. The adult might say, "That's not his name; tell him what you didn't like." Little children tend to think that labels they are given stick to them, so name calling is often unacceptable as it damages the self image.

Adults sometimes forget to give credit to the child who used to bite, hit or kick, when he or she uses colorful language instead. If words are to have an impact, the preschool child who is using them forcefully, is operating at a higher level than previously. After a child is well finished with an outburst, an adult might say, "You are really, really, angry. I can tell by your words. Do you know what I say when I'm really mad? I say, 'I'm furious about that,' or 'This is unacceptable.' I say it loudly, just like you did. I don't swear; I don't need to."

Not all children bite, scratch, kick, hit or push. Children are born with different temperaments and some are naturally positive in their interactions with others, some more demanding. Some are very physical and some more passive. Parents and teachers can find ways to help children learn acceptable behaviors.

Chapter 10
Preschooler Memory:
In One Ear
and Out the Other?

Neala S. Schwartzberg

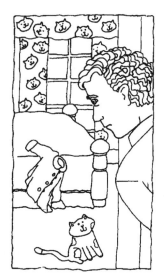

*Children have a hard time
remembering anything that
is uninteresting to them.*

"Don't forget to hang up your coat," reminded Monica's father as they came into the house from their walk. "Um," replied Monica as she went into her room. But when she took off her coat she was distracted for a moment by the thought of her favorite television show and dropped the coat on the bed. A few minutes later her father poked his head into her room, saw the coat half on the bed, half on the floor, and sighed.

If children can remember all the characters in all the cartoon shows they watch, why can't they remember to put away their toys? If they can remember that two weeks ago you promised them ice cream, why can't they remember that two minutes ago you asked them to hang up their coats?

Whether it's milk left out of the refrigerator, lost clothing, or forgotten chores, some days our kids don't seem to remember anything. That's not really true of course; it only seems that way to frustrated parents and caregivers. But if we look at how children's memory works (or doesn't work) we can understand why our kids are so forgetful and how we can help them remember.

In order to remember anything our youngsters have to *notice* the information, *process* it in some way, *store* it, and then *retrieve* it when needed. Failure at any point along the way results in that most famous excuse: "I forgot."

Noticing Information
Parents know that when a child wants a particular toy he will notice all the advertisements and hundreds of other cues which remind him to ask for that toy. Children and adults notice things that interest them. Unfortunately, chores rarely interest them, so they don't remember them. They won't recognize that things are out of place so they don't hang up their coat, or pick up their toys. And when we ask them, "Didn't you see...?" they look at us blankly.

Children have a hard time remembering anything that is uninteresting to them. In one study youngsters were asked to remind their parents to do different tasks. The tasks ranged from fairly boring to a child (like doing the laundry), to more interesting (like buying candy). These two-three- and four-year-olds could occasionally remind their parents to do the laundry, but they were much better at reminding their parents to buy the treats. In fact, the youngsters remembered to prompt their parents to buy candy 70% of the time. Unfortunately, children seem to see few cues to remind them to hang up their coats.

Processing Information

After a child has noticed something, or we have brought it to his attention, he has to do something with the information if he is going to remember it. Young children do not yet understand the *process* of how to remember. Their idea of trying to remember something is to listen very intently or look very hard. They don't realize that it would assist their memory process to repeat the information, or think about it, or do something with it. So it really does go in one ear and out the other.

Young children find it difficult to process more than one or two pieces of information at a time. If you ask an adult to do three things, the adult will probably remember by repeating the instructions and counting the number of things to be done and deciding what order to do them in. "Okay I have to do the laundry, load the dishwasher, and drive Sandy to her friend's house. First I'll put up the laundry, then drive Sandy. By then the laundry will be done and I can run the dishwasher." Can you imagine a child actually thinking about the things she has to do? They don't...so they don't remember.

• Four-year-old Sarah has just been asked to pick up her toys. She begs for a few more minutes of television and promises as soon as the show is over, she'll put them away. Does Sarah think to herself "Okay, I have to remember, after the show I'll put away my toys"? Probably not.

• Five-year-old Evan needs to clear his dishes from the table and put his dirty clothes in the laundry. Does he think about which to do first and why? Again, probably not.

Remembering to call grandparents. Getting things ready for school the next day. These things require our children to think about their responsibilities and plan how they will do them. And children just don't do that. They don't yet have the mental capacity.

Children also have a smaller base of information to use in helping them to remember. Part of the reason we remember things better than our children do is that we have greater knowledge which we use to make sense of our experiences. Our children don't have that background and experience, so things don't make as much sense to them, and they simply forget them.

When the situation is reversed and our youngsters are the ones with the superior background, they outshine us. Ask your youngster to generate a list of his or her favorite TV characters, or sports stars. Then see if you can remember these names. Unless you share this particular interest with your child, her memory will probably be better than yours, and you might silently think, "This from a kid who can't even remember to throw the laundry into the basket."

What does this mean in real life?
When we ask children to do several tasks, they listen to us, assure us they remember, and walk out of the room, forgetting almost instantly. Here are some ways to help them remember:

• Do it now. Time has little meaning for children and "later" is a convenient way for children (and adults) to put off something they have no interest in doing. If they need to clean up their toys, ask them to do it then and there.

• Do make sure you have your child's attention. Never compete with the TV, the dog, or a sister or brother. Get down to her level and maintain eye contact. Children have to notice something before they can remember it, and they have to notice us before they can listen.

• Try to avoid asking a child to remember several things at one time. If a child must remember to do more than one or two things, make a list using pictures to remind her. Toys, clothes, animal chores etc. can all be triggered using pictures. The last item on the list can be a treat for taking care of all those chores.

• Help your child process the information by rehearsing it. This forces your child to think about, and interact with, whatever it is she must remember. For example, tell your child, "There are two things you have to do. You have to set the table and take your toys out of the living room. Now you tell me — what are the things you have to do?"

• If your child does have to remember to do something later provide a good cue for recall. For things which are to be done at home, a timer or an alarm clock works very well. Explain that when the alarm goes off the child has to put the toys away, set the table for dinner, or even get ready for bed.

• Make things part of an automatic chain of actions in which doing one action acts as a cue to the next. Getting up in the morning might include washing up, brushing teeth, getting dressed, then going in for breakfast (or whatever your family morning routine). If this becomes the standard routine it is far easier for a child to remember to brush her teeth before getting dressed. If it is something your child can practice in advance, let him go through the actions several times while you watch to make sure nothing has been left out. You are creating links and associations between actions so that one action will lead to the next.

• Use external reminders. Put their lunch someplace where they can't miss seeing it. If you can, hang it from the doorknob, then when they reach for the door knob, there's the lunch box. Do they need to remember to bring things on a trip? Try taping pictures of the items on the door.

• Helping them remember things to do when they arrive at preschool — like giving a note to the teacher — is a little more difficult. Home and school are very different environments, with nothing in common to jog your child's memory. The solution? Tell your child, "When you see your teacher I want you to remember to give her the note." Giving a note to the teacher can be triggered by the sight of that teacher. As a backup strategy put the note where the child is sure to see it — like taped to the sandwich wrapper in his lunch box.

It is important to be realistic about our expectations. Young children's memory will slowly get better. But it is true that they are never going to remember easily to do things they find boring or trivial. However, there are things we can do to help them remember. And for us, a good sense of humor helps.

Resources for Section One: Guiding Young Children's Behavior

FOR ADULTS

Parents on the Spot! What to Do When Kids Put You There, by Judi Craig, Ph.D., Hearst Books/Wm. Morrow, 1994. This book is one of a series of Good Housekeeping Parent Guides, with lively, readable chapters dealing with real-life experiences. Includes articles on tantrums, hitting, biting, etc.

The Preschool Years, by Ellen Galinsky and Judy David. Ballantine Books, 1991. The authors, who co-wrote a chapter in this book, have written a monumental work using actual interviews with parents, combined with practical advice from child development experts. They discuss all aspects of young children's development including discipline, family relationships, schools and child care.

Guide to Your Parenting Concerns, by Linda Lewis Griffith. Kindred Books, 1996. This book is unique in that it contains short, how-to chapters on discipline, parent-child communication, holidays, etc., taken from the weekly newspaper column of a Family and Child Counselor.

Your Child's Emotional Health, by The Philadelphia Child Guidance Center Staff and Jack Maguire. Macmillan, 1995. A comprehensive family reference book on children's emotional well-being, from birth to adolescence, including information on discipline, play, sleeping, eating, and other important topics.

Understanding Young Children's Behavior: A Guide for Early Childhood Professionals, by Jillian Rodd. Teachers College Press, 1996. This guide provides information to early childhood educators about using positive strategies to manage young children's behavior in group settings.

Loving Your Child is Not Enough: Positive Discipline That Works, by Nancy Samalin with Martha Moraghan Jablow. Viking Penguin, 1988. In this helpful volume, Samalin, author of a chapter in this book, details her down-to-earth approach to discipline, which preserves the child's self-esteem, while setting clear and consistent guidelines.

The Discipline Book: Everything You Need to Know to Have a Better-Behaved Child — *From Birth to Age ten*, by William Sears, M.D. & Martha Sears, R.N. Little, Brown, 1995. The authors encourage parents to develop a philosophy of discipline and offer tools to help with child rearing. A chapter on *Disciplining Bothersome Behaviors* includes a discussion of biting, hitting, pushing, kicking and bad language.

Child-Wise, by Cathy Rindner Tempelsman. Morrow/Quill, 1995. In this reassuring guide, the author encourages readers to stop striving to be "perfect" parents, and to focus instead on accepting, knowing, and really enjoying their child.

Discipline: A Sourcebook of 50 Failsafe Techniques for Parents, by James Windell. Collier Books/Macmillan, 1991. Windell, author of a chapter in this book, suggests practical techniques for guiding the behavior of children from preschool age through the teenage years. He draws upon his long experience in working with families and uses many examples of parent/child dialog to illustrate his points.

8 Weeks to a Well-Behaved Child: A Failsafe Program for Toddlers Through Teens, by James Windell. Macmillan, 1994. In a series of lessons spanning eight weeks, Windell teaches parents how to be firm and consistent in their discipline while building a child's self-esteem and self-control.

FOR CHILDREN

School Isn't Fair! by Patricia Baehr. Aladdin, 1992. "Sometimes school just isn't fair," Edward complains. A girl spills juice and it gets on your shirt; the class won't sing the song you want to sing; you can't see the pictures in the book at storytime, and you get punished for something you didn't really mean to do. But sometimes — for instance when you can help a classmate — school can be fair, and even satisfying.

Anna and the Little Green Dragon, by Klaus Baumgart. Hyperion, 1995. Anna is eating her breakfast toast when the box of cornflakes tips over. It was tipped by a little green dragon, who then proceeds to make a mess, squishing through the butter, breaking an egg, and spilling Anna's cocoa. Her mother doesn't believe her story about the dragon — until the surprise ending.

One Bear in the Picture, by Caroline Bucknall. Puffin Pied Piper, 1993. Ted's mother wants him to stay clean at school today, because the photographer is coming to take pictures of all the little bears in his class. Like most young bears, Ted can't help getting messy, but he finds a way to clean up before mother sees him. (However, photographs don't lie, and in the final page we can behold the photo that mom will see, Ted with mud, paint, and all.)

My Brown Bear Barney in Trouble, by Dorothy Butler. Greenwillow, 1993. A little girl and her bear manage to get into mischief every day of the week. While things quiet down on Sunday, they look forward to Monday and the exciting week to come!

Pass the Fritters, Critters, by Cheryl Chapman. Four Winds Press, 1993. Brightly-colored cut cloth is the type of media used to illustrate this book, which teaches manners in a fun way. When a boy asks (in rhyme) for a food to be passed to him, he says, "Pass the eclair, bear." Each animal he asks refuses until he uses the magic word. When the boy says "Please," the book closes with a feast, and a surprise.

Annie and Cousin Precious, by Kay Chorao. Dutton, 1994. It's hard for Annie to be a good hostess when Cousin Precious comes for a visit, since her guest keeps bossing Annie and ruining her toys. How Annie and her cousin confront each other and (almost) get to like each other is the satisfying ending to this story.

I Want It (2nd rev. ed., 1996); *I'm Frustrated* (1992) by Elizabeth Crary. Parenting Press, Inc. These two Children's Problem Solving Books give parents and children the opportunity to read either from cover to cover, or as an alternative book, where children choose among a variety of alternatives and influence the course of the story. In the first book, two girls both want to play with the same truck and must learn to problem solve. In the second, a boy who is learning to roller skate feels very frustrated when he keeps falling, and has to learn how to deal with his feelings.

Clean Your Room, Harvey Moon! by Pat Cummings. Bradbury Press, 1991. This humorous story is told in rhyme. Harvey wants to watch his favorite programs on television, but his mother insists that he clean up his messy room first.

Bunnies on Their Own, by Amy Ehrlich. Dial/Pied Piper edition, 1992. When mother rabbit goes to market, she leaves the bunnies on their own. Larry and Harry behave very well, even cleaning up the kitchen. But their sister Paulette finds a bugle and wants only to play Ta Ta Ta TA!

Walter's Tail, by Lisa Campbell Ernst. Bradbury Press, 1992. Mrs. Tully gets a puppy for company and calls him Walter. He is cute, and his tail keeps wagging. As Walter grows bigger, that wagging tail causes many disasters, knocking over nails in the hardware store, lemon balls in the candy shop, and even a fancy wedding cake at the bakery. Everyone in town tells Mrs. Tully to get rid of that dog, until Walter becomes the town hero, wagging tail and all.

Owen, by Kevin Henkes. Greenwillow, 1993. Owen is going to start school. That's fine with him, as long as he can take along his fuzzy blanket. He had kept it close to him ever since he was a baby, and he isn't going to give it up. Nothing that Owen's mother or father can say or do will change Owen's mind. But Owen's mother solves the problem with an absolutely wonderful idea — and it works!

Grandma Gets Grumpy, by Anna Grossnickle Hines. Clarion, 1990. Five little cousins stay at Grandma's house overnight, and have a fine time playing. But when things get out of hand, and the children jump on the sofa and knock over the lamp, even a loving Grandma can run out of patience. Restoring Grandma's good humor is not difficult, once the children figure out what to do.

Three-Star Billy, by Pat Hutchins. Greenwillow, 1994. Billy, a monster, is starting monster nursery school but he doesn't want to go. His sister tells him that he will get a star if he's good. Billy doesn't want to be good. So he behaves monstrously, and gets a star for each misbehavior. At the end, like many preschoolers who are not little monsters, when his parents come for him, he doesn't want to go home.

It Was Jake! by Anita Jeram. Little, Brown, 1991. Danny loves his dog, Jake. But when Danny messes up his room, or digs up the garden to look for buried treasure, or gets the bathroom all wet, he tells his mother, "It was Jake!" Mother is clever enough to know the troublemaker was Danny. But in the surprise ending, when Danny's supper is gone, it really was Jake!

I Took My Frog to the Library, by Eric A. Kimmel. Puffin Books edition, 1992. In this funny book, a little girl takes her pets to the library with disastrous results: her giraffe tries to read over everybody's shoulder, her hyena laughs too loud during storytime, and her elephant...well he's just so big!

The Tantrum, by Kathryn Lasky. Macmillan, 1993. A little girl sits quietly remembering the tantrum she had earlier in the day. She describes in detail all the things she did, like screaming, and making scuff marks on the wall with her feet. She tells about how each member of the family reacted. And how she suddenly stopped and couldn't remember what her tantrum was about. She looks forward to being grown up, when she won't have tantrums any more.

Me First, by Helen Lester. Houghton Mifflin Sandpiper, 1995. Pinkerton is a little pig who always wants to be first: first in line, first to get off the bus, and first to eat. Until, on a picnic at the beach, he encounters a sand<u>witch</u> who teaches him that first is not always best.

Uh Oh, Baby, by Wendy Cheyette Lewison. Scholastic/Cartwheel Books, 1992. In this little book for the youngest preschoolers a toddler gets into trouble in routine activities, such as petting a kitten, drawing on paper, and racing a toy car. The reader can lift a flap to see where his actions lead him.

Boomer Goes to School, by Constance W. McGeorge. Chronicle Books, 1996. Boomer, the golden retriever, goes with his owner to school. He follows the routines along with all the children. Although sometimes a bit confused when getting acquainted with school, Boomer makes new friends and has a fun-filled day.

The Tale of Custard the Dragon, by Ogden Nash. Little, Brown, 1995. Nash, the famous humorous poet, tells the story of a brave little girl, Belinda, and her cowardly dragon who longs for a nice safe cage. But when a pirate threatens Belinda and her pet animals, Custard the dragon saves them all.

King of the Playground, by Phyllis Reynolds Naylor. Aladdin Books edition, 1994. Kevin is afraid to go to the playground if Sammy is there. Sammy is always threatening to tie him up with a rope, or put him in a cage with wild bears, or other scary things. Kevin's Dad helps him think of imaginative ways to answer Sammy's threats.

That Bothered Kate, by Sally Noll. Greenwillow, 1991. Kate's sister Tory wanted to do everything that Kate did. She tried to dress like Kate, and ordered Kate's favorite flavor of ice cream. All of that bothered Kate. Then Tory found some friends of her own, and stopped noticing Kate. And that bothered Kate too! But Kate finds that it's all part of growing up.

Eating Out, by Helen Oxenbury. Puffin, 1994. In this humorous book, realistic pictures and setting will get children laughing when the spaghetti spills on the perfectly behaved family at the next table. Parents can relate to the need to go out to eat and to try to relax, even when they find that going out with a preschooler is not as relaxing and enjoyable as they had hoped. Simple text adds just enough explanation to the expressive pictures.

Amelia Bedelia, An I Can Read Book®. by Peggy Parish. HarperTrophy edition, 1992. Lovable, willing Amelia Bedelia, is the heroine of many books by this author. This is the first in the series, introducing the literal-minded housekeeper who does exactly what her employers tell her to do, with hilarious results.

Mind Your Manners, by Peggy Parish. Mulberry edition, 1994. Manners do matter and this book, with its humorous illustrations by Marylin Hafner, gives children specific suggestions for telephone manners and table manners. It tells youngsters how to behave during sleep-overs, and what to do when somebody gives you a gift that you really don't like!

Benny Bakes a Cake, by Eve Rice. Greenwillow, 1993. In this charming story that toddlers will love, it's Benny's birthday, and he helps Mama bake his cake. But his dog Ralph has an eye on the cake, and when Benny and Mama turn their backs, Ralph has knocked the cake to the floor. Benny cries and cries, until Daddy saves the day with a new cake, and the story ends with everybody singing Happy Birthday.

Thomas's Sitter, by Jean Richardson. Four Winds Press, 1991. After his baby sister is born, Thomas' mother needs to go back to work. A babysitter must be found to take care of Thomas and his sister. When prospective babysitters come to meet him, Thomas purposely misbehaves, and the ladies don't want to cope with him. Then he is introduced to Dan, a young man who will take care of Thomas and his sister. Dan can make paper airplanes, play in the sandbox, and set up a swing — not a babysitter but a "Thomas sitter."

Monster Manners, by Bethany Roberts. Clarion, 1996. It seems that monsters know about good manners, and, while they sometimes forget to use them, at other times they display them beautifully, (just like some youngsters you may know).

Yettele's Feathers, by Joan Rothenberg. Hyperion, 1996. Yettele loves to gossip and her stories are not always true. "Only words," she says, but her words can hurt people's feelings. One day she is taught a lesson when the Rabbi asks her to perform a most unusual task. This wise and funny story was inspired by an old Jewish folktale.

Mrs. Morgan's Lawn, by Barney Saltzberg. Hyperion, 1993. A little boy tells how his neighbor, Mrs. Morgan, doesn't want anything touching her lawn. Every time one of his balls lands on her lawn, she keeps it. She now has a collection of them. When the little boy goes to her house to ask her for them, she says she has a cold. She's indoors for so many days that the leaves pile up on her lawn. The boy rakes the leaves for her, and when Mrs. Morgan is back outside, she returns all the balls, even the new purple-and-white soccer ball.

I Am Really A Princess, by Carol Diggory Shields. Puffin, 1996. A little girl who is tired of doing the everyday chores of everyday people, like picking up her clothes and feeding the fish, decides that she is really a princess. As such, she has more important things to do, like riding her pony and rescuing princes from firebreathing dragons. Won't her family be surprised when they find out who she really is! A humorous story about a little girl with a lively imagination.

Caps for Sale: A Tale of a Peddler, Some Monkeys and Their Monkey Business, by Esphyr Slobodkina. HarperTrophy edition, 1987. HarperChildren's Audio Book & Cassette, 1995. This book has been a favorite of preschoolers since it was first published in 1940. It is also available as a set with audio-cassette. It tells how a peddler carrying caps of many colors falls asleep against a tree-trunk. When he wakes up, he finds that monkeys up in the tree are wearing all of his caps. A wonderful story to dramatize.

The Lemonade Babysitter, by Karen Waggoner. Little, Brown, 1992. Molly thinks she's too big to have a babysitter, so when old Mr. Herbert from down the street comes to take care of her, Molly tries to think of things Mr. Herbert would never want to do, so that he won't come back ever again. But both the little girl and the old man find they have more in common than one would imagine.

Shy Charles, by Rosemary Wells. Puffin Pied Piper, 1992. Despite his parents' efforts to make him into a dancer or a football player, or even to say, "Thank you," to the local storekeeper, Charles is as shy as any mouse could be. However, when an emergency occurs, he comes through as a real hero. (But he still remains the same shy Charles.)

Big Black Bear, by Wong Herbert Yee. Houghton Mifflin Co., 1993. When Big Black Bear comes out of the wood, and visits the house on Sycamore Street, a little girl answers the door. Big Black Bear isn't polite, and won't listen to the little girl's rules about wiping his feet, or covering his mouth when he sneezes. But an even bigger black bear arrives just in time to teach him good manners.

Crazy Clothes, by Niki Yektai. Aladdin Books edition, 1994. When Patrick tries to show his mother how well he can dress himself, he tells her that his clothes are not behaving correctly and are going on all the wrong parts of his body. His mother laughs at first. He sorts them all out, and dresses properly before his mother can get annoyed.

Oh No, Nicky! by Harriet Ziefert. A Puffin Lift-the-Flap Book, 1992. The youngest preschoolers will enjoy this book about a kitten who gets into all kinds of trouble. They can lift the flaps to learn how Nicky learns to stay safe.

What's Polite? by Harriet Ziefert. A Puffin Lift-the-Flap Book, 1995. At a restaurant with his mother and father, Scooter, the little boy pig, learns about saying, "Please" and "Thank you" and what it means to be polite. Children will enjoy lifting the flaps as they read this story about a very polite family of pigs.

Section Two
Communicating
with
Young
Children

Section Two
Communicating with Young Children

Introduction

What joy there is in being able to communicate with another person! Human beings are *always* communicating, both in words and nonverbal messages (such as gestures, facial expressions, and tone of voice). When a mother smiles down at her baby and the infant responds, reflecting the smile back at her, communication is taking place.

To communicate well with a young child, listen to her words, look at her facial expression, and notice her body language. These observations can help you tune into the child's feelings. If a little girl says, "Megan won't play with me today," her mother can say, "That must have made you feel sad." If a preschooler declares, "I'm going to knock down this whole school," his teacher can reply, "You must be feeling very angry today." Negative *feelings* should be understood and accepted, although destructive *behaviors* must be stopped.

When communicating with young children, there are simple, appropriate strategies you can use, such as: speak to your child from infancy, offer specific praise, schedule time alone with each child, and send positive rather than negative messages. These and other constructive ideas are described by the authors on the following pages.

SECTION TWO
GUIDING YOUNG CHILDREN'S BEHAVIOR

Chapter 11
Constructive Communication with Your Preschooler

Elizabeth J. Webster

*Human beings of any age
always communicate
when they are with other people.*

Responding to unspoken messages is as important to good communication as responding to the words that people say. At two months old, Chrissy stopped crying, smiled and cooed as her smiling mother bent over her crib. Although no words were spoken, Chrissy and her mother were sharing a time of good communication.

In the following incident, five-year-old Johnny and his teacher use words as well as behavior to share a time of good communication. Johnny was the shortest child in his preschool class. When student teachers arrived to observe his group, Johnny promptly climbed up on a table. As he stared silently at the strangers, his teacher asked, "Feels good to stand on the table?" Johnny replied seriously, "Yup, you don't see so much feet!"

These children and adults were communicating because human beings of any age *always* communicate when they are with other people. They send messages through facial expression, body movements, and tone of voice, as well as speech.

The majority of preschoolers' messages are about their feelings. They slowly gain the language necessary to sustain expression of ideas.

Parents value good communication with their preschoolers. They also know that they must start early in their child's life to model and teach open, constructive communication skills.

The first ingredient in constructive communication is <u>trust</u>. Babies do not automatically trust their environment (for example, they fear falling). Parents start by helping infants learn to trust what they do as well as what they say. The following suggestions can help build communication that is productive and pleasant for both parent and child.

Respond to Meanings of Messages
Each message has both content (gestures, speech, etc.) and meanings or feelings that govern content. Each message a child sends is true to her feelings *at the moment* and as often as possible you should *try to understand* these meanings and *say aloud* what you think you understand. This helps the child find words for his feelings and ideas.

Sometimes it's easy to guess a child's feelings. Chrissy's mother in the earlier example might have said her understanding as, "You're so glad to see me!" The meaning of Johnny's behavior was harder to guess, but he could tell his teacher enough that she guessed he probably felt very small and possibly afraid.

It often is fairly easy to understand your child's positive feelings, but it is important that you let her know you also understand her negative ones, because feelings of anger, sadness, and unhappiness do not go away when ignored or denied. They will reappear, often in undesirable ways.

Note that although negative *feelings* should be understood and accepted, hurtful or destructive *behaviors* must be stopped. Allowing such behaviors to continue creates anger and guilt in both you and the child, anger at each other and guilt because no constructive communication is possible under these conditions.

Shorten Messages for Understanding

Although infants respond primarily to tone of voice, as they mature they need to hear words to supplement tone of voice. However, they can cope only with sentences that are just slightly longer than those they use. To insure understanding, break your statements into short units: instead of, "Take all your cars and trucks and put them in your room before you bring out other toys," divide it into, "First, put all cars and trucks in your room. Then bring out other toys."

Avoid lengthy explanations and instructions because extra words become noise to be tuned out. Incomplete sentences are useful in aiding meaning. Instead of, "You can't have candy before supper because you need to eat supper to stay healthy," try, "No candy till after you eat supper." Remember that when you are behaving reasonably you will communicate this to your child without a lot of explanation.

Use Praise Often

Preschoolers begin to develop their self-concepts from how they feel parents see them. They also learn to do what they feel parents like, so it is wise to start praising early.

Again, use simple specific language. You give her more information when you say, "I like having you sit so quietly," than with, "That's a good girl!" Likewise, an enthusiastic, "I like your help!" is better than, "You're such a big girl!"

The idea behind all these suggestions is that parents and children learn *together* to communicate constructively. They do so in ordinary everyday encounters as well as in more structured times such as those detailed on the following pages.

Activities to Promote Good Communication

It is easiest for parents and children to learn to communicate in situations that are structured to be pleasant. Such situations vary by family and these general activities can be modified to fit individual needs. Remember that it is less important that parents and preschoolers spend great amounts of time with each other than it is that their time together is of good quality.

Encourage Child Participation in Conversations
Children should not be talked *about* when they are present. To do so can hurt and embarrass them, or lead them to feel that they cannot speak for themselves. Rather they should be encouraged to enter a conversation and to take turns in it.

Parents also can arrange situations in which the child is the leader of the conversation. For example, in a family which is together at supper time, each one should have time to tell about the day's activities. Children can discuss pets or toys, or tell of a funny happening. All participants are encouraged to focus on the member whose turn it is and the preschooler is given the same attention as is accorded an adult. In another family in which the father is at home only on weekends, Sunday morning is family conversation time and is used as in the previous example.

In both the previous cases, parents enjoy the pleasant communication and the chance to learn more about their children's thoughts and feelings. The preschoolers enjoy having their share of the limelight and are learning the conversation skills of both talking and listening.

Time Alone for Child and Parent
Preschoolers need to have some time with a parent that is theirs alone, time they need not share with other people. The majority of parents do not

have large amounts of time to devote to each child. The important thing is that the parent can use the time to really focus on the child's ideas, feelings, and needs.

In one family, bedtime is the only time a parent and child have a few minutes to share together when the child can lead their conversation; in another, father gives each of his boys their baths and they use that time to talk. One woman uses the time when she is driving her daughter home from day care for what the child calls, "My alone time."

A woman who was raising six children by herself reported to a parents' group how she managed to give each child 10 minutes of her time each day. She worked as a waitress and arrived home, very tired, at about 4 in the afternoon. She went directly to her room to lie down. Then each child came in alone for 10 minutes with her. She said she took the youngest child first, "Because it's harder for her to wait." She also said each child had quickly learned to respect the importance of the time for the others and did not interrupt, and that, "After that refreshing hour I'm ready to get up, fix dinner, and see them all together."

Parents generally report that they enjoy the time alone with a preschooler when they permit him to choose what they will talk about or do together. They report that they learn more about their children's joy, sadness, creativity, and humor.

Reading Together

The situation in which a parent reads to a child is in itself conducive to good communication. They sit close together so that both can see the book or magazine; often the child is on the parent's lap or the parent has an arm around her.

It is desirable for the parent to go beyond just reading words from the page. The parent can ask, "What do you think could happen next?" "What would you do if that dinosaur came into your house?" Such questions help your preschooler express not only creative ideas but also feelings.

In this setting the parent is again saying it's all right for you to say your ideas and feelings — so, again, the parent does *not* say, "You shouldn't feel like that," or "It's not nice to say that." Also, it is the parent who gives the child words to express joy, anger, frustration, love, etc.

In all of the above structured activities, as well as in all parent-preschooler encounters, the parent is teaching the child how to communicate. The goal is to help him communicate in constructive, rather than destructive, ways. An added bonus is that he also learns language skills.

Chapter 12
Words to
Love By

Katrina Katsarelis

*Start a cycle of
loving words today.*

"Sticks and stones may break my bones but words will never hurt me." I remember hearing that phrase for the first time during second grade recess when I witnessed a girl being teased by a group of children who were calling her "flea bag." I was impressed by her defiant comeback until I got closer and saw the tears streaming down her face. Her tears told me how she really felt. I now know that words do hurt and children are sensitive little beings who take words to heart.

Parents who maintain an ongoing effort to use appropriate words and positive messages when speaking to a child establish a foundation for successful family communication. This is the best way to teach a child — by example — words to love by.

Form a connection from the beginning

Speaking to a child from infancy can start you and your child on the road to a lifetime of successful communication. Babies delight in drinking in the rich tones of parents' voices and you can see it in a baby's expression when you speak. The best way to communicate with an infant is in a face-to-face position which encourages eye contact and conversation. Hold the baby in your lap; look directly at him and begin to initiate a dialogue. You're almost certain to receive an instant response in the form of gurgles and coos indicating that the baby is communicating with you.

As your child grows into an active, curious preschooler, continue talking to him on this personal level. Set aside regular times for having parent/ child conversations, such as during car rides, meal times, or at bedtime.

Five steps to healthy communication

1. *Have an open-door policy.* From the beginning, always encourage your child to come to you with questions or problems of all kinds, no matter how embarrassing or silly they seem. You may feel uncomfortable answering questions about certain subjects, such as sex. But, remember that information coming from you is better than the misinformation he may receive from his peers. You are your child's best teacher. When your child comes to you with a question or problem, take the time to listen.

2. *Teach children effective communication techniques.* At the age of 22 months, Jenny developed an irritating communication pattern common to her age group. When an object was out of her reach she would simply point at it and let out an ear-piercing scream until her startled mother placed it in her hands. This screaming eventually became intolerable. Her parents consulted her pediatrician and explained that although Jenny could speak in simple sentences, she would scream more than she would speak. The pediatrician advised them not to react to the screaming but only to Jenny's use of words. By simply changing their response to, "Jenny, use your words and tell me

what you want..." Jenny's screams quickly transformed into simple requests. Teaching a child early on to "use words" when communicating and then responding positively when she does, encourages the child's use of language.

3. Have patience and good listening skills. Some preschoolers take a long time to express a thought or finish a sentence. Patience is a definite necessity when communicating with preschoolers. By far, the most difficult part of communication for busy parents is listening. No matter how tempting it is to interrupt, stop yourself. Let your child complete the entire thought before initiating your response.

4. Avoid empty threats. Many parents make the mistake of blasting out empty threats to get children to behave. Youngsters learn to recognize the empty-threat-game and eventually test you on it. Trent is a three-year-old boy who hates getting dressed. If he had his choice he would wear nothing but a smile every day. "If you don't put your clothes on right now you're not going to the birthday party," his mother warned him 15 minutes before they were set to leave. Having no intention of missing the party, she didn't follow through on the consequence.

Trent had heard this type of meaningless threat before, so he continued to dawdle around in his Power Ranger underwear, knowing full well he would get to the birthday party eventually. A great many well-intentioned parents also say, "I really mean it," then refuse to follow through on the consequences — sending mixed signals to a child. Trent's mother could have said, "It's time to get dressed so that you won't miss the games and the ice cream." Now it's up to Trent to get dressed or suffer the consequences. It's important for children to receive clear and concise messages from parents — ones they know can and will be enforced.

5. Be a positive communicator. Imagine you're a young child and you're told 20 negative statements throughout the course of one day, times 7 days a week, times 52 weeks a year. After adding the numbers, it's easy to see how communication can break down in a negative household. Look at the following examples.

Children take our words literally
Young children are like sponges absorbing and processing information all around them. Despite their apparent resiliency, they are very sensitive to our words and the manner in which we say them. Tara, a four-year-old girl has a golden retriever named Laddy. Any time the front door is opened, Laddy darts out the door and races around the neighborhood, up and down the streets. The family constantly chases the dog, trying to catch him before he meets up with the bumper of a minivan. The last time Laddy

escaped, Tara's father blurted out, "I'm going to kill that dog!" Later, the father found Tara crying on the sofa. When he asked Tara what was the matter, Tara's response was, "I don't want you to kill Laddy. I love Laddy."

History repeats itself
Think back to your childhood. Was your mother a screamer? Was your father the withdrawn and silent type? Was conflict resolved quickly or never dealt with at all? Poor communication patterns set forth by your parents when raising you will likely be repeated in your own family if you don't take steps to change them. If you came from a wonderful and supportive home, it's almost second nature to raise your own children the same way.

How to make changes for the better
• *Rearrange and reword.* Take some common expressions used in your own household and give them a positive makeover. "Quit whining" transforms into "Please use your regular voice so I can understand what you're saying." Keep practicing and soon it will come without thinking.

• *Don't talk when you're angry.* When you hear a negative comment coming out of your mouth, stop yourself. If you have to, leave the room so you won't say something harsh. It's okay to explain to your child that you're too upset to talk right now but you'll speak to her later. Give yourself a moment alone to plan gentler words.

• *Adopt a no-hurting policy.* Just as some families have a no-hitting policy the same goes for banning hurtful words by children and parents.

• *End the legacy.* Remind yourself that you are a separate person from your parents and you're committed to raising your child without harsh words, criticism, or screaming. Recognizing the poor communication patterns in your own childhood is the first step in knowing how to make changes for the better.

Start a cycle of loving words today
The words we are using on our children now will likely be spoken to our grandchildren in the future so it's our responsibility to start a cycle of generations of loving words.

Although we will all make mistakes during these precious years, it's important to keep the mistakes minimal and select appropriate words that will give our children self-esteem and confidence. Some of what you say now will probably be ingrained in your child's mind for years to come. Take the opportunity to create memories of warm conversations in a home filled with endless "I love yous."

Dos and Don'ts When Communicating with Preschoolers

• DO get down on a child's eye-level when talking.

• DO speak to your child as politely as you speak to other people's children.

• DO use "I messages" whenever possible. "I messages" keep the focus on what you need from the child and away from personal faults of the child. "I need you to put your toys away before dinner," gets more results than, "You always leave your toys lying around."

• DO speak to your child the way you would like her to talk. If you use slang or an occasional cussword you can almost guarantee your child will say it too.

• DO apologize to a child whose feelings you've hurt. If you've yelled, or said something you regret, tell your child that you lost your temper and that you're sorry.

• DON'T force an apology out of a child who has done something wrong. Just because he says the words doesn't make it true. Forced apologies aren't real apologies.

• DON'T compare your child with others.

• DON'T hurt your child with nonverbal communication. The rolling of your eyes or a frustrated sigh when he talks to you tells the child instantly that he's getting on your nerves.

• DON'T place labels on your child. Children who are labeled with bad descriptions generally see themselves that way and may conform to the label. Children who are labeled as being good may find it difficult always to live up to the high standards set for them.

• DON'T lecture. A simple explanation will do the trick. Children will learn to see a lecture coming a mile away and tune out.

Negative Messages

I'm busy now.

What's the matter with you?

No yelling in the house.

Don't talk to me while I'm on the phone.

Get off the table.

Positive Messages

Sure, l can help you with that puzzle just as soon as I finish writing this letter.

Will you tell me with your words why you're so upset?

Please use your indoor voice.

I can talk to you about that as soon as I'm finished with this call.

Tables are not for climbing. I need you to get down.

Resources for Section Two: Communicating with Young Children

FOR ADULTS

"Not in Front of the Children..." How to Talk to Your Child About Tough Family Matters, by Dr. Lawrence Balter, with Peggy Jo Donahue. Viking Penguin, 1994. In this valuable parenting guide, Dr. Balter explains how to approach such topics as divorce, sex, illness, and death, with children of different ages. He gives practical suggestions about appropriate ways to talk to toddlers, preschoolers, and older children about these and other difficult subjects.

How to Talk So Kids Will Listen & Listen So Kids Will Talk, by Adele Faber and Elaine Mazlish. Avon Books, 1982. This popular book promotes effective parent/child interaction, offering mothers and fathers the skills to help children identify their feelings and solve their own problems.

Between Parent and Child: by Haim G. Ginott. Avon, 1976. This book has become a classic, showing parents how to talk to their child in language the child will understand.

P.E.T.: Parent Effectiveness Training, by Thomas Gordon. Plume paperback, 1975. In this important work the author details ways parents can listen "actively" and use language for better parent-child understanding.

Parent & Child: Getting Through to Each Other, by Lawrence Kutner, Ph.D. Avon Books, 1992. An authority on parent/child communication, the author provides comforting advice about understanding children of different ages.

The Unspoken Language of Children, by Suzanne Szasz. W.W. Norton, 1980. Children's emotions, both negative and positive, are powerfully depicted in this beautiful book of photographs. There is also a section on the effects of parents' body language on children. The photographer/ author uses brief text to explain and clarify what is happening in the pictures.

FOR CHILDREN

Willie's Not the Hugging Kind, by Joyce Durham Barrett. HarperCollins, 1989. Willie's friend, Jo-Jo, tells Willie that hugging is silly, so Willy doesn't want his family to hug him any more. Willie's sister comments, "You're just not the hugging kind then...if that's the way you feel." But it's not the way Willie feels, and when he realizes that he loves to hug and be hugged back, Willie can tell Jo-Jo that he's the one who's silly.

Let's talk About Feelings: Ellie's Day, by Susan Conlin and Susan Levine Friedman. Parenting Press, 1989. A little girl, Ellie, has many different feelings in one day, as she responds to different experiences: excitement, sadness, fear, happiness, etc. Each page of the book ends with a question to the reader, which could promote discussion of feelings.

Chatting, by Shirley Hughes. Candlewick Press, 1994. The little girl in this story loves to chat. She chats with the cat, with friends in the park, and on the telephone with Grandma and Grandpa. The author/illustrator is well known for her Alfie books, and her pictures are filled with affection and understanding for family life.

Tell Me a Story, Mama, by Angela Johnson. Orchard Books, 1989. In this delightful book, winner of the Ezra Jack Keats award, a young girl wants to hear her favorite stories about her mother's childhood. Mama is willing to tell her, but the girl knows the stories so well, Mama hardly has to say a word.

On Monday When It Rained, by Cherryl Kachenmeister. Houghton Mifflin, 1989. Photographs of a little boy with an expressive face illustrate a wide range of emotions throughout the week: from Monday when it rained and he couldn't play outside (disappointment), to Sunday when he had nobody to play with (loneliness) and beyond... Children will enjoy reading the text, guessing boy's feelings, and turning the page to see the unspoken message in the photograph.

Alexander and the Terrible, Horrible, No Good, Very Bad Day, by Judith Viorst. Macmillan, 1972. On a day when everything goes wrong for Alexander, he realizes that bad things can happen to others, too. This story invites children to imagine what better things will happen the next day.

I Like to Be Little, by Charlotte Zolotow. Crowell, 1987. In a loving dialog between mother and daughter, the little girl describes the joys of being a child.

When I Have a Little Girl, by Charlotte Zolotow. Harper Trophy, 1988. A mother listens with understanding as her little girl tells how different the rules will be when she has a daughter. Her little girl will be able to wear party dresses to school, have a friend overnight whenever she wants, and go out in her nightgown to watch the sun come up.

Section Three
Teaching
Children
Responsibility

Section Three
Teaching Children Responsibility

Introduction

Should I take that job? Should I buy a house? Should I give up smoking? Surely serious decision-making is a feature of the adult years, not of early childhood.

But how can we make thoughtful choices as adults if we have no experience with decision-making in our early years?

Young children can learn to make decisions by practicing that skill with events that have meaning in their lives: What kind of juice do I want to drink for breakfast? What story would I like to hear at bedtime? What toy will I choose to buy with the money grandma gave me?

One method for teaching responsibility is to assign preschoolers some household chores. There are tasks that can be done by young children that are appropriate, safe, and not just busywork: setting the table, watering plants, folding laundry, feeding pets, and other simple chores.

The authors provide many examples of teaching responsible behavior. And one writer notes that, "When you teach children the skills they need to make good decisions and to act responsibly, you teach a basic skill for successful living."

Chapter 13
Guiding Preschoolers
to
Behave Responsibly

Cynthia Burns

*Responsibility means understanding
that it makes Jason happy
when you share your tricycle.*

Johnny is an active three year old. He takes all of his toys out of the brightly colored plastic bins his mother bought for sorting and doesn't put them back. He leaves his clothes wherever he happens to take them off. His exasperated mother laments that he's young and can't be expected to pick up after himself.

Johnny has a four-year-old cousin named Michael. Michael is a great help around the house. He picks up his toys before he goes to bed and he puts napkins and forks at each place at the table before dinner. He even puts his socks and underwear away in his dresser.

You've met children like Johnny and Michael. It's not that one is good and the other isn't. It's just that Michael is in the beginning stages of learning to be responsible while Johnny has yet to receive guidance on responsible behavior.

Having a responsible child isn't the luck of the draw

Most child development experts agree that it is the parents' job to teach responsibility. But what does that mean? Responsibility is instilling a set of values that will stay with your child even when you're not there. Let's face it, there's a lot to be responsible for:

Possessions: putting away toys, putting dirty clothes in a hamper, or not leaving a jacket at a friend's house.

Work: helping to set the table and doing other simple household chores.

Actions: understanding that it hurts Lisa when you hit her, or that it makes Jason happy when you share your tricycle.

Character: treating others with care and consideration.

Linda and Richard Eyre, authors of *Teaching Your Children Responsibility* (see Resources, page 112), believe children learn responsibility in a sequential order.

• Responsibility to parents (obedience).

• Responsibility to society for who you are and what you do (morality).

• Responsibility to self (discipline).

• The highest level is to be responsible to and for other people (service).

They also believe that children start learning responsibility before they start school.

Dr. Kevin Leman, author and family counselor, says that you give children responsibility and let them learn how to handle it through trial and error. And, when they make errors, there are consequences. This way, children can learn that choices must be carefully considered because the results cannot always be readily reversed.

Teaching responsibility at different developmental stages

By understanding what a child is capable of at different stages of development, parents can provide opportunities for their children to learn responsibility. Even two-year-olds can understand that their behavior can help or hurt themselves and others. Children begin to understand the concept of responsibility at about 2 1/2 years old. On the simplest level, responsibility is listening to parents and caring for possessions.

In nursery school, Linda and Karen, who are both three, know that they must put away the blocks before they can go to the table for snacktime, and that puzzles go back on the shelf before they can sit on the rug for a story. They have the ability to listen to the explanation of the rules and comply with them because they understand the reasons for them. They use simple social skills such as taking turns.

In the class of four-year-olds, the children learn cooperation and share more readily. They know to wait patiently to take a turn stirring the pudding the class is making, and that they each have two minutes to ride the trike before letting the next child ride it. If anyone doesn't follow the rules, it is often the children, not the teachers, who set the offending child straight.

You can spot a responsible child. He or she has a strong sense of self-esteem, a positive belief in himself, can empathize with others, has good judgment, contributes his fair share, and understands the consequences of behavior.

Although a tall order, you can help create a responsible child by teaching values a day at a time through your words and by your example. Giving children responsibility and providing an opportunity for them to demonstrate responsible behavior is a delicate balance. You don't want to give them more than they can handle, yet you don't want to inhibit the progress they've made. It is important to let children prove they can handle a new task in your presence before letting them do it alone.

Assigning household chores

Begin teaching responsibility by assigning household chores to your child. Preschoolers like to help. They feel great satisfaction just from the doing. It helps them know that they are needed and appreciated.

The chores should be appropriate to your child's age and capabilities. You would not want your three year old carrying knives or glasses to the kitchen table, but he can certainly handle napkins, spoons and plastic cups. Don't worry about efficiency; it's not important if the napkin isn't folded to your liking.

Try providing child-sized tools such as a small broom or rake, a lightweight watering can, or a low stepstool to reach the sink. It is also helpful to establish a checklist. Letting your child check off a chore or place a sticker next to a job description when it is completed gives her a sense of accomplishment. (This still works for me!)

Let your child pick jobs he or she wants to do. When possible, give her a choice of chores, such as watering the flowers or setting the table. To be sure your child knows how to do the chore, do it with her several times. Emphasize that once responsibility is accepted, she is expected to follow through. It isn't something to do only when she feels like it.

There are some things for you to keep in mind:
• Don't rush in to take responsibility away because you're behind schedule.
• Ask or request rather than order or demand.
• Learn to use natural or logical consequences as a teaching tool, not as punishment. When three-year-old Angela deliberately breaks her toy drum in a fit of anger, she realizes that she can't play it anymore. She has to live with the consequences of her actions.

How Parents Can Foster Responsible Behavior

Developing responsibility is a gradual process. Begin by giving your child chores to do around the house.

Let your **two or three year old** choose from these household chores:

√ pick up toys and put them away
√ put books on a low shelf and magazines in a rack
√ sweep the floor
√ put napkins, plates and silverware on the table
√ put dirty clothes in a hamper
√ clear one's own place at the table
√ brush teeth, wash and dry hands and face and brush hair
√ put away folded clothes in drawers
√ help with baking or cooking under adult supervision
√ put groceries away in the pantry

Let your **four or five year old** be responsible for several of these additional chores:

√ put items in the grocery cart
√ feed pets
√ water house plants
√ help with yard and garden work
√ help make the beds
√ help do the dishes or load the dishwasher
√ dust the furniture
√ make a sandwich
√ match socks according to color
√ polish shoes

Responsibility As Compassion

At age two, Megan can express concern for Jake when he falls down, or ask why Sara is absent from a play group. By three, Megan can soothe Jake with hugs and pats. She feels sorry for Jake and feels remorse if she caused the crying.

Two-and-three-year-olds are capable of understanding that they can hurt other people's feelings. Parents can promote sharing and not hitting. Three-year-olds are more cooperative than two-year-olds. They are old enough to learn basic manners, to say, "Please" and, "Thank you" and to understand that good manners make others feel good.

By four, kids are ready to participate more actively in a project that demonstrates social responsibility and compassion. This is a good time for your child to help you bag old clothes and toys, and go with you to donate these items.

Four-and-five-year-olds try to do what's right to please their parents. A five- year-old can respond to a question like, "How would you feel if someone wouldn't play with you?" with an answer such as, "It would hurt my feelings."

Money and Responsibility

Learning the value of money and how to handle it is another area of responsibility. Beginning at age three or four, let your child buy something for 50 cents or less. Work with him so that he can learn the names of coins and bills. At this age, children understand that parents give people in stores bills and coins in exchange for food and other items.

At some point you may want to add money for doing certain chores — not only to sweeten the pot, but to develop another facet of responsibility. Three-year-olds enjoy earning money. Try providing a clear plastic bank to store shiny pennies. Kids may not understand the value of money, but enjoy being rewarded for work. Four-year-olds love to earn money — pennies, nickels and dimes — for their jobs. They understand enough about money to use it to buy something they want.

Giving your child an allowance provides practice using money. The amount is determined by your finances, standards, and what the money is expected to cover. Some people believe that children should be able to spend the allowance any way they see fit. This allows them to enjoy what they bought or to learn from purchasing mistakes.

Responsibility At School

Patti Greenberg Wollman, a preschool teacher and an author, says responsibility is an internal mechanism. At a young age, responsibility for social behavior begins with the ability to control impulses. In preschool social skills are emphasized and children are reminded not to hit and not to hurt. In her classroom, she promotes the concept of good citizenship and responsible, positive behavior.

Chapter 14
Responsibility
vs.
Obedience

Elizabeth Crary

In order to develop responsibility,
a child must have the choice
to decline the task.

Four kindergarten girls were walking home after school. A man drove up and asked them to get in his car. They said, "No. We're not supposed to go with strangers."

The man replied that their fathers had sent him. Three of the girls got in the car. The fourth girl continued home and told her mother what happened. The other girls were quickly recovered.

When asked why she didn't go with the man too, the fourth girl replied, "My Daddy always tells me to think. I didn't think he would send someone to get me if he didn't tell me first."

This story illustrates a big difference between <u>obedience</u> and <u>responsibility</u>. *With obedience, the child is expected to do what he or she is told. Obedience needs no agreement on the part of the child. The decision and motivation come from outside the child,* (*Pick Up Your Socks*, by E. Crary, p. 7). Responsibility, however, is the <u>thoughtful</u> acceptance of a task or obligation, regardless of who suggests it.

Oftentimes when parents say, "I want my child to be more responsible about picking up his toys," what they really want is obedience. For example, if you told your daughter, "Put your toys away now," and she did, that would be obedience. If she did not put them away, that would be disobedience.

In order to develop responsibility, a child must have the choice to decline the task. If you **ask** your son whether or not he wants to help you set the table for dinner, he may say *yes* or *no*. *Either* answer would show responsibility. It's only irresponsible if he says, "Yes" and does not follow through. However, there are certain areas where parents must retain control. For example, Adam may not play in the street, or walk two blocks alone to a friend's house. The challenge for the parent is to sort out what decisions a child may be responsible for.

Our society needs people who can exercise both obedience and responsibility. If a person is only obedient, he becomes a target for peer pressure and cults. However, if everyone insisted on making *every* decision to suit himself, life would be chaotic and the highways unsafe as people drove every which way.

Responsibility is not an "all or nothing" skill. It develops over time. The **first step** is for a child to help with a task, (for example, your toddler can help you tidy up her room, picking up the playthings and putting them on a shelf); the **second step** is to do the task when reminded (such as reminding your preschooler that it's time to put away her toys before going to sleep); and finally, the **third step** is to take full responsibility to do the task without supervision or reminding (this last step usually occurs after the preschool years).

The average age when children help get themselves dressed is two-and-a-half. They get dressed when reminded at about five, and dress without being reminded at about ten. Since these are averages, many children dress earlier and others later. In either case, there is a large gap (of several years!) between when the child can *physically* do the task and when he can be *responsible* for doing the task alone.

You can encourage the development of responsibility by teaching children ways to motivate and remind themselves, as well as by letting them make some of their own decisions. The activities that follow offer a variety of ways to build a sense of responsibility in young children. When you teach children the skills they need to make good decisions and to act responsibly, you teach a basic skill for successful living.

Activities That Help Build Responsibility

The way you interact with your child affects what they learn about responsibility. The following are some simple things you can do to encourage responsibility.

Distinguish between questions and orders.

Ask questions that can be answered **yes** or **no** — *only if the child has a real choice.* Don't ask, "Do you want to get dressed now?"—*if the only acceptable answer is* **yes**. Your child may assume that either **yes** or **no** is acceptable. If you phrase your orders as though they were requests, and reject your child's answers time after time, he will have difficulty learning to make good decisions.

Alternate types of praise.

Children need encouragement. When you say, "I'm glad you picked up your toys so quickly," children sense your pleasure. You are offering them praise from an external source. As children grow older they need to feel the pride in accomplishment themselves. Gradually you can reflect their internal satisfaction, for example, "I bet you're proud of how quickly you picked up all your toys."

Picture your child being responsible.

Draw pictures or take photos of the tasks your child is supposed to do. Hang the picture on the child's door or in a family "hall of honor."

Let children choose their areas of responsibility.

List several tasks you would like your children to do. For example: pick up belongings, put dirty clothes in laundry area, fold clean laundry, hang up clothes, set the table, bring in the newspaper, feed the pets, etc. Let them pick which ones they will be responsible for.

Reward responsible actions differently from obedience.

If you give your preschooler one sticker for picking up her toys promptly when requested, give her two stickers for picking them up without being reminded. Everyone likes recognition for what they have done, particularly when they are learning a new skill or habit.

Establish clear criteria for success.

How clean is clean? How soon is soon? Often the standards are clear to the parent, but not to the child. If you don't want your child simply to learn by <u>failing</u> to do the task as you expected, you need to make your messages as clear as possible. For example: "I want you to pick up those toys soon!" is not a clear message, as "soon" may mean 5 minutes to you, but it probably won't have the same meaning to your preschooler. However, if you say, "You need to pick up those toys before you have your milk and cookies," your preschooler will have a better understanding of your expectations.

Model the behavior you want. Parents delay responding to children's requests for help with, "In a minute," or "When I'm done here." But somehow that time never comes. Set a timer and tell the child, "I'll come when it rings," and then do it, whether it is convenient or not.

Play "What would you do if...?"
Most preschoolers are taught a set of rules rather than the principles behind them. If they run into a new situation, they don't know what to do. You can teach them to think by asking, "What would you do if...?" (What if we were in a shopping mall and you got lost? What if you see a wire hanging from a pole? What if you found something on the ground that looked good to eat?) Respect whatever answer the child comes up with.

When you goof, share with your child
how you plan to do better next time.
Sometimes children feel overwhelmed by all that is expected of them. They need models more for how to improve, than how to be perfect. If you forgot to take an important paper to work you can say, "Darn! Next time I had better write a note and tape it on the door so I will remember."

Help your child find ways to motivate himself or herself.
In the beginning parents may need to provide the motivation (rewards) to children. However, it is useful for children to learn to praise themselves and give themselves treats. You might say, for example, "What would you like to do as a special treat when you get all your toys picked up?"

Teach children ways to make unpleasant tasks fun.
One characteristic of successful people is the ability to get themselves to do things they don't really want to do. You might explain to your preschooler, "Sometimes it's easier to do a job if you do one part of the job at a time—so let's fold only the clothes that are the color red first. Then we'll do each color by itself."

There is no one way to be responsible. Children need a variety of tools to use in different situations. You can expand upon these ideas to give children the skills and experiences they need to be responsible.

Chapter 15
Helping Children Develop Self-control

Neala S. Schwartzberg

*Adults who model self-control
help youngsters
develop self-control.*

The chocolate-chip cookies have just come out of the oven. Three-year-old Sarah watches as her mother sets them on the counter. The doorbell rings. As mother leaves to answer the door, she says, "Don't touch the cookies; they are too hot to eat. As soon as they cool off we'll have some with milk." With her mother gone from the room, Sarah eyes the cookies.

Johnny, who is five, is angry. His little brother, Tim, has just taken his favorite book and ripped out two pages. Johnny knows Tim is too young to know better, and has been told repeatedly never to hit him. Now faced with the mutilated book Johnny has called for his father. But he is still very angry and is ready to retaliate.

Sarah's mother has just told her not to eat the cookies until they cool. Johnny knows that he is not allowed to hit his younger brother. But without parental supervision will they obey the rules? Will Sarah stop herself from eating a cookie? Will Johnny resist the temptation to hit his brother? It is not too difficult for children to obey the rules when adults are watching them. They know if they misbehave they will get caught and punished. But we can't always be there to monitor a child's behavior. At some point children must be able to control their own behavior without relying on adults to do it for them. That is the essence of self-control.

Shifting the Source of Control from Outside to Inside
Sarah's mother has clearly set up a situation in which Sarah can sneak a cooky now or obey her mother and enjoy sharing cookies and milk with her later. How can Sarah control herself until her mother returns?

Before the age of 30-36 months, children can't seem to wait even one minute for something they want. After that there is a clear improvement in the ability of youngsters to delay gratification (like waiting for the cookies to cool). But even then about two minutes is all they can wait. Part of the reason for the improvement lies in their increased ability to use language. They need to be able to take the adult commands like, "Don't touch" and use them as guides to their own behavior, repeating the rules softly as a reminder.

Older preschoolers use a variety of strategies to help them resist temptation. Psychologist and researcher Walter Mischel has been studying the way children delay gratification. In a typical study, preschool children are given a choice between a small candy now, or several pieces later on. The children want to wait, but how can they bridge the time gap? One very effective technique was to distract themselves. The youngsters created their own diversions like singing and playing games. In another technique the children focused on how good it is to wait, or they imagined the candy was something less attractive. One technique which *didn't* work was to think about their delight in the reward. In adult terms, it is is like putting up a large picture of the dream vacation you are saving money for. On the one hand it reminds you why you are saving, but it also reminds you that you don't have it. A better solution would be to chart progress towards a goal rather than focussing on the goal itself. For adults this might mean depositing the money each week into a special vacation account, and watching as the balance goes up... and up. For a child like Sarah, who has to wait several minutes for a special treat, a simple timer may be the solution. She can see the time go by and maybe even hear it through the clicking. It would also be a good idea to put the cookies out of sight.

Johnny's problem is a little more complicated. Although he is not delaying gratification, he is showing self control by not hitting his younger brother.

Children's aggression changes with age. Children below the age of three are more likely to act aggressively on impulse. As they get older, they become better able to judge the other child's intention. Therefore, the innocent actions of Tim would be less likely to provoke an aggressive response. Actions perceived as deliberate, however, would still be seen as a reason for retaliation. Older children can also express their anger verbally which can help reduce their physical outbursts. They have also learned the rules against physical aggression. In Johnny's case he can still use language to remind himself, "I'm not allowed to hit Tim; he's too little to know better."

Adults can help youngsters to develop self-control, even when the child is provoked. Clearly state the rules and the reasons for the rules, but also acknowledge the youngster's feelings. "I know you are angry at Tim because he ripped your book. It is OK to be angry, but it is not OK to hit Tim. He's too little to know better and you could really hurt him. When Tim does something to make you mad, remind yourself 'I'm not allowed to hit Tim; he's too little to know better.' Then come and tell me and I'll handle the situation."

Helping Children Build Self-Control
Adults who model self-control help youngsters develop self-control. Every day before my son leaves for school, he asks me if I will be playing our new game on the computer. Every day I remind him that as much as I'd like to play the game we bought, I have to wait until my work is done. Rules such as, "Work comes before play" can guide not only a child's life, but should guide the adult who is his role model. Verbalizing how you are saving up money for special occasions is another example of how you can demonstrate and reinforce the lessons of self-control.

The way we handle children's transgression also sends them a message. Adults get very angry but we don't strike out. We calm down and discuss the problem behavior with the youngster. If we feel that we are beginning to lose our self-control we leave the room to "cool off." When adults use self-control children not only learn the "how to" but also that being in control of their own behavior is the mature "adult" way to behave. The children learn that they can be angry without striking out, and the ways to handle that anger.

Provide a few simple, basic rules for behavior and explain why they are important. These rules should be truly necessary rather than based on convenience:

• Do not go into the street alone. Always hold an adult's hand in parking lots and when crossing the street. Cars may not see you or you may not see the car. It's just too dangerous and you could be seriously hurt.

• Be gentle with pets. Pulling ears and tails is no fun for an animal. You can hurt them, and they could bite you.

• Wash your hands after using the bathroom. There are germs on your hands and you need to wash them away with soap and water, otherwise you could get sick.

There are many rules adults would like children to follow, but most are based more on our convenience than the children's health and safety. Putting toys away when they are finished playing is an important rule, but if you react with the same intensity to both blocks on the living room floor and wandering away from an adult in the department store, how will a youngster know which is truly important? It is important to recognize and praise children when they do show self-control. When Johnny's father comes in and sees that, although sorely provoked, Johnny has not hit his little brother, a hug and a good word help let Johnny know he did the right thing. Sarah's mother can also praise Sarah for waiting, even giving her an extra cookie for being so patient.

Have reasonable expectations. Young children are easily tempted, so try not to set standards too difficult for them to meet. Help them control their behavior by giving them tools and techniques (See Tools and Techniques page 105).

It is helpful for adults to monitor situations where problems are likely to occur and be ready to step in and gently remind children of the rules. No matter how much play material is available, two children are likely to want to play with the same red shovel. When one child is tugging it away from the other youngster, and a fight erupts, be ready with, "We don't hit; there are better ways to settle problems." Ask the children about ways to settle the dispute and remind them of how to solve the problem for next time. They won't learn immediately, but the final goal is to help them control their own behavior when you are not there. Teach them with patience and understanding and your rules will become their own internal rules. And that is the real source of self-control.

Tools and Techniques

Tools and Techniques

The essence of self-control is to stop and think, then act.

1. Strong emotions well up quickly, but dissipate with time. The key is to help the youngster become aware that she is getting angry and upset, and then to allow herself the time to calm down. Discuss with the child how she feels when she begins to get angry. When she recognizes that feeling what should she do? Counting to ten is an old standard technique for giving ourselves a chance to calm down but for young children taking several deep breaths might be better.

2. Think before acting. What are the rules? What am I supposed to do? Make the rules easy to verbalize so the youngster can use them as a guide (see example about being gentle with pets, page 103). You can even practice situations which are particularly troublesome (hold hands while pretending to cross the street).

3. Changing the focus of attention is an important technique. Children have to wait for many things. They have to wait until all the children have their coats on to go outside and play. They have to wait until the toys are put away to have snack time. And waiting is very hard for youngsters. Learning how to distract themselves by singing a little song, looking around to see what is new and interesting are just two of the ways children can change the focus of their attention.

4. Break the connection between stimulus and response. Sometimes youngsters react out of habit. They see something and they grab for it. For example, a child who sees another child with an attractive toy and snatches it away is acting on impulse. Stop the action. If you can, stop it even before the youngster gets his hand on the toy, certainly before the child has the chance to play with it. Then remind the child of the rules, "No — no, that's not your toy. What do we do when we see a toy we want but someone is playing with it?" Then state the rule with the child: "We ask for a turn."

Chapter 16
Learning
to Make
Decisions

Pegine Ecchevaria

*Decision-making is a learned
skill that will be
refined and developed
as children grow and mature.*

Jan is driving to the toy store with her two children, Zack, 5 1/2 and Ariel, 3 1/2. Each child has been saving money for a toy, and it is their choice as to what they will buy. Zack has been wanting an accessory for his train set, or another dinosaur to add to his collection, or a new game for his computer. Ariel has an equally long list of things. Each child has only a limited amount of money to spend. Each is excited about making his or her own decision.

Learning to make decisions

How do children learn to make decisions? How can parents and professionals assist children in developing their decision-making skills? Decision-making is a learned skill that will be refined and developed as children grow and mature. When we give young children opportunities to make simple decisions, they are practicing the skills they will be faced with as adults every day. From simple decisions like, "What are we going to have for breakfast?" children will grow up to face the more complex and difficult ones such as, "Should we buy the house?" "Should I change jobs?" etc.

The decision-making process

Making decisions is such a valuable skill that it may be helpful to see how Jan prepared the children to make up their own minds as to which toy they would buy.

• *First, we need to be clear about our options.* Jan made sure to discuss their options with Zack and Ariel. Before they left to go shopping, each child dictated a list of their possible choices, which Jan wrote down.

• *We need to be aware of the limitations.* Jan set limits as to safety and appropriateness for the toys chosen by the children.

• *We need to be aware of the costs.* Next to each item on the list, Jan wrote the cost that she had seen in advertisements or catalogs. The children compared the cost with the amount of money they had saved.

• *We need to make comparisons.* Jan discussed each item with the children as she read the list to them, so that they could examine the good points and the bad. For Zack that meant looking at the play time involved. On a typical day does he spend more time playing with his dinosaurs than his train? When was the last time he played his computer game and why does he want another one?

• *We need to avoid being distracted by items that we don't really want, but seem attractive at the moment.* Jan told Zack that he may only choose between the train equipment, a dinosaur, or a computer game. It was made clear that when he goes into the store he must not get distracted by the hockey sticks, action men or bicycle paraphernalia. The same goes for Ariel; she may only choose from the list she has prepared.

• *After all the above points are adhered to, the final decision is the child's.* Jan can mention the toy that she thinks Zack would enjoy most, and point out her reasons for making such a choice. For example, "Zack, I think you would enjoy the train accessory most because you play every day with your trains. By adding to your collection you can build bigger and better things!" But she has to respect Zack's final decision.

Living with the consequences of your decision

As parents we can also point out the consequences of making a decision. This is a tough idea for children younger than four to understand. In Zack's case, Jan reminded him that once he started to play with the toy he bought he wouldn't be able to change it for something else.

For children 2 1/2 to 4 the concept of consequence (cause and effect) is developmentally just beginning to play a part in their lives. For these youngsters, choices should be limited to those items that would be appropriate. For example, when allowing Ariel to choose her clothes during the winter time, Jan asks Ariel, "What would you like to wear — a skirt with warm stockings or pants?" If she had said, "Ariel, time to get dressed. It is cold outside; what would you like to wear?" Ariel might choose her favorite summer dress. She would not understand the consequence of wearing a cotton dress on a cold winter day. Therefore, Jan allows her to choose only within the category of warm clothing. This allows Ariel to make the decision — yet does not create a problem of allowing her to choose inappropriate clothing. (If convenient, you should remove all summer clothing from the child's room and pack it away for the winter — and do the same with the winter clothing during warm weather.)

After making the decision

Once the decision is made there is usually a sense of relief and happiness. It is also the time to be reflective. For children this is the time when we can help them see the process of their decision making, pointing out the different phases: 1) We need to be clear about what we have to decide. 2) We have to consider the things that will influence our decision. 3) We have to think about the consequences of our decision. We can also talk with the children about the different emotions that they felt throughout the process.

Children cannot suddenly learn to make decisions when they reach eighteen if they haven't had the opportunities to do so as they grow up. The above examples of the decision-making process with regard to buying toys and choosing what to wear are not theoretical. Children can learn to make decisions from a very early age. You can limit the selection that they can choose from, but they can decide :

• what kind of cake they want at their birthday party
• what story they want you to read at bedtime
• whether they drink their juice from a pink cup or a yellow cup

Importance of the decision-making process

Decisions are an integral part of every human life. Each day we go through hundreds of decisions, from small (I'm hungry, so I will eat) to large (I'm going to apply for that job). By teaching our children how to make decisions, we are giving them a firm, secure base that will enable them to be *independent, courageous,* and *responsible.* *Independent* because they will be able to be secure in their own decision-making process and not rely on others to make the decision for them. *Courageous,* because having acquired a solid base in the decision process gives the child the confidence to make a difficult decision and be aware of the risks involved. *Responsible,* because once they have been given the opportunity to make decisions they also become responsible for the consequences of the decisions.

Decision-making Tips

About one year old

• Limit choices between two simple contrasting items (example: a toy car and a tambourine). One-year-olds are not mature enough to be able to choose between a red car and a blue car. (See SCENARIO.)

• Be aware of their limited attention span (5 minutes on average).

• When we give choices we must be clear that it is the child's choice, <u>not ours</u>. Often we want them to choose what <u>we</u> would like rather than accepting whatever their choice is.

SCENARIO

Tommy (14 months) just woke up from his nap. After mommy cuddled him and gave him a snack she said, "Tommy, look I have a car (she holds it in one hand) and look I have a tambourine (she shakes it in the other) what does Tommy want?"

About two years old

• Two year olds can remember favorite places they like to visit. Let them choose their next outing. However, if they are to choose a particular place, the child must be able to recall and identify the site.

SCENARIO

Cristina (2 years old) loves to go out with her mother. She has two favorite outdoor parks, one with a large slide and the other with a sandbox. Mommy says "Cristina where do you want to go, to the park with the sandbox or to the park with the big slide?"

About three years old
• Three-year-olds begin to distinguish between colors, shapes and sizes.
• Encourage your child to use words to verbalize his thinking process about his choices.

SCENARIO
Jemal asked for a glass of milk. "Do you want the red glass or the blue one?" his mother asked. "The blue one," said Jemal. As he drank his milk his mother smiled and asked, "Jemal, why did you choose the blue one?" "You know why mom; blue is my favorite color!"

About four years old
• Four-year-olds usually want to be as independent as possible. This is the time for parents to allow children to make more decisions (within   reasonable limits) about clothing, food, or games to be played.

SCENARIO
Jeffrey opened up one of his birthday presents. It was something he had wanted for a long time: a pair of Superman pajamas. He put on the pajamas immediately. Later, his mother said, "Jeffrey, it's time to get dressed. Company is coming." Jeffrey replied, "Today, I want to wear my Superman pajamas all day." His mother allowed him to do so.

About five years old
• At five, children are bombarded with choices every day. School, friends, and outside activities begin to play an important role in the decision-making process. Five-year-olds have decisions to make about which friend to play with, and which activity to choose in class. Parents and professionals can help by discussing the decision process at home and in class, and by talking about options and consequences.

SCENARIO
In the kindergarten classroom, the children are sitting around the morning activity board. Each child has the opportunity to choose an activity. The choices are: painting, block play, dress-up, science area, and arts and crafts. It's Katie's turn. Her favorite was dress-up clothes. Then she remembered that it was her mother's birthday and she'd like to paint a picture for her. "I'll take painting," she decided.

About six years old
• At six children become more social and develop strong friendships. Often their interests are based on being with their friends.

SCENARIO
George wants to join Cub Scouts. He is already enrolled in an after school computer class and science club. He was given a choice by his parents, "If you want to join Cub Scouts, you have to drop one of the other two." George decided, "I want to be in Cub scouts because Patrick is there. I really like my computer class so I'll drop science club for now."

Resources for Section Three: Teaching Children Responsibility

FOR ADULTS

The Moral Intelligence of Children, by Robert Coles. Random House, 1997. In this inspiring and highly readable book, the Pulitzer Prize-winning author of *The Spiritual Life of Children,* uses stories and incidents from his own experiences as a teacher and child psychiatrist to illustrate his beliefs about "the way character develops in the young; about the way they obtain their values; about what makes a good person, and about how we might help shape a child's moral intelligence." An important book for teachers and parents.

Pick Up Your Socks...and other skills growing children need, by Elizabeth Crary. Parenting Press, 1990. This practical guide to raising responsible children, by the author of a chapter in this book, distinguishes between responsibility and obedience, and explains why both are necessary in different situations. It provides guidelines, exercises, and useful charts— such as a job chart illustrating at what ages children can do specific house-hold chores.

Teaching Your Children Responsibility, by Linda and Richard Eyre, Fireside/Simon and Schuster, 1994. The Eyres identify twelve simple kinds of responsibility and provide simple, practical games and activities that you can use to teach your children these concepts.

Children Learn What They Live, by Dorothy Law Nolte and Rachel Harris. Workman Publishing, 1998. The poem by Dr. Nolte, which begins, *If children live with criticism, they learn to condemn...* has been an inspiration to parents and teachers since it was published in 1954. Each of the 49 couplets of the poem becomes the focus of a chapter in this insightful book.

FOR CHILDREN

No Jumping on the Bed! by Tedd Arnold. Puffin Pied Piper, 1996. Walter ignores his father's warning to stop jumping on the bed in this imaginative look at the consequences of unacceptable behavior. As a result, his bed crashes through the floor to the downstairs neighbor's apartment! Down and down he goes, carrying the neighbors with him to each floor below. Is it all a dream? No matter. Walter decides, "No more jumping on the bed for me." But what about his brother Delbert? Watch out below!

The Little Red Hen, by Byron Barton. HarperCollins, 1993. With bright, childlike illustrations, the author/illustrator retells the classic story of the hen who asks her friends for help with planting, threshing, and grinding the wheat. "Not I," says each of them. When it is time to eat the bread she has baked, the little red hen tells the other animals the result of their uncooperative behavior — they will not share in the eating!

Arthur's Birthday, by Marc Brown. Joy Street/Little, Brown, 1989. What a dilemma! Arthur's birthday party and Muffy's birthday party are being held on the same day! Which one should their friends attend? Some super problem-solving skills help to give everyone a happy celebration.

Kinderkittens: Who Took the Cookie from the Cookie Jar? by Stephanie Calmenson. Scholastic Cartwheel, 1995. The kittens love to sing their song about *Who Took the Cookie from the Cookie Jar?* and the school principal comes by to listen. At snacktime, a cookie really is missing! Who is the culprit? Includes words & music to the song and a cookie recipe.

Shortcut, by Donald Crews. Greenwillow, 1992. A group of children are taking a shortcut home by walking along a railroad track. "We should have taken the road. But it was late, and it was getting dark, so we started down the track." The author/illustrator helps you feel the danger in the air as they jump off the track when the train rushes past them. And you know they mean it when they say, "We walked home without a word.... And we didn't take the shortcut again."

Hunky Dory Ate It, by Katie Evans. Puffin Unicorn, 1996. In this book with simple rhyming text, the mischievous puppy, Hunky Dory, eats everything in sight. As a result, he gets very sick, and must go to the vet for help.

Jamaica Tag-Along, by Juanita Havill. Houghton Mifflin, 1990. Jamaica's older brother, Ossie, doesn't like her to tag along when he plays basketball in the park with his friends so Jamaica goes sadly to play in the sandbox. A toddler wants to play with her, but she doesn't want him to mess up her sand castle. However, when she sees that she's treating the toddler the way her brother had treated her, she lets him help build a beautiful castle. Even her big brother is impressed when he sees it, and joins them in their construction.

The Carrot Seed, by Ruth Krauss. Harper & Row, 1945. In this classic story, a little boy plants a carrot seed, waters it, and pulls the weeds every day. And, despite his family's doubts, the little boy's efforts are rewarded by an enormous carrot.

Mrs. Toggle's Zipper, by Robin Pulver. Aladdin 1993. When Mrs. Toggle arrives to teach her class that winter morning, she can't take her coat off, because the zipper is stuck. The children, the principal, the school nurse, everybody tries to help. Ah! but Mr. Abel, the custodian, uses a little common sense, and finds just the right tool to open the zipper.

The Big Storm, by Rhea Tregebov. Hyperion, 1993. Everybody in Jeanette's family has a job in the delicatessen that the family owns. Jeanette sweeps the floor, her brothers help with deliveries and even the cat takes responsibility for keeping the mice away. One stormy night, Jeanette forgets about her faithful cat waiting out in the snow for her. But Jeanette cares about her pet, and the cat is saved by the loving treatment she receives.

Alexander, Who Used to Be Rich Last Sunday, by Judith Viorst. Aladdin Books edition, 1988. Last Sunday, Alexander's grandparents gave him a dollar, and he felt rich. But somehow the money disappeared, and Alexander doesn't feel rich anymore.

The Biggest Bear, by Lynd Ward. Houghton Mifflin, 1952. This favorite story tells of a little boy's pet bear, who grows so large and unmanageable that the boy, Johnny, is told by his father that he must bring his pet back into the woods. But the bear keeps coming back home, and Johnny's father decides that the bear must be shot. A Caldecott Medal winner, this book is full of suspense, with a surprising happy ending.

Follow Me! by Harriet Ziefert. Puffin *Easy-To-Read Level 1, 1996.* Lee listens carefully to his mother when she takes him shopping. "Follow me!" she says, and gets into the elevator. The doors close before Lee can get on. But the child remembers what his mother had told him she was going to buy, and is able to find her.

Section Four
Coping
with
Stress
in
Special
Situations

Section Four
Coping with Stress
in _Special_ Situations

Introduction

Young children like the comfort of routine. They like to be assured that — in the structure of their day — first comes juice and cookies, then comes a story, then comes naptime. They feel safe when the pattern of each day is familiar and predictable.

The intrusion of a change in routine may throw them for a loop. Plan even a pleasant diversion like a birthday party or a family trip and your youngster may behave in ways that make you wonder, "What's become of my cheerful, well-behaved child?"

If even happy interruptions to the regular routine are stressful, how much more so when the situation involves a move to a new home, a divorce, or a death in the family. The authors of this section provide valuable advice about how to cope in these special situations.

SECTION FOUR

COPING WITH STRESS IN SPECIAL SITUATIONS

Chapter 17
Helping Preschoolers Cope with Stress

Aletha J. Solter

*Any major change
in a child's life
can be
a cause of stress*

Tommy, recently toilet-trained, begins wetting and soiling himself after the birth of his sister.

Three-year-old Vanessa starts having nightmares after watching a scary program on TV.

Five-year-old Michael picks fights with other children at school when his parents begin talking about getting a divorce.

These children are all exhibiting signs of stress.

Causes of Stress
Any major change in a child's life can be a cause of stress. In addition to the birth of a sibling or the parents' divorce, stress can be caused by a move to a new home, a death of a relative or a pet—or any firsthand experience of violence or a natural disaster. Sometimes, just hearing about such events or watching them on TV can also produce anxiety.

Young children also experience stress when they are pressured to succeed or when parents are overly strict and inflict frequent punishment. Separation from their parents for more than a few days can also cause stress in some children.

It is impossible to avoid all stress. Frustrations and conflicts occur daily even in the most stable and loving environment. Children's inexperience in understanding the adult world can result in confusion, misconceptions, and disappointments. These various feelings can accumulate and contribute to a general feeling of stress.

Signs of Stress
Some children under stress become very agitated and impulsive while others become quiet and withdrawn. Additional signs of stress include lack of appetite, overeating, nightmares, bedwetting, headaches, sleep troubles, stomachaches, and a regression in toileting habits. Children under severe stress may have a lower resistance to infectious diseases and become ill more often than children who are less stressed.

Stress can also lower their attention span as well as their tolerance for frustration, thereby interfering with children's ability to think and learn. Clinging, whining, and resistance to separation can occur. If medical and nutritional causes have been ruled out, these various symptoms probably mean that the child is experiencing an accumulation of stress. Young children cannot easily verbalize their feelings or give the reason for their behavior, but the actions can be a clue for parents that something is wrong.

How Children Overcome Stress

Children have various ways of dealing with the painful feelings that result in stress. One of these is through play. Spontaneous fantasy play often includes elements that, in real life, are frightening or confusing to children. If a little boy sees his parents quarrel, he may later act out a quarrel with puppets. A girl who hears about an airplane crash may recreate an accident with a toy airplane.

This kind of fantasy play is extremely important because it helps children to understand distressing events and gain some control over them. It also allows them to laugh, and laughter is an important tension-release mechanism that helps children deal with anxiety. Play and laughter are therefore excellent antidotes to stress.

Another important tension-release mechanism is crying. Children will spontaneously cry when they have experienced a distressing event. Crying is a natural healing process that allows children to rid themselves of feelings of sadness, frustration, or fear. It is an essential part of the normal and healthy grieving process.

Researchers have found that crying produces beneficial physical and chemical changes in the body, and symptoms of stress have been found to decrease dramatically when children are able to release their feelings through crying. If parents can be tolerant and accepting of their children's tears, the painful feelings will have an outlet. In this way children can keep themselves stress-free. Although it is tempting to distract or scold a crying child, a more helpful approach is simply to allow the child to cry as long as needed.

Parents can play an important role in helping children cope with stress by providing a supportive atmosphere for their children's natural tension-release mechanisms of play, laughter, and tears.

Strategies to Deal with Children's Stress

Try to minimize ongoing sources of stress.
If your child is showing signs of stress, the first step is to figure out the cause. Is there tension in the family? Is your child being mistreated by other children? Are your expectations for your child's behavior too high? Is she watching too much violence on TV? Sometimes the source of stress is not readily apparent from outside circumstances, and you may need to probe into your child's inner world of feelings. Does she have some new fears, misconceptions, or guilt feelings? By talking with your child and observing her in her play, the causes of stress may become more apparent.

If the cause of your child's stress is an ongoing one, it is often possible to reduce or eliminate it. For example, if you have observed that his school or daycare center is overly strict, you can remove him from the school and look for a better setting.

Prepare your child for upcoming stressful events.
Preparation is extremely important in helping young children adjust to potentially stressful future situations, such as the birth of a sibling, a move to a new home, or the child's hospitalization for surgery. You can inform and prepare your child for the event by talking about it openly, answering questions, reading picture books about the subject, and role-playing. It is also helpful to bring the child to locations where stressful events will be taking place, such as a hospital or new school. A three-year-old's preparation for the dentist might include looking at books from the library about going to the dentist, visiting the dentist's office ahead of time to see the room and equipment, and rehearsing the visit at home by role-playing it in an atmosphere of fun and laughter.

Encourage fantasy play about stressful events that have occurred.
Once your child has experienced a stressful event, you can help him deal
with it by encouraging him to act it out through play. If your child seems
very disturbed after a fire in the neighborhood, you can give him a toy fire
engine and join him in playing with it. Following hospitalization, your
child will make good use of a doctor's kit and doctor play with you,
yourself, playing the role of the frightened patient. While playing with
your child in these fantasy situations, try to encourage laughter, because
this will help your child release tensions and fears.

It is beneficial for children when adults playfully pretend to be weak,
ignorant, or scared. This allows the children to gain some objectivity about
their own feelings of powerlessness or anxiety, and to laugh heartily about
them.

Accept your child's feelings.
Children need to have their entire range of feelings heard. If your son says
he hates his baby sister, he will feel truly understood if you say, "You are
feeling very angry towards your sister." He needs to know that it's okay to
feel that way, but that he must not hurt her.

Children's fears also need to be acknowledged rather than denied or
belittled: "I see that you are really frightened about going to the hospital.
It is scary, but I will be with you."

Very often children's expression of feelings is not with words at all, but
through tears. Crying allows children to heal themselves from the effects
of distressing events. The next time your child starts to cry, if your usual
approach is to ignore, scold, or distract him, try saying instead, "I see you're
very upset right now. If crying makes you feel better, go ahead and cry. I
will stay with you until you are done."

Violence towards others must, of course, be stopped, but harmless crying
with no attempt to hurt anybody is best accepted. We all need a loving
shoulder to cry on, and children are no exception.

Sometimes the crying will seem reasonable to you, but at other times it will
appear to be totally unjustified by the situation that triggered it. I call this
the "broken cookie phenomenon." A cookie breaks and the child cries as if
her whole world has fallen apart! This kind of crying and raging is just as
important to accept as the kind that seems more reasonable, because
children accumulate painful feelings and then release them all at once in
intense crying sessions triggered by small events.

Children do not usually verbalize the real issue they are crying about, but
this is not necessary for the crying to be beneficial.

The following true incident illustrates this. Six-year-old Sally cried and raged loudly for half an hour after school, when her mother told her they would be going to the circus that evening instead of that afternoon. Her mother did not understand Sally's overreaction to what seemed a minor disappointment, merely a change in time. Nevertheless, she calmly accepted Sally's outburst. After crying, Sally was in a wonderful mood and greatly enjoyed going to the circus in the evening. The next day her mother learned from Sally's teacher that Sally had been badly teased and rejected by some children at school the previous day. Sally had saved her painful feelings until she found an opportunity to release them in the safety of her own home.

A parent's attitude of love, understanding, and acceptance is of primary importance in helping children get through difficult times.

Chapter 18
Choosing
Child Care

Betty Farber

*You want a place where
your child will be happy, safe,
and lovingly cared for.*

A Visit to a Child Care Center

There were so many little people in the room, I thought I was in Munchkin Land (from the <u>Wizard of Oz.</u>) But these little people were **babies**. One was being held by a young woman; others were walking, creeping, wandering from room to room in the small ranch house.

I was visiting a potential child care setting (for infants to five- year-olds) to explore the kinds of child care services that were available to care for my granddaughter while my daughter works.

A tour of the house revealed an empty crib in each room. Yet one six-month-old baby was lying on his back on the double bed in the master bedroom gazing at television. "He can turn from his stomach to his back, but not the other way," explained the caregiver, "so he's safe in the middle of the bed." We left him there alone, as we continued our tour. I felt troubled and I thought, *What if today is the day he learns to turn onto his stomach, and what if he keeps rolling right off the bed?*

In the poorly lit basement, a tangle of toys on the floor was the "play-room" with two four -year- old boys watching a cooking program on TV. There were no adults downstairs supervising them. In fact, all the adult supervision was handled by these two caregivers, one of whom was holding the infant on the first floor, and the other, giving us the tour.

Out in the backyard, four toddlers were unsupervised, in an area that contained climbers and a sand box, out of sight of the caregivers.

Although the two women seemed relaxed, and responded in a kindly manner to the children, the setting was unacceptable in terms of physical setup, safety, supervision, and number of adults available to care for the children.

What you need to know about quality child care for your preschooler.
When you look at which child care program is best for your child, there are several considerations.

You want a place where:
• your child will be happy, safe, and lovingly cared for
• your preschooler will learn to get along with other children
• your youngster will participate in interesting and creative activities

You need a program that is:
• convenient to your home or business
• affordable

You want to find the type of setting that suits you best:
• When you need all-day child care, look at *group daycare, family daycare,* or *in-home care.*
• If you want your child to be in a preschool program for just a few hours a day, search for a *nursery school* or *parent cooperative* to fill your need.

How to Evaluate Child Care Facilities

Observe the program
To find the setting that is best for your child, spend a few hours at potential sites to evaluate each program. On your visit, your best strategy is to **Look, Listen,** and **Ask questions.**

LOOK:
• Is the environment bright and cheerful?

• Is there enough space for the number of children, or do they seem crowded together?

• Are there indoor and outdoor play areas?

• Is the equipment kept in good repair?

• Are toilets and sinks easy for children to use?

• Is there a variety of materials on open shelves so the children can reach them?

• Are they selective about television or is it used as a baby sitter?

• Are all the activities chosen by the teacher, or are children allowed to make some choices?

• Are "interest centers" set up for the children such as a Book Corner, a Housekeeping Area, a Block Corner?

• Do the children seem happy and involved in what they are doing?

LISTEN
• **Listen** to the way the teachers talk to children in their care. Are their voices warm and caring? Do they look at the child as they speak? Do they seem genuinely concerned about what the child is saying?

• **Listen** to the way the children talk to each other. Do they seem friendly to one another? Do they respect one another's rights? (If the teachers are doing a good job, the atmosphere will be congenial.) Note: Observe the children *in general,* as there may be some children who misbehave no matter how good the teacher is.

• **Listen** to the way the professionals talk to each other. Do they seem sensitive to each other's needs? Teamwork is important in an early childhood center.

ASK QUESTIONS
(A well-run center will welcome questions about its program.)
• **Ask** about the background of the director, teachers, assistant teachers, aides, or family day care provider. What experience have they had in working with young children? Have they degrees or training in early childhood education?

• **Ask** how many teachers are in each classroom. In group day care there should be at least one teacher and an assistant with every group of children.

• **Ask** how many children are under the care of each adult. Although there is no absolute rule as to the proper ratio of adults to children, the following guidelines have been suggested by the National Association for the Education of Young Children:

infants up to 1 year: 1 adult to 4 infants;

1 to 2 years: 1 adult to 6 children;

3 year olds: 1 adult to 8 children;

4 to 5 years: 1 adult to 10 children.

• **Ask** how they handle discipline. Their answer will give you some clues as to whether their values are similar to yours. Professionals should be able to manage the children in their care without using physical punishment.

• **Ask** if there is a brochure describing the program's philosophy.

• **Ask** if they have written lesson plans. Find out what a typical day in the program would be like.

• **Talk** to parents who have children in the program. Find out how satisfied they are with the care their children are receiving.

Types of Child Care Settings

Early childhood programs are called by many different names:

Preschool: A general term for an early childhood program for children who are not yet of school age.

Group day care or center-based day care: Children are gathered for a full day, in group settings, at a day care center. Responsibility for licensing rests with the states. Child care centers may be sponsored by government or community groups, or private schools. Commercial day care programs are managed as a business and may be part of a franchise. Some industries provide child care for their employes, and universities may offer that service to their staff and students.

Family Day Care: Children are kept in the home of another person who usually cares for a few children of different families. Family Day Care may be licensed in some areas.

In-home care: Children are watched over in their own home, by someone who is hired for that purpose, or by a relative.

Nursery School: An early childhood program where preschoolers are enrolled for two to five days per week, usually for a morning or afternoon session. The emphasis is usually on enrichment and socialization.

Parent Cooperatives: A program where parents hire a person trained in Early Childhood Education to serve as head teacher. Parents themselves participate by assisting the teacher in the classroom and administering the program.

Head Start: A federally sponsored program for preschoolers from low-income families, combining early learning experiences with an emphasis on health, nutrition and parent participation.

Kindergarten: A program for five-year-old children, sponsored by public or private schools. Its purpose is to promote the social and emotional development of five-year-olds, and to introduce them to the academic skills needed in first grade.

Preparing Your Child
for a Preschool Experience

You can help prepare your youngster for a preschool experience by teaching skills that encourage independence and responsibility. It is very helpful for your child to be able to do some routine things for himself, as the teacher is sometimes too busy. In addition, the ability to do some of these tasks will enhance your preschooler's sense of self-esteem. (Ages when most children can accomplish these tasks are in brackets.)

• Let your child scribble with thick, nontoxic crayons (1 to 2 years).

• Give your preschooler opportunities to unzip his own clothes (1 to 2 years).

• Let your child remove her own shoes, socks, and sweater, after you have untied or unbuttoned them (1 to 2 years).

• Let your child help you set the table with napkins, spoons and other nonbreakable and safe objects (2 to 3 years).

• When your child is finished playing with her toys, have a "cleanup time" and help her to learn to pick up the toys and put them away (2 to 3 years).

• Using an unbreakable pitcher containing a small amount of liquid, let your youngster pour her own juice (3 to 4 years).

• Help your child to learn to wash and dry her hands by herself (3 to 4 years).

• Give your child opportunities to button, zip and snap his clothes (3 to 4 years).

• Teach your child to use the toilet independently (3 to 4 years).

• Print your preschooler's name on a piece of paper and hang it on the wall in her room and on the refrigerator, so that she begins to recognize it (3 to 5 years).

• Help your youngster to learn his first and last name, address and telephone number (4 to 6 years).

• Teach your preschooler to lace and tie his shoes (4 to 6 years).

Chapter 19
Traveling
with
Your Preschooler

Paulette Bochnig Sharkey

*When traveling by car,
a shoe bag hung on the back
of the front seat holds toys,
tissues, and other small articles.*

"Are we there yet?" It's a familiar cry to every parent who has traveled with children. But traveling successfully with preschoolers is not only possible, it can be fun *(really)*. It does require careful planning and flexibility on your part. And you should be realistic about the limitations and needs of your child. We hope that this chapter will help you on your way to discovering the joys of family traveling.

What to Expect from Your Child During Travel

If you can cope with all the necessities you must lug along, traveling with an infant is relatively easy. The toddler stage, however, can be more difficult. Your two-year-old may find it hard to tolerate long periods of inactivity, such as a cross-country airplane flight. You can try to avoid problems by changing the pace often, alternating social activities between you and your and child with games and toys your youngster can enjoy alone. Things usually improve by the older preschool years, when your child may be more ready and willing for the new experiences that travel brings.

Car Travel

Make car travel *safe* travel. Keep your child in an approved car seat at all times (preferably one that allows him to see out the window). Set a good example by buckling up yourself.

Allow enough time for a leisurely journey, with frequent stops to give your child a chance to exercise and work off excess energy. You might make a simple map that she can follow as you go. Mark the stops you are sure of, and tape the map to the car ceiling for quick reference. A child's portable toilet is handy to have along in the car, and a shoe bag hung on the back of the front seat holds toys, tissues, and other small articles.

Air Travel

When arranging for air travel with your child, ask for the seats with the most leg room, usually the front row of the coach section (sometimes called the "bulkhead" seats). Children younger than two years may travel free on domestic flights, but they are assigned no seats of their own and are expected to sit on a parent's lap (unless the plane is not full and a flight attendant helps out). By calling the airlines at least 24 hours ahead, you can order a children's meal that may appeal to your preschooler more than the regular airline meal. Once you are on board, be sure to ask for an "entertainment" packet for your child.

Train Travel

A short journey by train can be lots of fun for a small child. Longer trips of a day or more are not recommended because of the lack of space to run and exercise. But there are benefits of train travel over car travel. Here your toddler has the option of sitting on a seat or curling up on your lap. Parents, without the responsibility of driving, have the time to play with youngsters. Also, trains have bathrooms available, so a special stop doesn't have to be made. Most children enjoy looking out the window and watching the scenery gliding by. And, if you tire of sitting, there is always the possibility of a walk down the aisle to the snack bar.

Traveling Together: The Good Parts
Traveling can help children become more open to new and different people, places, and ideas. Their natural curiosity also makes travel a great educational experience. And seeing the world through the eyes of your child is a rich experience for you, too. Happy traveling!

Practical Suggestions

Packing
It's hard to travel light with children, but imaginative packing pays off. Consider a separate suitcase for your child. Making a checklist as you pack and taping the list to the inside of the suitcase might prevent his favorite teddy bear from being left behind in a motel room.

Dress your child in old, comfortable clothes for traveling. Jogging suits work well — they are warm and they don't bind (important in case of stomach upsets). If you want your child to look fresh and neat when you arrive at your destination, pack extra clothes for changing into at the last minute, or have her wear a large bib or sleeveless apron during the journey.

Health Considerations When Traveling

If your child gets motion sickness:
• Avoid odors of strong-flavored food or tobacco, as well as greasy foods that may upset the stomach.
• Offer pretzels, crackers, hard lemon candies* or chewing gum*, to relieve mild queasiness.
• If traveling by car, direct your child's attention to things outside and *far off,* rather than focusing on the side of the road. Open a window for fresh air.
• Don't let your preschooler do close work, such as coloring.
• When nausea is severe, have your child sit with head resting back and eyes closed.
• Ask your doctor about giving your child an over-the-counter drug for motion sickness, but remember that it will be effective only if taken before the trip.

What about earaches during air travel?
To reduce pressure on your child's ears during airplane takeoffs and landings, offer something to suck on or chew — a bottle or pacifier for younger children, sugarless lollipop*, or chewing gum* for older preschoolers. Yawning or swallowing hard can also help.
(* caution: these items may not be appropriate for very young children — check with your doctor.)

Remember to travel with a first aid kit, and pack any medicines your child takes routinely.

Games and
Toys for Travel

Travel Games
There are many games you can play with your preschooler to help pass the time on long journeys. Here are a few to consider:

"I spy"
Choose a color such as red. Count how many red items you can see out the window, as you drive along. Change to another color after a time.

"First One to See"
Agree on one thing you are likely to see along the highway (for example: cement mixer, cow, boat on top of a car, moving van, etc.). The first one to see this chosen object gets to name the next thing to watch for.

"Broadcast Game"
Give an older preschooler a pretend microphone (a hairbrush is good) and let him sing, tell a story, etc., while everyone else acts as the "audience." Set a time limit, however, or this game could go on forever!

"Missing Words"
An adult reads a familiar story, recites a nursery rhyme, or sings a favorite song, leaving out a key word now and then. The children take turns filling in the missing part. Many variations of this game are possible. For example: instead of leaving out a key word, *replace* the word with a similar one, (such as "Jack and Jill climbed up the *mountain"*) and have your preschooler give you the correct word.

"Categories"
Pick a category, such as musical instruments, and have each player name something in that category, such as trumpet, piano, etc. Continue until no one can think of anything else in that group; then start a new round with a different category.

"True Stories"
Children love to hear their parents tell stories that begin "When you were a baby...." They delight in your reminiscences about their favorite toys and food, first words spoken, etc. It can also be entertaining (and a good memory-stretching exercise) to have your child tell *you* a story about a past experience.

"Break the Silence"†
Here is a wordless game that will no doubt be started by the driver! At a signal, everyone tries to remain quiet for as long as possible. Whoever makes a noise is out and will then try to make the others talk. The one who keeps silent the longest wins.

"Singing in the Car"†
Singing passes the hours quickly. When you tire of your favorites, make up your own travel songs to go with familiar tunes. Here is an example, to the tune of *Frere Jacques:* "We are driving, we are driving,/ To the beach, to the beach..." (†These are two of the many travel ideas in *Purple Cow to the Rescue,* by A. Cole, C. Haas, and B. Weinberger. Little, Brown, 1982.)

Versatility is a key factor in choosing toys for your trip. Select those that can be played with in more than one way. Of course, taking compact items will allow you to pack a larger variety, but avoid toys with lots of pieces that could easily get lost. You might want to invest in a "lap desk," a flat hard tray attached to a bean bag pillow base. It provides a stable play surface and doubles as a pillow for rest times.

Bringing little surprises and unwrapping them along the way brings great pleasure to a small child and costs very little. If you choose toys from home, do so several weeks before you leave and put them away just for the trip. That way they will have fresh appeal.

Here are some toys that usually work well on trips:
√ Crayons, pencils, paper: draw pictures, play tic-tac-toe, invent a dot-to-dot for your child to complete
√ Activity books, coloring books, mazes, and sticker books
√ Colorforms®: soft plastic figures or shapes that stick to a scenery board in endless combinations
√ Magnetized drawing boards such as Etch-a-Sketch® or Magic Slate®
√ Magnet board with magnetic shapes, letters and/or numbers
√ Sewing cards
√ Books, story and music tapes, headphones
√ Hand puppets or finger puppets
√ Jump rope or inflatable ball for active play during breaks in car travel

Chapter 20
Moving
with
Young Children

Paulette Bochnig Sharkey

*"When I move away,
will I still be me?"*

"But where's the canopy bed that was here?" my three-year-old daughter wanted to know, "and that little play stove?" Jessa had expected these things to be at our new house when we moved in. After all, they were there when she saw the house before the previous owners left! It turned out that Jessa had lots of expectations about our recent move that I didn't realize until it was too late to avoid the disappointment. I am wiser now, having moved with a preschooler.

Preschoolers may feel anxious and uprooted

Infants are not likely to be affected by a household move if their routine is undisturbed and the people in their lives remain constant. Toddlers and preschoolers, however, like to do the same things in the same way, day after day. Losing the old familiar surroundings is distressing for them. Like adults, young children fear the unknown; changes can be frightening. They may have anxieties about changing preschools and finding new friends.

The distance you move is largely irrelevant to young children, since their understanding of geography is very limited. A preschooler, not yet allowed to cross the street alone, probably won't feel better being told that his new house is only a mile away! A move within the same city can be every bit as upsetting as one across several states.

How will your child react to a move?

Your child will probably have many questions as he tries to understand what a move means: *Where will my room be? Will I have a friend to play with? When I move away, will I still be me?* Sadness, confusion, and irritability are all common emotional responses of children to a move. It is not unusual for preschoolers to feel temporarily ill or experience sleeping problems. Be prepared for some regression, too, in areas like potty training and weaning from a bottle.

What you can do to help

TALK to your child about your plans to move about a month before the change. Remember that preschoolers' sense of time is undeveloped, so don't mention it <u>too</u> early. Explain *why* you are moving (e.g., Daddy's new job in another city; the need for more room for the family, etc.). Reassure your child that he is indeed coming along with you on the move. Many young children fear being left behind, especially as they observe old household items being sold at a garage sale in preparation for a move.

EXPLAIN how the move will occur. You may find yourself answering the same questions over and over. "Yes, we will take all your books and clothes and toys. We'll pack them in boxes and the movers will come to the house in a big van to pick them up..." "No, we can't take the lilies in the flower garden, but you could help me plant some different ones to enjoy next year." This repetition is important. Each time your preschooler hears about the upcoming move, it will become a little more real in his mind.

LISTEN to your child so that you can understand how she is feeling and correct misconceptions. Acknowledge her fears and anxieties about moving and gently counter with plans for new and exciting experiences to come. Reassure her that many routines will be the same.

INVOLVE your youngster in the move as much as you feel is practical, including a little of the packing. Although you will be busier than ever, you child will want and need to spend more time with you as he prepares for this big change in his life. Your presence will offer a sense of security.

A three-year-old might "help" with the packing by crumpling newspaper to stuff in boxes. She will better understand that moving does not mean leaving possessions behind, and she will be reassured to see her belongings carefully packed and labeled: "Jessa's Room." But don't pack your child's favorite blanket or stuffed animal — she'll need to carry that herself!

Finally, be positive about your move. Your child will look to you for clues about how to react. If your attitude is positive, he is likely to respond the same way.

Strategies to Help Prepare Your Child for a Move

• Help your preschooler make a scrapbook of the old neighborhood. You could include a flower from the yard, and pictures of special friends and places. This book will be looked at again and again as your child reminisces later. Snapshots of new friends and activities can gradually be added to bridge the gap from old to new.

• To reduce the fear of the unknown, arrange to take your child to see the new home and neighborhood before you move. If that is not possible, bring back pictures of not only the house, but the ice cream parlor, library, playground, and other places that will be important in your child's life.

• If your youngster attends preschool and participates in a "show-and-tell" session, you might have her share a photograph of her new home while she tells her friends about the upcoming move.

• If you are moving into a new community, you could subscribe to the Sunday newspaper for a few weeks before your move. Besides looking at the real estate section for a home or apartment, watch for announcements of children's plays, museums, gymnastics, dance classes, etc. This will enable you to sign up your child for a favorite activity in advance to help him feel more a part of the new community when he arrives.

• Help your preschooler find a suitable home for any pets you can't manage to transfer, such as goldfish.

• Let your youngster choose some special treasures to move in person (in the car or on the plane) to your new home.

• Children often use play to overcome their anxieties. If your child is pretending to be "moving," encourage his play by suggesting props such as empty boxes, newspapers, and a wagon or truck as a moving van.

Adjusting to a New Home

The time after the move will be a major adjustment period for your child. My three-year-old daughter suffered a case of post-move blues that required extra hugs, patience, and attention from me for several weeks following our family's relocation across the country. Here are some suggestions that helped my child to adjust:

As soon as you get into your new surroundings, set up your child's room first. Try to make it similar to his old one, for the sake of continuity. Your child will be comforted by what is familiar, so this is not the time to throw out the old bedspread and start redecorating, or to move your child from a crib to a bed. In fact, it can be helpful to go through the entire house with your child, pointing out similarities between old and new. For example, in the living room you may have the same furniture, just arrange differently.

Try to settle your youngster into a daily routine that is similar to his life before the move.

If you have only moved a few miles from your former street, go past your old home a few times after the move. This will help your preschooler understand that friends and familiar places are still nearby.

Help your child to make new friends. One way to do this is to get involved in an outdoor activity that kids can't resist, such as setting up a swing set. You will have instant visitors! Or go to the neighborhood park or playground. Your preschooler may carry a bag of cookies to share with new friends, with their parents' permission. (Be sure it is after lunch, so the other children can partake in the treat.)

Walk with your child and talk to neighbors to find out where potential playmates live. Notice toys left out in yards as clues to the ages of children who live there.

Attend Parents' Meetings at preschool. There may be potential friends living just around the corner that you hadn't discovered. Call your local library about story hour and other programs for preschoolers. Contact your local community center about "Mommy and Me" programs.

When Friends Move Away

When a friend moves away, your child may experience feelings of loss, rejection, and sadness. Some older preschoolers may even doubt their own self-worth ("Why doesn't Adam want to play with me any more?") Here are some ways you can help:

√ Point out the reasons for a friend's move in a way that your child can understand, e.g., "Seth's mother got a new job so they will be living in another city, close to her work."

√ Don't downplay your child's anger or hurt feelings. Help her realize that in time she'll find other friends, but they won't _replace_ the old one moving away, because friends are not like replaceable parts.

√ Help your child say goodbye to a friend who is moving away. Exchanging "going away" gifts can serve as a sign of continuing friendship and a reminder of shared times.

√ Encourage correspondence (children can send drawings and dictate a letter to be written by a parent) after a friend moves away. Buy your child his own brightly colored note cards or stationery and markers.

Chapter 21
Helping Children Cope with Divorce

Bruce V. Hillowe

*Divorce has emotional and
behavioral consequences,
even for well-adjusted
preschoolers.*

How was preschool today, Danny? *I had fun, mom, but my friend Marsha was sad all day long. She said her mommy and daddy are getting divorced. She said her daddy is leaving because he doesn't love her any more. Will you and daddy get divorced?*

You may be faced with the same situation that Danny's mother had to confront. How well you handle the explanation can determine how well your child can react to his friend's problem.

You can reassure your child that you and his father have no plans to divorce, that you both love each other and him very much, and that you are going to continue living together as a family. You can explain that his friend's parents will always be her parents, and will always love and take care of her, even if they don't live in the same house.

Although your first reaction as a parent might be to try to shelter your child from his friend's painful experience, you can better help him become a more caring person by encouraging him to be extra friendly during this difficult period. You can try to explain that sometimes bad things happen to friends, even though they are nice people. When this happens, you can look for ways to help them feel better.

Children's reactions to their parents' separation
Divorce has emotional and behavioral consequences, even for well-adjusted preschoolers. Both long-term and short-term consequences are inevitable, but with proper understanding, much can be done at the time of divorce to help children adjust. Although most children do adapt eventually to the new family situation, the time of change is extremely stressful. Preschoolers will have different reactions to the news that their parents will be separating.

Fear and anxiety
Three-year-old John became scared his mother would not return from work, and clung to her as she left. Children feel unprotected and worry about who will feed, protect, and take care of them. They may become anxious about their future relationships with their parents, thinking that if marriage can be broken, so can parent-child bonds. They may fear that they will be abandoned by both parents. They may worry about their parents' welfare and their parents' inevitable distress. Their whole idea of parents and adults may change as they see their parents as vulnerable individuals and not as a unit.

Sadness

Tommy's teacher noticed that he often seemed on the brink of tears, and one day found him, embarrassed to be seen, crying alone. Many preschoolers also become sad at the time of divorce. They may become tearful and moody. For many, this sadness specifically revolves around their loss of a full-time father. They may yearn for him and feel that they need a daddy. From these sad feelings may arise fantasies of reconciliation. Some children may deny altogether that divorce is occurring and live in a fantasy of a restored family, or where children take care of children and parents are uninvolved and unimportant.

Conflict of loyalty

Karen's teacher was disturbed when Karen drew a picture of a child being pulled in opposite directions by two adults. Divorce can also be a time of conflicted loyalty. Youngsters may feel that by moving closer towards one parent, they betray the other. Some choose aloneness and try not to be close to either parent out of love for both. Others may resolve this difficulty, if their parents are in open conflict, by joining in with one and becoming angry at the other.

Guilt

Roger told his neighbor that his father had left because he had made his father angry when he played in the street. Children may feel guilty at this time, believing that they are to blame for the disruption. They may feel that the parent's departure is directed at them, not at the other parent.

Regression

After the divorce, four-year-old Nathan began looking for the security blanket that he had given up a few months ago. Children's behavior will reflect their emotional distress. Preschoolers may become clingy and anxious and not want to go to nursery school or day care. To cope with the anxiety associated with divorce, most preschoolers will move backward in development in order to gain some strength. It is difficult for them to comprehend the change. Their concepts of dependability and personal ties have been deeply shaken. The regression children may show may be sucking a thumb, asking to be fed, wetting the bed, physical complaints, separation fears, or tantrums. They may be easily frustrated or take longer to fall asleep. Generally, though, these common and quite normal reactions are transient and gone within a few weeks.

Pseudo-adult behavior

Five-year-old Bonnie had no apparent emotional reaction to the divorce, but she did start to imitate adult behavior in the way that she scolded and lectured her three-year-old brother. Some children's behaviors change by their adopting pseudo-adult behaviors. These children usually have the idea that their parents want support and reassurance from them because their parents cannot cope or are lonely. These super-children may try very hard not to display any of their own painful feelings.

Withdrawing from play

In the weeks following the divorce, four-year-old Mark would sit quietly in a chair watching his friends play, a stark contrast to his earlier enthusiastic self. The sadness that children feel may diminish their capacity for play and pleasure and they may not be able to concentrate and may be preoccupied in their play with themes of looking for lost loved ones. Such grief or sadness will gradually improve, especially as the child sees that the absent parent is still involved.

Parents can do a great deal to help their children cope with divorce.

For very young children, the most important factor in their adapting to the divorce is the capacity of their parents to continue to be competent and attentive parents.

Children adapt best to divorce when they are able to maintain contact with both parents and when conflict in their parents' relationship is minimized. In order to maintain contact with both parents in a meaningful way, children should be encouraged to feel that they will now have two families and two homes. They need to be reassured that their parents both love them and are committed to being their parents forever.

Practical Advice for Parents

Telling the children

It is best to tell the children before the separation, but only after a definite decision has been made. Telling them too long before may only lead to prolonged pain. A few weeks is usually adequate. Ideally, parents should inform the children together, with all the children present. Be direct and truthful, but avoid any gory details. You might say, for example, "Daddy and mommy have decided not to live together in the same house and we won't be married anymore. We are getting divorced. We are sorry it has to be this way, but mommy and daddy think it is best for everyone. Although mommy and daddy don't love each other anymore, we will both continue to love you. You'll be staying with mommy from Monday to Friday and with daddy on weekends." Giving concrete details about the upcoming changes can minimize the children's anxiety. Be honest, simple, and brief.

Feelings
Don't deny your own or the children's feelings. It is okay to let the children know if you are disappointed, angry, or hurt. In doing this, however, it is important that they know that these feelings are a grown-up matter and have nothing to do with them. It is also important for the children to know that their parents did once love one another. Acknowledge the children's anger and sadness. As children grieve for the loss of their family, repeated discussion may be needed as a kind of emotional desensitization, and to reassure the children of their parents' continuing interest.

Changes
Children cannot tolerate too many changes at once. If dad is going to move out, it may be best to wait a while before mom moves. If the children can stay in the same house in the same neighborhood and continue to attend the same preschool, that would be best. A stable environment outside the home can be a safe haven for children undergoing drastic changes at home. In the second home being developed by the parent who is moving away, it is important that the child have his own space with his own belongings. In order for the second home to feel like one, the child should be familiarized with the house, apartment and neighborhood and a sensible routine should be worked out there. In both homes, routine, order and rules are needed to show the children that you can cope and that you are in control.

Guilt
The guilt children often feel serves a function for them of gaining control. They feel that if they have caused the divorce, then they can reverse it somehow. Reassuring them that they are not at fault may be futile. Instead, it is best to help the child appreciate that there are certain things she can control, but there are others she cannot. For example, she does control who she is going to play with and what she's going to play, but she can't control things like the weather or that her parents are getting a divorce.

Troublesome behavior
The regressive behaviors described on page 145 are common and normal. It is best to allow some gratification when these behaviors first appear. For example when a child demands extra attention, give it. But gradually expect your child to recover from the regression.

Expectations
Don't give children false hopes of reconciliation and don't lean on them. Some parents, under the stress of divorce, may look to their children for support and reassurance, operating under the misapprehension that their children are their emotional equals. Children are simply not equipped to handle adult traumas and such role reversals are not healthy.

Seeking help
Although children do ordinarily adapt to divorce, some develop acute or chronic difficulties and may need therapy. The keys to deciding whether therapy is needed are the intensity and duration of the symptoms, and how generalized they are. For example, long crying jags or disruptive behavior that lasts more than six weeks may indicate a need for outside assistance. It can be expected that a child's cooperative behavior at home may diminish, but if this is also the case at school and with peers, treatment may be indicated. Continuing indications of anxiety and depression, such as irritability, temper tantrums, sleeping problems, excessive crying, and physical complaints are indications, if they last longer than a year or so, of the need for therapy.

Don't interfere with the other parent's role
Encourage your child to talk over problems they are having with the other parent. However, don't say bad things about the other parent, even if sorely tempted. Do not use the children as messengers. Do not ask your children about the other parent's life. Respect differences in child-rearing methods. Be orderly and businesslike in your dealings with the other parent; even rigid adherence to schedules may be necessary at first.

Parents sometimes have a difficult time putting marital disagreements aside and working together as co-parents. They usually have to build up a new parenting relationship. They may need to remind themselves that their ex-spouse is also their child's much needed other parent.

At the time of divorce, children need as much affection and time as their parents can give them. Children do best during and following divorce, when their parents continue to spend time with them, make them feel loved and wanted, keep them out of the middle of any conflicts and allow them to have independent relationships with each parent. With parents' help, children can be remarkably adaptable and, in time, will overcome the stress and problems of divorce.

Chapter 22
Helping Children Cope with Death

Fredric C. Hartman

*Children know how to mourn
because they can appreciate
what it means to change.*

Did you ever play "peek-a-boo" with your baby? Remember how he stared, wide-eyed, when your face disappeared, and giggled with joy when your face came back into his sight? One researcher has traced a distinct fascination with death back to six months of age when the infant responds to appearance-disappearance games like "peek-a-boo." Adah Maurer traced the term "peek-a-boo" back to Old English and Scottish words meaning "alive or dead?" The researcher suggests that the fascination with these games is an attempt to master the mysteries of being and nonbeing.

Death as change

What death really amounts to for all of us who are alive is a change, and children know about change because they are in the middle of a process of dramatic change. Their universe is changing at an enormous rate. In the course of a month or so, they can outgrow their wardrobes and see the world from new heights. Likewise, their ability to solve problems and their capacity for new and deepened feelings can enlarge practically before our eyes. They may not be able to express their feelings about these changes in ways we adults readily understand, but they do know they are changing. They feel it in their very bones, and they can cope with it in astonishingly sophisticated ways if we let them.

Children know how to mourn
because they can appreciate what it means to change

This may seem surprising at first. We're used to seeing our child as new to the world and as unfamiliar to something as momentous and final as death. Although children do not conceive of death and express their feelings about it in exactly the same way as we adults might, they most definitely are equipped with a highly sophisticated capacity to mourn a death when it does occur.

Keep in mind the idea that death is an event which causes a change in ours and our children's lives, and that it is change which brings on a potentially highly creative process—called mourning. We can then be aware that poignant feelings of loss can follow not only the actual death of a pet, a friend, or a relative, but it can also follow a move from one home to another, or the birth of a baby brother or sister, or the end of a vacation, or even the end of a touching movie. Your child may experience these changes as though a real death had actually occurred.

The kinds and intensity of feelings your child experiences during the mourning process will depend upon how attached your child is to what has been lost or changed. Some of the feelings that may be evoked in a young child during this process include anxiety, fear, confusion, insecurity, helplessness, frustration, anger, sorrow — even hope and wonder.

Adults also mourn change

Which parent could deny experiencing moments of actual mournfulness when he or she realizes that their son's or daughter's childhood is beginning to grow to a close and their child already bears some growing outlines of the adult he or she will soon become? These poignant feelings of loss and mournfulness attest to the similarity between death and change and how integral this mourning process is to normal and healthy growth.

Parents need to believe in their children's ability to mourn

The most important thing you, as parents, can do to help your children deal with a loss or a change is simply to allow them to express their feelings to you without feeling that you must make them feel better. Simply listen and receive the communications in what they are saying and in the way they are playing. Children know how to mourn their losses. Each child will discover remarkably creative ways to express his complex feelings about the death or the change he is struggling to accept.

When you as a parent believe in your children's ability to come to terms with a death and are attentive and try to understand their expressions of mourning, it can transform your children's pain and doubt into strength, self-confidence, and faith in people which can significantly enhance their development in many ways and endure for their lifetime.

Ways to Help Your Child Cope with Death

Each child has a different way of expressing his or her feelings of mourning. One child may behave as though the death of a special grandparent never occurred and will be unresponsive to questions about it. Another child who lost an uncle may seek to engage a parent in a highly abstract conversation, asking many disturbing questions about death. Another may cry with heart-rending sorrow over the death of a pet. Another child whose friend's parent died violently in a car accident may engage in play with toys that seems frighteningly morbid and violent. Another child whose brother died may become agitated and disruptive to the point of throwing objects and hitting people. What could parents do in these instances to help their child? Following is a list of the things I have found to be the most important.

• Examine your own feelings
It is crucially important for parents to examine their own feelings about death. The way you interact with your grieving child sets an example and models for the child how he is to mourn his losses. If you deny that a death or a significant change has had any real impact and are uncomfortable with your child's expressions, you are teaching your child to deny his feelings as well. If you can recognize feelings and can acknowledge the feelings in your child as they occur, your child will learn to do the same, becoming increasingly resilient in the process. It is worth devoting a considerable amount of time undergoing this self-examination even if it means seeking the assistance of a professional for a brief period of time.

• Let your child express his feelings

It is important to let children express the widest range of feeling when they are mourning *up to the point where they are at risk of harming themselves, others, or of destroying property.* In the case of the child who throws and breaks objects and hits others, the limit should be firmly but lovingly set in this regard. If your child continues to hit or throw and break objects, he may need to be physically restrained. While holding your child, acknowledge his pain but let him know that he is not allowed to hurt himself or others, or to break things, and that he needs to find another way to express his feelings. You may have to do this several times before your child will understand the limit.

• Understand your child's play behavior

Children up to the age of about twelve tend to express what they are thinking and feeling through play. It is a somewhat different language from the one using words. It is more indirect and ambiguous. What is important to do while watching children play is simply to try to understand the themes in the play. For example, a child mourning the loss of a grandparent may enact an elaborate funeral ceremony with dolls. All a parent would have to do to help this child is to be there if the child wishes, and to say aloud in a neutral but interested tone what is occurring during the funeral. It would be important not to suggest how the funeral should be conducted. The child should be allowed to decide every event however nontraditional it might seem, and everything that may be said by each one of the dolls. If your child wants you to play the role of the priest, minister or rabbi while manipulating a doll you should do that, and perhaps deliver a eulogy while remaining responsive to the child's feedback and wishes. A grieving child is helped immeasurably by being in control of the play and hearing an adult showing understanding by reflecting in words the events which they are creating. Sometimes the play is more difficult to follow and doesn't seem to be related to the loss you know has occurred. Letting the child control the play and while you say what is happening and what is being expressed goes a long way in helping the child feel understood while going through the mourning process.

• Let your child know it is okay to be sad

The child who behaves as though nothing has occurred and is unresponsive to questions about it may need to be allowed his or her space for a time. What might help the child is for the parent to express his or her own feelings about the loss in a way that conveys to the child that it is okay to feel pain and express such feelings, and that it may lead to feeling much better. Sharing these feelings with your child can help him overcome inhibitions and significantly deepen your relationship as well.

• **Let your child attend the funeral**
If there is a real funeral to attend try to involve the child in some way. Contrary to common belief, it is not helpful to the child to be spared the experience of a funeral and excluded from the event. Children are likely to feel more confused by the death if they are left out. Giving them a simple role in the funeral or wake helps them to mourn, and feel that important sense of belonging at a difficult time, as it does the adults who participate in it.

• **Answer questions about death truthfully**
Don't be afraid to say you don't know to the child who asks disturbing questions about death. The fact is that death is a bewildering mystery and all we have been able to do about it since the beginning of time is to regard it with awe and wonder. To say to your child that you don't know and yet praise and support the child and wonder along with him in his quest to understand the mystery can deepen your relationship profoundly. I have found in my clinical work that while I cannot always give answers to their questions, what is more gratifying to children is my response of support and approval of their questioning.

Resources for Section Four:
Coping with Stress
in _Special_ Situations

FOR ADULTS

Good Day Bad Day: The Child's Experience of Child Care, by Lyda Beardsley. Teachers College Press, 1990. Writing about two fictional child care programs, the author uses her experiences as an early childhood consultant and researcher to compare the child's experience in a superior program to one in a low-quality center.

Sharing the Caring: How to Find the Right Child Care and Make It Work for You and Your Child, by Amy Laura Dombro and Patty Bryan. Simon & Schuster, 1991. A valuable resource for parents, offering practical advice about how they can work effectively with caregivers to ensure a positive experience for their child. (Out of print, but look in your library.) Amy Dombro is also an author of a chapter in this book.

The Hurried Child, 2nd ed., by David Elkind. Addison Wesley, 1988. A major cause of stress in children is our tendency to hurry them emotionally and intellectually. The author describes the harm caused by expecting too much, too soon.

Ties that Stress: The New Family Imbalance, by David Elkind. Harvard University Press, 1994. The modern American family is under enormous stress. It is out of balance — failing to meet the needs of children. The renowned child psychologist and author describes what has happened to the American family, and looks at the possibilities of a new balance between the needs of the children and the needs of the parents.

The Parents Book about Divorce, by Richard A. Gardner. Creative Therapeutics, 2nd ed., 1991. Sensitive, sensible, and comprehensive, this is a valuable guide for divorcing parents on how to be understanding parents during and after the divorce.

Talking About Death: A Dialogue between Parent and Child, by Earl A. Grollman. Beacon Press, 1991. This book contains a children's read-along, an extensive parents' guide for explaining death to children of all ages, and a thorough listing of nationwide resources.

Before the School Bell Rings, by Carol B. Hillman. Phi Delta Kappa Educational Foundation, 1995. This paperback discusses child's play, learning environments, outdoor exploration, and other important topics in early childhood to help caregivers fill young children's lives with healthy and joyful experiences.

Helping Your Child Handle Stress, by Katharine Kersey, Ed.D. Berkley Pub., 1995. This book offers common sense advice for parents about a wide range of topics from sibling rivalry to sexual abuse.

Starting School: A Parent's Guide to the Kindergarten Year, by Judy Keshner. Modern Learning Press/Programs for Education, 1992. The author provides parents with helpful suggestions to prepare their children for a happy, successful school experience.

After Death Communication: Final Farewells, by Louis E. LaGrand, Ph.D. Llewellyn Publications (St. Paul, MN), 1997. Dr. LaGrand is a grief counselor, educator, and lecturer. He discusses the varied experiences described to him in his counseling practice in which a person who suffered a loss feels the presence of the loved one who has died. These encounters usually bring comfort and solace and help the bereaved person to go on with his life.

High Risk: Children Without a Conscience, by Ken Magid, Ph.D. & Carole A. McKelvey. Bantam Books, 1987. Anything that disrupts the parent-child bond (early separation, divorce, illness, neglect) is a source of stress for young children. The authors explain how this can lead to emotional and behavioral problems, and propose suggestions for prevention and cures.

Resources for Early Childhood: A Handbook, edited by Hannah Nuba, Michael Searson, & Deborah Lovitky Sheiman. Garland, 1994. This comprehensive guide to early childhood contains informative essays about all aspects of child development, along with annotated resource lists helpful to parents and educators.

Scenes from Day Care: How Teachers Teach and What Children Learn, by Elizabeth Balliett Platt. Teachers College Press, 1992. The author records in detail the small events that happen in day care in order to focus on the question, "What kinds of experiences should occur in quality day care?"

How to Take Great Trips with Your Kids, rev. ed., by Sanford Portnoy and Joan Flynn Portnoy. Harvard Common Press, 1995. A comprehensive guide to planning, packing, and en-route problem solving.

The Aware Baby: A New Approach to Parenting, by Aletha Solter, Ph.D. Shining Star Press, 1984, PO Box 206-85, Goleta, CA 93116, web site: <http://www.sb.net/awarepar/>. Dr. Solter, who wrote a chapter in this book, focuses here on the emotional needs of children up to two-and-a-half years of age and provides useful insights into the causes and remedies of stress early in life.

Helping Young Children Flourish, by Aletha Solter, Ph.D. Shining Star Press, 1989. A sequel to *The Aware Baby*, this book concentrates on the emotional needs of children from 2 to 8 years of age. The author emphasizes the importance of allowing children to express their feelings fully in order to keep themselves free of the effects of stressful experiences. She discusses a wide range of topics, including causes of stress, fears, alternatives to punishment, helping children learn, visits to the doctor, sibling rivalry, and bedtime problems.

Necessary Losses, by Judith Viorst. Fawcett, 1987. This is an excellent book for parents to read about "the loves, illusions, dependencies, and impossible expectations that all of us have to give up in order to grow." This book will help parents explore their own feelings and thoughts about death, change and loss. It is beautifully written and thoroughly researched.

Second Chances: Men, Women and Children a Decade after Divorce, by Judith Wallerstein and Sandra Blakeslee. Houghton Mifflin, 1996. This book presents, in highly readable fashion with many examples, the results of a major pioneering study on both the immediate and long term consequences of divorce. It offers guidance on ways to lessen the potentially harmful impact of divorce on children.

Kids on Board: A 10-City Guide to Great American Family Vacations, by Ken and Marilyn Wilson. Warner Books, 1989. "Each chapter in this book is a presentation of a major American city, its amenities and the attractions it offers parents and their children." This comprehensive guide offers information on where to go, what to see, and where to stay, in order to enjoy your family holiday.

Behind the Playdough Curtain: A Year in My Life as a Preschool Teacher, by Patti Greenberg Wollman. Charles Scribner's Sons, 1994. An engaging story of a dedicated preschool teacher and the children and families that her life touches.

FOR CHILDREN

My Visit to the Aquarium, by Aliki. HarperTrophy, 1993. A little boy encounters a myriad of colorful aquatic creatures on a visit to the aquarium.

We Are Best Friends, by Aliki. Mulberry Edition, 1987. When Robert's best friend, Peter, moves away, both are unhappy. They learn that they can make new friends while remaining best friends with each other.

Airport, by Byron Barton. HarperTrophy Edition, 1987. Bold color illustrations and large text capture the excitement of an airport, from the time a plane is prepared for flight until it moves down the runway.

When Daddy Came to School, by Julie Brillhart. Albert Whitman, 1995. A little boy tells in rhyme about the wonderful time he had on his third birthday — when Daddy came to spend the day at his preschool.

Dinosaur's Divorce: A Guide for Changing Families, by Laurene Krasny Brown and Marc Brown. Atlantic Monthly Press, 1986. A simply written, lively, illustrated "lap book" designed to be read by parents to their young children. It is full of suggestions for handling the new situations and difficulties such as spending holidays in two separate households, and adjusting to a stepparent.

When Dinosaurs Die: A Guide to Understanding Death, by Laurie Krasny Brown and Marc Brown. Little, Brown, 1996. This wise and comforting book explains in simple, honest language what it is to have a loved one die, and explores the feelings of those who have lost someone dear to them.

The Dead Bird, by Margaret Wise Brown. HarperTrophy, 1995. This is a beautifully simple and moving story about a little girl and her friends who find a dead bird and encounter death for the first time. In a poignant episode they create funeral and burial ceremonies and accept the finality of death.

The Accident, by Carol Carrick. Clarion, 1981. Chris' dog, Bodger, is killed when he is hit by a truck. The boy displays many difficult feelings, particularly anger directed at his father for not yelling at the truck driver. Chris' parents remain patient and supportive. Finally it is with his father that he is able to let out his sorrow. When they choose a grave marker together, Chris' tears begin to flow and his anger disappears.

The Foundling, by Carol Carrick. Clarion, 1986. Chris, the protagonist of The Accident, (see above) is having nightmares following his dog's accidental death. His parents try to get Chris to adopt a dog from a nearby animal shelter, but Chris is not ready. When he is, he finds an ownerless dog in his neighborhood and takes him in. The theme of this book, gently conveyed, is that grief works itself out in its own time.

I Had a Friend Named Peter, by Janice Cohn. Wm. Morrow, 1987. When Betsy learns from her parents that her friend Peter died in an accident, she has many disturbing thoughts and feelings. She wonders if she will die too. She if afraid that she somehow caused the death. And she has bad dreams. But her parents and her teacher listen to Betsy's questions and answer them with honesty and sensitivity. She begins to understand what her teacher says—that even when people die, they stay in the memories of the people who loved them.

The Boy with a Problem: Johnny Learns to Share His Troubles, by Joan Fassler. Behavioral Publications, 1971. A boy with a secret problem (not mentioned in the book so that children with a variety of problems can relate to it) feels better after he pours out his troubles to a friend who is able to listen well.

The Train To Lulu's, by Elizabeth Fitzgerald Howard. Bradbury Press, 1988. Two young sisters travel all by themselves on a train from Boston to Baltimore to stay with their great-aunt Lulu for the summer.

When You Go to Kindergarten, by James Howe. Mulberry Books edition, 1995. This book is an ideal introduction to a new experience. With color photographs of boys and girls in real school activities: playing with blocks, painting, reading, and making friends with everyone including the teacher, who will be "your best grown-up friend at school."

Round Trip, by Ann Jonas. Greenwillow, 1983. Text and black-and-white illustrations record the sights on a day trip to the city and back home again to the country. In this unusual book, the story runs from front to back, then upside down from back to front!

Hotel Boy, by Curt & Gita Kaufman. Atheneum, 1987. Illustrated with appealing photographs, this book is about Henri, who had to move with his mother and brother to a hotel room when a fire left them homeless. Henri must make friends in a new school. It all ends happily with Henri and his family moving to an apartment where he looks forward to making friends all over again.

Best Friends, by Steven Kellogg. Dial, 1986. Kathy feels lonely and betrayed when her best friend goes away for the summer and leaves her alone.

Going to My Nursery School, by Susan Kuklin. Bradbury Press, 1990. With color photographs of young children at a quality nursery school, photojournalist Kuklin follows a four-year-old boy through the activities and routines of the day. Includes an informative section for parents entitled, *What to Look for in a Nursery School.*

One April Morning: Children Remember the Oklahoma City Bombing, by Nancy Lamb and Children of Oklahoma City. Lothrop, Lee & Shepard, 1996. Reading this book is an emotional experience best described by the author: "[The children] demonstrated a wisdom beyond their years as they told me about feelings, taught me about healing, and showed me a path to acceptance."

We're Going on a Trip, by Christine Loomis. Morrow Junior Books, 1994. What can you expect when you travel by car, airplane, and train? Children can be happily prepared for their next family vacation by reading this informative book. There is also a section called Notes for Parents with helpful advice on packing and vacation planning.

What You Know First, by Patricia MacLachlan. Joanna Cotler Books/HarperCollins, 1995. In poetic language, the author of Newbery Medal winning novel, *Sarah, Plain and Tall*, tells how a little girl feels when her family must move away from the prairie she loves.

School, by Emily Arnold McCully. Harper Trophy edition, 1990. In this wordless book, the littlest mouse in the family decides to follow the older mice to school to see what it is all about.

First Flight, by David McPhail. Little, Brown, 1991. A naughty teddy bear, in contrast with his well-behaved owner, ignores all the rules and disrupts their first airplane trip.

Annie and the Old One, by Miska Miles. Little, Brown and Co., 1985. An Indian girl's dying grandmother gives her a weaving stick. The grandmother will die when the rug has been woven. The girl tries to prolong her grandmother's life by undoing the rug. But the grandmother explains to her that the order of nature cannot be changed. The grandmother dies and the story ends with the girl accepting the death and going on with her life by taking her place at the loom.

Monster Goes to School, by Virginia Mueller. Albert Whitman, 1991. Schools for monster children seem filled with familiar activities. The children have playtime, storytime, music time, and naptime. Little Monster makes a clock, showing all the different "times" they have at school. Lynn Munsinger's drawings of the monsters show them to be appropriately weird yet appealing.

The Big Hello, by Janet Schulman. Dell, 1976. A little girl encourages her doll to be brave about the family's move cross country, and shares with the doll her triumph at learning how to find new friends.

I Am Not A Crybaby! by Norma Simon. Albert Whitman, 1989. A description of a variety of situations that make children want to cry, with the message that crying is normal.

On Divorce: An Open Family Book for Parents and Children Together, by Sara Bonnett Stein. Walker, 1984. Two books in one — photographs and a simple text for the child, along with more detailed discussion to help parents answer questions arising naturally from a child's curiosity about divorce.

Mom and Dad Don't Live Together Any More, by Kathy Stinson. Annick Press, 1984. A book with a clear message: "I love my mommy and my daddy. My mommy and my daddy love me too. Just not together."

The Tenth Good Thing About Barney, by Judith Viorst. Atheneum, 1971. Barney, the cat, dies. His young owner tries to think of ten good things to say at the funeral, but he can only think of nine. While helping his father in the garden, the tenth good thing occurs to him—Barney will now help things grow.

The Hating Book, by Charlotte Zolotow. HarperTrophy, 1989. A story about a little girl who feels hurt because she thinks her best friend hates her.

My Grandson Lew, by Charlotte Zolotow. HarperCollins, 1974. Lew's grandfather died a few years before this story takes place. Lew is suddenly missing his grandfather. The tenderness that comes through this story is in the relationship Lew has with his mother with whom he shares his memories of his grandfather.

The Quarreling Book, by Charlotte Zolotow. HarperTrophy, 1989 During a stressful day, a chain reaction of unpleasantries starts in a family when the father forgets to kiss his wife goodbye on his way to work. Eventually the situation is reversed and a chain of pleasant events occurs.

CATALOG

Centering Corporation, 1531 Saddle Creek Road, Omaha, NE 68104, offers a *Children and Grief Resource Flier* of books and videos for children and adults. Telephone: 402-553-1200 • Fax: 402-553-0507 • E-mail: j1200@aol.com.

Section Five
Coping
with Stress
in
Everyday
Situations

Section Five
Coping with Stress
in _Everyday_ Situations

Introduction

Today's families are under enormous stress. Mothers and fathers work hard, yet financial security is often unattainable. There are demands and pressures on adults that are always present in modern life — dealing with issues of health, discipline, time schedules, safety, housework, separations, and so on.

If the anxieties of everyday life are difficult for adults, how much harder they can be for young children who have no skill to deal with stressful situations, and few words to express their feelings.

The tensions of a daily routine that is complex and demanding can make young children angry and fearful. The educators and psychologists who wrote the chapters in this section offer guidance to parents and teachers on coping with difficulties such as separation, sleep problems, and common fears. They also look at approaches to developing good family TV habits.

And finally, one author helps parents with the often unnerving experience of conferring with the professionals in their children's lives.

COPING WITH STRESS IN EVERYDAY SITUATIONS

Chapter 23
Dealing with
Children's Anger

Michael K. Meyerhoff

*"I hate you!" No other words
uttered by a preschooler
can cause as much damage
to the morale of
her mother and father.*

"I hate you!" No other words uttered by a preschooler can cause as much damage to the morale of her mother and father. After all the nurturing, worrying, and encouraging, parents are always prepared for an "I love you" and a warm hug. But they rarely are ready for—and thus are extremely vulnerable to—any kind of angry attack from their child. A thousand expressions of affection never seem to compensate for the terrible pain that results from a single expression of anger.

Prior to one year of age, an infant will become upset from time to time, and will express her distress in no uncertain terms. But at this point in development, her feelings are largely reflexive and her reactions are not directed at any one person. Therefore, while her behavior may generate concern, it usually will not cause dismay .

After the first birthday, things change. Gradually, a toddler starts to formulate genuine discontent, and she begins to direct her displeasure toward particular people. As her physical and mental capacities grow, and as her social and emotional experiences become more complex, her expressions of anger steadily increase in variety and sophistication. Consequently, from their two-year-old's tantrums, through their four-year-old's sulking, to their six-year-old's verbal assaults, mothers and fathers can suffer from all sorts of unpleasant behavior from their young children.

Dealing appropriately with a child's anger is an important and difficult task of parenthood. Proper coping involves different considerations and calls for different strategies at different stages of development. Mothers and fathers should strive to keep in mind the following fundamental principles at all times.

• *Don't take it personally.* Although parents are typically the target of a preschooler's anger, they rarely are the real root of her problem. As a sense of self emerges, your preschooler is psychologically compelled to test her personal power against that of other people. Unfortunately, since her mother and father exert the most control over the child, they become her favorite "opponents." In addition, while constantly improving, a preschooler's mental capacities are not fully mature or refined. As a result, they often come into conflict with the realities of the world around her. Again, since her parents are perceived as all-powerful, she unreasonably regards them as the best place to vent any and all frustrations.

• *Do take it seriously.* Parents sometimes dismiss the ill-feelings of their preschooler because they consider them to be illogical. But it is critical to realize that the child's emotions are very real to her, and that they are perfectly legitimate from her point of view. They won't just go away if they are ignored, scoffed at, or ridiculed. And, the longer the underlying issues go untreated, the more they will fester and the worse they will become.

• *Educate as well as eradicate.* Having respect for a child's expressions of anger does not mean permitting inappropriate behavior. However, curbing misbehavior ultimately will be counter-productive if suitable alternatives are not provided. While parents should make it clear that unacceptable activities simply will not be tolerated, they also must take the time and make the effort to teach their preschooler how to convey her discontent constructively—and then praise her lavishly when she does so. For example, preschoolers often bite other children to express frustration or hostility. When this occurs, the offending child should be restrained and denied any positive attention while the offended child is comforted and compensated. After she has calmed down, the biter can be told, "You will not be allowed to hurt other children. If you want something, ask for it. If you don't like something, say so in words. If you need help, come to me." Then make sure that any appropriate behavior she subsequently exhibits is rewarded with a "Very good!" and a hug.

• *Don't hold a grudge.* Since they can be so hurtful at times, a preschooler's expressions of anger can easily poison the entire parent-child relationship. But, as intense as a child's displeasure may be, it also tends to be momentary. Given her relatively limited attention span and memory capacities, she probably will have long forgotten a particular conflict over which her mother and father are still agonizing. Her parents are a preschooler's primary source of love and support as well as her favorite opponents, so it is critical that they don't allow the occasional negative interactions to undermine the good that they provide through positive interactions.

• *Anticipate problems and avoid confrontations.* There is no way to escape unpleasantness completely. However, recognizing potential sources of a preschooler's ill-feelings will enable parents to eliminate a fair amount of trouble and thus maintain a predominantly friendly atmosphere in the home. It also will allow them to minimize the need for corrective action. For example, the introduction of a new sibling often produces intense feelings of jealousy and hostility in a preschooler. By being careful not to make a big fuss over the baby in front of her, and by making sure to give her a half-hour or so of undivided attention every day, parents can reduce a lot of the rivalry that would otherwise occur. Dealing with a child's anger will be easier and more effective if it requires only periodic lessons in civility instead of constant battles.

Strategies That Can Help

Prior to 1 1/2 years.

A child's first genuine feelings of anger are typically due to frustrated curiosity. Because she is rather naive, her explorations can lead her toward danger and destruction on occasion. And when her parents are thus forced to impose restrictions, she may express her displeasure by screaming, hitting, and biting.

The best preventative medicine is to make the home as safe as possible for the child's explorations, which will eliminate the constant need to say,"No." "Stop." "Don't touch." etc. Then, when she still manages to violate one of the few remaining restrictions, simply remove her from the offending situation and direct her toward more appropriate items and activities. She also can be given a chance to vent her frustrations in a more proper manner by hitting a pillow, biting a teething ring, etc.

1 1/2 to 2 1/2 Years

This is the period when the child's sense of self explodes and her inclination to test her personal power is overwhelming. This developmental compulsion often manifests itself in *negativism* — the tendency to refuse all requests, violate all restrictions, and ignore all warnings. Many mothers and fathers make the mistake of trying to appease their child, which only serves to encourage her and strengthen her determination. Then, when her behavior becomes totally intolerable and they finally attempt to curb her, she is likely to react quite violently with a classic temper tantrum.

The most effective strategy involves accommodating rather than appeasing the child's need to exert personal power. Whenever possible, she should be given suitable choices instead of direct instructions. For instance, during a dressing session, rather than issuing direct instructions, one can say, "Do you want to put your shirt or your pants on first?" This allows the child to have some control without having to contradict the will of her parents.

When confrontations do inevitably occur from time to time, simple distraction and re-direction probably will no longer work very well. Unfortunately, since she is yet not a particularly rational creature, extensive explanations that appeal to reason won't work. Instead, remove her from the offending situation and hold her with a firm hug for several minutes until the message sinks in that unacceptable behavior will not be tolerated.

This may be tough and time-consuming, and it may be embarrassing if it occurs in public. However, by remaining calm as they retain control of the situation, parents can provide their child with an excellent model for proper behavior during interpersonal disputes.

Finally, it is a good idea to temporarily put off toilet training or any other procedure that necessitates a lot of compliance on the part of the child.

2 1/2 to 4 Years
At this stage, a child does become comparatively "reasonable." However, her mental capacities remain rather immature, and her logic is extremely basic. Consequently, she often will become angry when the irregular world does not conform fully to her rigid expectations. The situation is further complicated by her *egocentrism* —her belief that everyone else is seeing and thinking precisely what she is seeing and thinking. As a result, after a brief outburst, she may start sulking or engaging in some other form of uncooperative behavior as if to say, "Well, you <u>should</u> know what's bothering me, so I'm not going to tell you!"

The first step in coping with such problems is to keep all rules, routines, obligations, etc. as simple and consistent as possible. Then, when a difficult situation does arise, use explanations that are well within the child's limited realm of experience and that don't overload her simple thinking processes. If she is reluctant to interact, take advantage of the fact that children at this stage greatly enjoy role-play and fantasy activities. By using dolls, "pretend" games, drawing materials, etc., it may be easier to have her express her feelings.

4 to 6 Years

This is the period when a child ordinarily begins to receive extensive instruction in everything from sports to academic subjects. Some children are likely to meet challenges for which they not ready developmentally. This can produce repeated failures; and since the child now is in competition with her peers on a regular basis, her disappointment may be all that much harder to take. She may subsequently suffer from low self-esteem, and she may turn her self-hatred around on occasion. The result is an apparently "unprovoked" attack on her parents, in which she uses the full extent of her ever-growing verbal abilities — including "cuss words" and other inappropriate language.

The first task for parents at this point is to ensure that their child has as many successful experiences as possible. This may mean ceasing certain types of instruction temporarily and then reintroducing them at a later, more developmentally suitable date. It also may mean scheduling extra sessions for activities she has mastered, so as to give her plenty of opportunities to feel good about herself.

When an inappropriate expression of anger does occur, parents should refrain from overreacting to the outburst, as this aggravates the situation. They should try to remain calm and encourage the child to talk about what is *really* bothering her. This won't always be easy, and it may sometimes require independent investigation. Once the real problem has been addressed, they can discuss with the child various ways in which she can get directly, quickly, and efficiently to the root of her difficulties and thus avoid a lot of unnecessary unpleasantness for everyone *the next time this happens.*

At Any Age

Remember to regard a preschooler's expressions of anger as a signal of psychological pain rather than as a personal rebuke. Keep cool, and speak to the child in language (both words and actions) she can understand. And always let her know that although you may disapprove of her inappropriate behavior, you still love and cherish her.

Chapter 24
When Parents and Children Get Angry

Toni H. Liebman

Nothing is more frustrating to parents than a disobedient or defiant child over whom they seem to have no control.

A typical morning scene:

It's almost time to leave the house to drop Daddy at the train station and Jeffrey at preschool before Mom goes to her office — but Jeffrey refuses to get dressed. "Hurry Jeffrey or we'll make Daddy miss his train, and you and I will both be late,"says Mom. "I don't care," says Jeffrey who is still feeling sluggish, "I'm not ready to get dressed." "Yes you are!" shouts Mom. "No I'm not," he shouts back. And so it goes...their voices getting louder and louder. "You're a bad Mommy...I hate you!" yells this now out-of-control four-year-old. "How dare you speak to me like that!" retorts his frustrated mother.

Anger, a legitimate emotion

Anger is a legitimate emotion and yet it is probably the one which causes the most difficulty for parents — especially mothers. Let's examine why.

Traditionally, most of us were never taught how to deal with anger. Women in particular were reared to think it "unfeminine" to express their anger. "Be nice!" was the common admonition from <u>our</u> mothers! And so, we were made to feel guilty if we felt angry. Many people equate angry feelings with a destructive rather than a healthy emotion. But it is important to differentiate between *destructive* and *constructive* anger.

We generally treat anger in one of three ways: 1) deny and repress it only to have it surface in unhealthy ways at a later date; 2) vent it in destructive ways that may be hurtful to others or damaging to people and property; or 3) manage it in acceptable ways to solve problems, right a wrong, or motivate positive behavior.

Why children get angry and how they respond

From infancy on, children become angry for many reasons:
- their physical or emotional needs are not met
- they feel frustrated because they are unable to accomplish something and cannot put it into words
- they are denied something they want
- they are striving for independence and feel overly controlled
- they are frightened, feel abandoned or have been treated harshly (verbally or physically)

It is interesting to note that, for children, sadness and anger are closely associated. What an adult experiences as sadness may be felt and expressed as anger in a child. Children tend to get angry most easily when tired, ill, stressed or bored.

Children's response to anger depends upon their age and/or developmental stage as well as the physical situation and the persons involved. The youngest will typically bite, cry, scream, pout, kick, yell, or all of the above (a full blown temper tantrum). As they reach four and five, their anger may be expressed by sulking or pouting or the use of angry words. In fact, getting youngsters to use words instead of physical outbursts is the goal of most early childhood educators. Most parents have heard expressions such as: "You're a doody-head." "I hate you." "I wish you were dead." (Occasionally a precocious four-to-six-year-old comes out with appropriately timed "adult" four letter words to everyone's chagrin.) More than likely, expressions of anger occur where children feel safest: at home, in the presence of parents, or at an early childhood program where they feel very comfortable.

Why parents get angry at their children and how they respond
Adults usually believe that they can, or are supposed to, control children. Nothing is more frustrating to parents than a disobedient or defiant child over whom they seem to have no control. Sometimes parents *can* tolerate the whining, the accidents, the excessive noise and mess. But often the failure to cooperate, the lack of appreciation, the battle of wills, or out-of-bounds behavior is more than parents can bear. The resulting sense of utter helplessness and humiliation makes parents feel they have "done something wrong."

When *parents* are tired, ill, stressed or bored, the problem is compounded and reactions are less controlled. Parents yell, scream, threaten, punish, scold, hit, isolate, deprive. While it may temporarily stop a child's negative behavior and/or make a parent feel better, a constant diet of such out-of-bounds behavior on the part of adults will not likely have a positive impact and may, in fact, cause long-lasting negative results. It is generally accepted that children who have been harshly treated at home are most likely to become the bullies of the school yard and punitive parents to their own offspring.

Parenting is probably the most difficult job any adult can have. Children are unpredictable. The conflicts between children's needs and parent's needs are universal and never-ending. There are no easy answers...and even the most capable parents must deal with troublesome events and misbehavior. But the way parents react to such situations determines whether or not their children will learn positive ways to express their anger and become self-controlled individuals. It is important to understand that discipline is a long term learning process by which children adopt their parents' values and attitudes and develop the inner controls so desperately needed to become well-functioning adults. The manner in which parents speak to — and listen to — their children is a critical part of this process.

Ways for Parents to Prevent Angry Confrontations

Be a good detective: Read your child's signals so that you know when he or she is tired, ill, bored, sad, or frustrated. Behavior gives the clues to what a child is thinking and feeling, especially in very young children. Even older children cannot always put their feelings into words.

Be accepting of your child's thoughts and feelings: No one can, or should, control what another person, including a child, is thinking or feeling even when those thoughts or feelings seem "foolish," "childish," or "inappropriate." A child must not only be allowed to express feelings, but encouraged to do so! In the incident mentioned on page 173 when Jeffrey refused to get dressed, his mother could have said, *"I know you would rather not get dressed right now — but we have to leave for the station or we'll all be late. I'll help you so you can do it faster."*

Other examples are: Michael is shopping with his mother and demands that she buy several toys he had seen advertised on TV. His mother could say, *"I know you would like to buy all those toys, but we don't have enough money right now. When we get home we'll write them on your wish list. Then we can choose what to buy you for your birthday."*

Aisha is having an argument with her younger sister. Her father sees Aisha making a fist and gently stops her and says, *"It looks like you are very angry with your sister right now, but I can't let you hit her...that hurts, and we don't hurt each other."*

Be positive: Tell children what they can do and praise them for their efforts. Instead of *"Stop bouncing that ball in the house, "* offer an option: *"The ball can be bounced outside, but not inside."* Catch a child doing something good: *"You're doing a great job putting your toys away...or dressing yourself...or setting the table."*

Instead of getting angry when your child misbehaves — try these strategies.

Treat a "mistake" as a chance to learn: *"Looks like you forgot the rules about not playing ball in the house. Please try to remember next time."*

Show faith in his/her ability to improve: *"I see you don't feel like sharing that bike right now, but I'm sure you'll be ready to share in a little while. Please let Ericka know when it's her turn."*

Provide logical consequences
Consequences should be:
1) In proportion to the behavior — not every deed is a major offense.
2) Related to the behavior — removing crayons for a while has more to do with learning not to crayon on the walls than denial of TV.
3) As soon as possible after the incident so that the child connects the consequences to the behavior.

Speak as calmly as possible. Let the child know why you are angry: Choose words which focus on the *behavior,* not the child as a person. *"I don't like it when you spill your milk on the floor; it makes a mess,"* rather than *"You bad girl, you always spill your milk on the floor. You're so messy."*

Be willing to admit a mistake
Reassess what might be unrealistic expectations on your part and tell your child if *you've* made a mistake. For example: *"Jane, I'm sorry that the bag of groceries fell on the floor. I didn't realize that it was too heavy for you to carry."*

What to do when you start to feel really angry at your child
Calm down...and, depending upon how angry you are:
• Take a deep breath and remember, you are the adult.
• Count to 10...or 100.
• Think through the alphabet...forward...backward.
• Remove yourself from the situation...take a "Time Out!" Splash some

water on your face; take a bath; hug a pillow. Listen to your favorite music.
• Try to think clearly, "What is happening here...do I know what actually happened?"
• "What am I *really* angry about...my child's behavior, or something larger?" "Will I be sorry if I take a particular course of action?" *"No trip to the beach tomorrow,"* may punish you as well as your child...and by tomorrow, she may forget why she's being punished.
• Be willing to apologize. Say, *"I'm sorry"* about words used or action taken in the heat of your anger.

What not to do when you start to feel really angry at your child
Don't inhibit your child's angry feelings by ignoring, denying, or punishing them. Ineffective responses are: *"How dare you talk to me like that." "I never want to hear you say those things again." "I'm going to spank you if you ever get this angry again."* Instead, find out why he/she is so angry...and try to help solve the problem.

Don't take it personally when your child argues, talks back, or refuses to do something. Children have always balked at parents' authority...it is quite normal that they do not want to do everything asked of them. Sometimes they are just trying to assert their independence. However, parents also have a right to assert their authority as long as they are fair and considerate, and have expectations that are appropriate to the age of their child.

Don't problem solve or set a punishment in the heat of anger: *"We'll have to discuss this in a few minutes when I'm not so angry,"* may be better than jumping to a conclusion immediately.

Children can learn to understand the dangers of repressing their angry feelings and the importance of learning to express them in constructive ways if parents are good role models in this area. Parents can learn to accept their child's anger as a natural emotion which, if expressed in socially acceptable ways, can lead to a healthier life.

Naps, Bedtime, and Dreams

Paulette Bochnig Sharkey

Sleep — if only
small children liked it
as much as
their weary parents do!

Sleep — if only small children liked it as much as their weary parents do! In most households, getting the children to sleep and keeping them asleep is a major effort. In fact, sleep problems are the most common concerns that parents voice to pediatricians.

How Much Sleep Does Your Preschooler Need?
Your preschooler may seem to be in perpetual motion, too busy exploring the world to take time out for rest. It is up to you to establish a daily routine to ensure that your child gets the rest he needs. But how much is that? Although the amount varies from child to child (and is often not as much as parents would like), most preschoolers need about 12 hours of nighttime rest.

Naps
Naps are an important part of the sleep picture. Somewhere around 15-18 months, most toddlers go through an awkward phase in which two naps are too many and one nap is not enough. By age two, a single late-morning or early-afternoon nap is usually sufficient. At around three-years-old, however, daytime naps may interfere with going to sleep at night. Many children are now ready to give up naps completely. They can then rest without sleeping by having a "quiet time" by themselves to listen to music or look at picture books.

Bedtime
The problem of getting off to sleep is actually a problem your child has, in learning to separate from you for the night and starting to grow toward independence. Your youngster will feel more secure about this separation if you establish a regular routine as he prepares for bed.

Bedtime Rituals
Keep bedtime at about the same time each night and keep your ritual simple. A bath, then perhaps a soft song and a story provide the quiet time needed to prepare most children for sleep. Television shows usually have a stimulating rather than a calming effect, and rough play just before bedtime will excite your youngster and make it harder for her to fall asleep. Be firm and consistent about your expectations for bedtime, even if your child resists. Help her see that bedtime is a happy, normal way to end the day.

Combatting Fears and Loneliness
Small children often feel afraid or lonely in a dark room at night. Providing a night light may help combat these feelings. The presence of a pet dog or cat sleeping beside the bed is also reassuring to youngsters. Most preschoolers are comforted by voices of family members and other sounds of domestic life drifting through their open bedroom door. Some

children like to listen to music as they fall asleep, or find the hum of a fan soothing during warm weather.

You don't want your child to need *you* in order to go to sleep. If your child is used to having you rock him, pat him, or lie down with him until he falls asleep, he will need you to repeat those actions in order to fall back to sleep any time he awakens during the night. Instead, encourage your child to select a special stuffed animal or a treasured blanket for bedtime. That object will then be associated in his mind with sleep, and if he awakens during the night, he will be able to fall back to sleep by himself, as he hugs his special bedtime companion.

To "wean" him away from needing your presence in the room, you might try this method: after you have finished your bedtime routine, say good night. Then leave the room for five minutes, saying, "I'll be back soon," and return as promised. If he is still awake, leave again, telling your child, "I'll check on you in a few minutes," and make the absence a little longer. If your child hasn't fallen asleep by the time you return, repeat this last step, checking occasionally to make sure nothing is wrong.

It's a fact of life that most parents spend some of their wee hours dealing with the sleep problems of their wee ones. But take heart, your child will outgrow it. And the day will come when you'll wonder how to get your sleepy-headed teenager out of bed on Saturday morning!

Helping Your Child
with Sleep Problems

Sleep Disruptions

If your child wakes during the night but has no problem, he should be able to fall back to sleep without parental attention. Although the experts don't always agree on how to deal with crying at night, most suggest to ignore the first whimper, but to respond to continued crying. However, after you've made sure that there is nothing really wrong, stay only a few minutes, until your child is reassured.

Nightmares

Young children often become their most fearful at night when they are tired. When your child's fears, either real or imagined, become part of his dream, the dream turns into a nightmare. Preschoolers often have bad dreams in which they are being chased by animals or monsters.

Nightmares are a normal part of childhood. They may result from daytime stress such as a change in preschool, a new baby brother or sister, or a move to a new home. Your child may also have bad dreams when running a high fever.

When your child has a nightmare, go to him immediately. Hold him and assure him that it's all right now, and stay until he is calm. The next day, you might want to talk about the fear. Having your child draw a picture of what frightened him can also help sort out reality from fantasy. Above all, *don't* undermine your child's confidence by dismissing a bad dream as "silly."

While nightmares are not usually something for parents to worry about, there are some things you can do to lessen their occurrence:

• Don't use sleep as a punishment. If your child associates going to bed with being bad, the anxiety may cause nightmares.

• Be careful about what you say at bedtime. The innocent remark, "Good night, don't let the bedbugs bite," may make your child wonder just where those creepy-crawlies are!

• Monitor what your child watches on TV. Imaginations can work overtime, especially at night.

• Your child doesn't need the added worry about wetting the bed, so don't make toilet-training an issue at night.

Night Terrors
Your child has just drifted off to sleep when you hear crying and screaming. You run to find her sitting up in bed, eyes open, trembling with fear. She doesn't recognize you and refuses to be comforted. The sobbing continues. Your child is having a *night terror.*

Many people confuse night terrors with nightmares, but they are actually very different. Night terrors occur within the first 2 hours of going to bed, in the deepest part of sleep. Despite her wide-eyed look, a child having a night terror is not awake, and sleep experts agree that trying to wake her only makes things worse. A night terror may last as long as half an hour, but as heart-wrenching as it is for a parent to watch, your child will remember nothing about the incident the next morning. Most children outgrow night terrors by the time they start school. If you suspect that your child suffers from night terrors, talk to your pediatrician.

Sleep — Health and Safety Considerations
√ Never tie a pacifier around your child's neck or use a long string to attach one to the side of a crib. It might get tangled and cause strangulation.
√ Remove all toys that are strung across the crib as soon as your child is beginning to push up on hands and knees or when he is five months of age, whichever occurs first. These toys can cause strangulation, according to the Consumer Product Safety Commission.
√ If your child develops the habit of climbing out of a crib, it's safer to start leaving the sides of the crib down. And maybe it's time for the big move...

From Crib to Bed: Easing the Transition

There is no set "correct" age when you should move your young child into a bed, although most preschoolers are ready between 2 and 3 years of age. This is an important milestone for your child. Here are some ways you can help:

• If you're buying a new bed, let your child be part of the process by going along with you for the shopping.

• Consider putting the new bed in place in your child's room along with the crib for awhile (space permitting). You can introduce the bed gradually, perhaps using it at first only for naps, and let the crib's importance gradually phase out.

• Make the bed inviting by selecting bright sheets and pillowcases. A small bedside table equipped with lamp, cassette or record player, and picture books will add to a "grown-up" atmosphere that will delight your child.

• Don't change your bedtime ritual when your child moves from crib to bed. For example, be sure it's understood that the new lack of physical barriers is not an open invitation to get up and play, or come to your room.

• If you have a new baby on the way, move your child into the new bed well ahead of the baby's arrival. Leaving the crib empty for a couple of months may lessen your preschooler's feeling of resentment toward the baby who will sleep there.

Early Waking

Small children often wake too early in the morning. If you want to grab a few extra minutes of sleep, you might try tucking a couple of books into your child's bed after he's asleep, or installing light-blocking window coverings. Some parents set a clock-radio, telling their preschooler, "You'll know that it's morning when you hear the music."

The Family Bed

One of the most controversial questions surrounding sleep is that of the "family bed," allowing small children to sleep with their parents. Some argue that it provides warmth and security for the child, while others worry about how it affects the parents' privacy and the child's independence.

If your child climbs into your bed at night, most child development specialists recommend that you walk him back to his own bed, tuck him in, give him his favorite toy to hold, reassure him, and return to bed.

Chapter 26
Summer Nights,
Summer Days

Betty Farber

*Sometimes they cannot believe
that it's time for bed,
because they know they go
to sleep at night —
and night means that it's dark...*

Summer Nights — Problems at Bedtime

The sky is still light—no moon or stars…people lounging outdoors…voices of older children playing ball. But it's bedtime for your preschoolers, tired after a long day of outdoor play.

Sometimes they cannot believe that it's time for bed, because they know they go to sleep at night — and *night means that it's dark.*

Children are governed by their perceptions, rather than by logic. When they see the sun shining in the sky, they believe it is daytime, because their perceptions tell them so. The fact that summer days are longer because of movements of the earth around the sun will probably not make sense to them until they are older. So when parents say it is bedtime, some children complain, "It's not bedtime! I don't have to go to bed yet!"

This is not a new complaint. Back in the late 1800's, Robert Louis Stevenson wrote in *A Child's Garden of Verses:*

Bed in Summer

In winter I get up at night
And dress by yellow
candle-light.
In summer, quite the other way,
I have to go to bed by day.
* * *
And does it not seem hard to you,
When all the sky is clear and blue,
And I should like so much to play,
To have to go to bed by day?

Problems at Bedtime

If bedtime is a problem for your preschooler, there are some strategies you can use to make going to bed more relaxing. After your child is in his pajamas, read a quiet story such as *Goodnight Moon* (See Resources, page 213). This practice is appropriate any time of the year. Children often enjoy hearing a soft lullaby or a poem that is pleasant and rhythmic.

Another device is to set an alarm clock for the hour of bedtime. Tell your child that the clock is saying that it's time for bed. This avoids a confrontation. Often children are more ready to respond to a mechanical object that is an impartial "third party." You and your child can read the time on the clock together.

If your child has difficulty sleeping because of the light coming in, try putting a dark curtain on the window. It may be hung on a spring-rod which can be removed, or tied back during the day. Or you can have room-darkening shades installed.

If your child is afraid of the dark, a night-light or a glow-in-the-dark toy may be a comfort. If your preschooler has fears of monsters, tell him that you are going to spray the room with anti-monster spray. Go through the motions of spraying with an imaginary spray can. Your youngster may be amused, but may also feel safe enough to go to sleep.

Summer Days: What'll We Do Now?

Summer days can be the best of the year for children. It is the magical vacation time when children and parents can share in the wonders of the countryside or the seashore. You and your child can share in the joys of this poem about summer. Involve your preschooler in the reading by letting him complete the unfinished lines.

Summer Song
by John Ciardi

By the sand between my toes,
By the waves behind my ears,
By the sunburn on my nose,
By the little salty tears
That make rainbows in the sun
When I squeeze my eyes and run,

By the way the seagulls screech,
Guess where I am? *At the ...!*
By the way the children shout
Guess what happened?
School is ...!
By the way I sing this song
Guess if summer lasts too long:
You must answer Right or...!

(from: *The Man Who Sang the Sillies,* Lippincott, 1961)

But summer can also be a lonely time—the preschool may be closed— friends are away— it rains and you can't play outdoors.

Here are ideas for activities indoors, outdoors and on the road.

Indoor Activities:
A rainy summer day. *What'll we do now?* Prepare for the inevitable rainy day while the weather is pleasant. Have your children collect materials such as sand, shells, rocks, pebbles, and leaves to make creative projects indoors when it rains.

For all of the activities that follow, cover a table with newspaper and tape down the edges to anchor it, for easier cleanup.

1. Sand pictures. Materials: Sand (1 cupful), cardboard or construction paper, white glue, disposable spoon, disposable cake pan (ages 2-6). Child squeezes out glue on to the cardboard or construction paper, making a design with the squiggles. Place the paper or cardboard into the cake pan. Use the spoon to sprinkle the sand over the paper so that the sand sticks to the glue. Shake off excess sand into the pan and let the picture dry while you make another.

2. Beach sculpture. Materials: Shells, pebbles, glue, cardboard, or wood (ages 3-6). Use shells and rocks collected at the beach. Glue them to a piece of wood or heavy cardboard for a three-dimentional collage.

3. Faces made from rocks and shells. Materials: Rocks and shells that are shaped like heads, watercolor markers, or paints and brushes (ages 3-6). Draw or paint eyes, noses, mouths, ears, teeth, horns, etc., on the rocks and shells to make strange and interesting faces.

4. Leaf rubbings. Materials: Leaves from trees or bushes, light weight paper, crayons (ages 3-6). Place the paper over a leaf. Remove covering from the crayon. Place the crayon flat (horizontally) on the paper and rub over the area where the leaf is. The shape of the leaf will appear. Use several leaves and different colors of crayons.

Outdoor Activities:
On a hot summer day, children cool off best with "water play" — using water as a play material. Water is not only cooling, it is calming and satisfying. It also offers opportunities:
• to **socialize** with other children
• to use thinking and reasoning abilities **(cognitive skills)** with concepts such as *float and sink* or *empty and full*
• to enhance **gross motor skills** (using the large muscles)
• to enhance **fine motor skills** (using the small muscles of the fingers).

The activities that follow all use some form of "water play."

HINTS:Your preschooler may wear a bathing suit, so that getting wet is part of the fun. You may want to wear one too !

1. Paint with water. Materials: Large paint brushes, bucket of water (ages 1-5). Have children "paint" the garage, fence, steps, etc. with water.

2. Exploring the ways of water. Materials: Large plastic water tub, unbreakable cups, squeeze bottles, funnels, strainers, egg beaters (ages 1-5). Place the plastic tub of water on a bench or low table so that children standing next to it can easily reach in with their hands. Let children explore the ways the water acts, using the different materials.

3. See what floats and what sinks. Materials: Plastic tub (see above), water, corks, toy boats, Ivory soap, rocks, buttons, cardboard rolls from used paper towels (ages 2-6). Children try placing various objects in the water to see which of them can float. They use the paper towel rolls to act as "the wind" and blow the floating objects along in the water. Children may try to predict whether a new object added to the water will float or sink. (SAFETY NOTE: Avoid using small items that young preschoolers may put in their mouths.)

4. This is the way we wash our clothes. Materials: Plastic tub (see above), water, liquid soap, doll clothes, washable dolls. String (for clothesline.) Clothespins are optional (ages 2-6). Let children wash their dolls and their doll clothes. Hang the clothes on a line—use string tied to the backs of two chairs.

5. Soap Bubbles. Materials: Liquid detergent, unbreakable cup, pipe cleaner (ages 2-6). Add a small amount of liquid detergent to a half cup of water. Stir. Twist pipe cleaner to form a circle at the top. Dip into soapy water and blow gently through circle.

6. Fill 'er up. **Materials: tricycle, waterproof container with cover** (such as a Cool Whip container), and watering can (ages 3-6). Punch two small holes in the bottom of the plastic container. Punch one hole on each side of the container and tie a string through it, like a bucket handle. Replace the cover on the container. Hang it on the back of the tricycle, behind the seat. The child riding the trike stops at the "gas station." The gas station attendant removes the plastic cover from the gas tank and fills the container with water, covering it when full. The driver rides around around until the "gas tank" is empty. (The gas is used up as the water leaks out of the holes in the bottom of the plastic container.) After a time, the roles may be reversed and the gas station operator becomes the driver.

7. Transferring Liquids. Materials: Plastic eyedropper, 2 bowls, food coloring (ages 3-6).Put food coloring in bowl of water. Child transfers liquid to the other bowl using eyedropper.

Activities on the Road
"Half the fun is getting there!" But not unless you have something to do in the car as you ride. Here are some ideas for activities as you journey toward your destination.

1. Bring along plenty of paper, a hard surface (such as a book) to write on, and thick, non-toxic, crayons for small fingers. Hint: crayons melt on the upholstery if left in a closed car on a hot day. Count your crayons and remove them from the car when you reach your destination (ages 1-6).

2. Play "Simon Says." Think of things your youngster can do while sitting. For example: Simon says, "Clap your hands." Simon says, "Close your eyes." Simon says, "Put hands on your head." (ages 1-5).

3. Bring a battery operated cassette recorder:
• Children can listen to tape recordings of their favorite stories and songs (ages 1-6).
• Children can talk into the recorder about what they're seeing as they ride— recording the history of the trip (ages 3-6)
• A child can play "Talk Show Host" and interview members of the family (ages 4-6).

4. Using the books, *I Read Symbols* and *I Read Signs,* by Tana Hoban, Greenwillow, 1983, find the signs or symbols pictured in the books (ages 3-6).

5. Make a list before you start of things you might see on your trip: for example: a dog, a cow, a dump truck. Check the item when somebody sees it. When the list is completed, everybody wins (ages 3-6).

Chapter 27
Helping Preschoolers Cope with Fears

Fredric C. Hartman

*Young children
are continually
facing the unknown.*

Preschoolers live in worlds of enchantment and mystery. What we adults see as ordinary and harmless, they might experience with downright terror: hearing a flushing toilet or a police siren, seeing ocean waves, animals at a zoo, or a parent leaving a room.

Young Children Are Continually Facing the Unknown.

The world is all new to them, huge to begin with, always expanding and ever changing as they themselves are dramatically changing and growing. And when a child is changing and growing so rapidly, he is continually encountering the unknown. Each moment his world is a different world and holds suspense and discoveries which can *terrify* as well as delight. Because their understanding is limited and their imagination is vivid, children tend to distort and magnify things. It takes time for them to learn to judge things and to put them into realistic perspective.

Young Children Need Their Parents' Patience and
Love to Help Them Gain Mastery Over Their Fears.

Fear, in young children, indicates the beginning stage of an accurate appreciation of the immense powers in the world, and represents a potentially highly creative struggle to gain mastery over what is frightening them. It is crucial that parents appreciate this important necessary creative act that shows itself as fear.

Children May Not Express Their Fears Outwardly.

Young children may not express their fear in any apparent way. They may harbor fear within themselves, and only give subtle cues as to how they are actually feeling. It may be because they do not know how to label their feeling as fear—or because they dread being criticized or shamed for having fears. It is important for you, as parents, to learn to be attuned to your child's unspoken expressions, and to be able to "read" them accurately.

General guidelines in dealing with your children's fears

What not to do when your child is afraid:
• Don't assume that it is necessarily your fault that he is afraid.
• Don't make light of — or fun of — his fears.
• Don't shame him before others because of his fears.
• Don't become impatient and treat him as if he were babyish because he is afraid.
• Don't force him to face the thing he fears before he is ready to do so.

Doing any of these things habitually will definitely hamper your child's ability to cope with fears and impede the development of a strong sense of self-esteem.

What to do when your child is afraid:
• Respect your child's fears as though they were your own.
• Allow your child a reasonable period of withdrawal from feared things before you attempt to help him adjust to them.
• Give your child a chance gradually to get used to what is fearful to him.
• When he actively desires to approach a formerly feared object, help him to have the desired experience, but only under your supervision.
• Keep in mind that your preschooler will likely outgrow most of his fears.

Try to understand your child's fear in relation to her personality, and, within reason, to spare her the situations which you know will cause fear. If your child is fearing an unfamiliar situation, such as attending a new preschool for example, try to analyze the problem to find out what is causing the fear. If your child's fears are excessive and become chronic — and you are unable to find the cause and help relieve the fear — consider seeking professional advice. Chronic fear can wear down a child's confidence and hinder her functioning at home, at school, and at play with others.

Children need their parents' wisdom, patience, comfort, and love in order to help them achieve the mastery over their fears — and make this mastery a permanent part of themselves. In this way, they will be better able to face the unknown and solve the problems to be faced later in life.

Common Fears and How to Handle Them

The Body. Children will learn to view their bodies in much the same way that their parents view their own bodies. If parents are unduly concerned with their own physical health or their child's health and surround the child with a sickroom atmosphere or smother him with anxious questions, the child may become preoccupied with his own health and develop fears about his body. Moderate concern and periodic visits to the pediatrician will be the best way to prevent fears from developing in your child about his body. The same applies to the curiosity in children that increases as they grow older. Children will explore their bodies to understand themselves. When parents are overly anxious about their child's interest in his bowels or genitals, the child may develop shame or fear of these body parts and their functioning. If a child becomes preoccupied with any part of his body, a limit can be placed on any unacceptable behavior, in a gentle manner without causing fear or shame to develop.

Sleeping. What do you do if your child says, "I'm afraid of the dark! Please don't turn off the light!" or, "There's someone hiding under the bed. I can't go to sleep." First of all it is important to take your child's fears very seriously and to respect them. If your child fears the dark, leaving a night light on may give the child the confidence she needs. Or you may provide a small flashlight under the pillow. This will help your child feel a sense of control over the dark and help her gain mastery over it. If there are shadows on the wall in your child's bedroom it may be helpful to provide curtains or to rearrange your child's room so he isn't as disturbed by them.

If your child feels that there are creatures under the bed or in the closet, it may require some imaginative ritual engaged in with the child to exorcise the ghosts and the demons. These collaborative efforts, if they are done in a spirit of patience, love, and concern, help foster in your child a sense of mastery over what he fears.

Nightmares. To help a child who wakes from a nightmare, parents can turn on the light, be with him for a short while, and let him see he is in a safe, familiar place. In general, nightmares can be reduced when children have a free, active play life but are not overstimulated by play or story time before bed. It will also help for parents to identify the causes of nightmares if they become persistent. Sudden changes in the home situation may set off periods of nightmares—such as a move to a new home, the presence of a new sibling, an illness in a parent, the death of a close relative, or a sudden change in the amount of time a parent spends with a child. If nightmares persist, professional advice may be needed.

Animals. Most fears of animals, particularly dogs and cats, are temporary. You can help your child deal with these fears by gradual and gentle familiarization. If a child is afraid of dogs, a small dog can often be tolerated when large dogs cannot. Some children have to start by playing with a toy animal or by reading books about the feared animal. With many children, having a puppy or a kitten is the best way to overcome fear of dogs and cats and other animals as well.

Water. The earliest fear of water comes in the form of being bathed. When this fear occurs, it is important to respect it. Discontinue the bathing routine that the child is objecting to for a few days, and perhaps give sponge baths instead. If sponge baths are given, always approach the child with the washcloth from the back and not from the front. Reduce even the sponge baths if necessary until the child is no longer alarmed at the prospect of a bath. It also is possible that the child could tolerate being bathed by someone else. Fear of the water at beaches, lakes, and pools ought to be dealt with by means of gentle encouragement without applying any real pressure. (Encouraging the child to take the plunge works with some children but not with most.) It is very important to allow the child to find her own most comfortable way to cope with the situation with the help of her parents' gentle support.

Fire. Fear of fire in young children is not uncommon particularly when there has been an unpleasant experience. The way to help a child to overcome a fear of fire is gradually to familiarize the child with fire in pleasant situations such as the family barbecue, the living room fireplace, a campfire, or even the burning of a birthday candle. Visiting a firehouse and speaking with firemen may also help increase your child's sense of security. Children who have too great a fascination with fire can be helped similarly by familiarizing them with the dangers as well as the positive uses of fire.

Physicians, Dentists, and Hospitals. Again, as with all other fears your child experiences, it is important to respect him, to avoid putting pressure on him, and to gradually familiarize him with the necessary settings and procedures. Visit dentists' and doctors' offices and the nearby hospital even before it is necessary to go. When it is time to go and your child expresses some fear and resistance, it may be enough if you just take a firm but gentle stand by simply saying that the work has to be done. With children who are more frightened, offering a meaningful reward may help. In some cases, it may be necessary for the dentist or doctor to befriend the child in order to relieve her fear.

However, in some instances, if possible, it will be necessary to postpone the appointment to relieve your child. In the event of an emergency when it will not be possible to ease the child into the fearful situation, a comforting, patient parent who can communicate love and support to the child can have a decisive influence on comforting and relieving the child's fears. Always be truthful in these situations. Don't promise the child that there will be no pain, because there might be, or that you won't leave him because you may have to. Plan in advance with the child for some nice thing to happen afterwards. Above all, allow your child to talk about the experience as often as is necessary. This too will help her master the feelings and fears that were experienced.

Separation. For children under six, perhaps the greatest fear of all is losing the closeness of their parents. Children know they are completely dependent upon their parents. Anything that threatens the parent-child bond can arouse intense helplessness and fear. Physical separations of any duration particularly with very young children need to be handled with the knowledge of your child's personality in mind. How you depart, the tone of voice you use, how long you are away and how you return ought to be geared as much as possible to the child's comfort until he is more used to your absence. It should be made quite clear to the child what is happening, where you are going, and how long you will be away. Objections on the part of your child should be answered simply and firmly and a clear idea given of when you will rejoin the child. Being honest with your child, and feeling confident yourself that leaving the child is okay will help your child accept your temporary absence.

Reference: <u>The Gesell Institute's Child Behavior from Birth to Ten</u>, by Frances L. Ilg. M.D. and Louise Bates Ames, Ph.D. Harper & Row, 1955, and <u>The Child from 5 to 10</u>, by A. Gesell, F. Ilg, L. Bates Ames, & G.E.Bullis. Harper & Row, 1977.

Chapter 28
Separation:
Saying Goodbye
is Often Difficult

Nancy Balaban

*Separation experiences
happen in
all phases of our lives...*

Joyce has just left three- year-old Henry at nursery school. Even though he has been happily attending school for two months, he now clings to her legs and begs her not to leave. She is both puzzled and annoyed. Why is he doing this now? Just when she had her morning all planned...

There are so many reasons for preschool children to resist separation from their parents, whether it's to go to school, stay with the babysitter, be left at a birthday party, spend the day at their grandparents, or go to a friend's house. Mainly, saying goodbye is often tough — not only for children but for adults as well — because it arouses a mixed bag of feelings: sadness, grief, anger and, at the same time, anticipation.

Separation Experiences Are Universal
Separation experiences happen in all phases of our lives beginning with birth when we leave the familiar, warm, protective, nine-month environment for a world of bright lights, noise, and changing temperatures. Separation occurs when we change jobs, move to a new home, take a trip, graduate from high school or college, get married, get divorced, or lose a loved one through death.

There is a common thread that runs through all these events. We must give up something familiar and face the unknown. And there's the rub — the unknown. What will the new job, the new neighborhood, the new school be like? The unknown brings both the excitement and the adventure of the new along with the pull back to the familiar. It is this bittersweet mixture that causes us — and our children — pain.

Parent/Child Attachment
The roots of these feelings about separation lie very deep in the attachment that infants form with their parents during the first year of life. This matures into a tie that binds child to parent across both space and time. It is this attachment that prompts a parent to rush to the bedside of a sick child, though the "child" be adult, the parent elderly, and the distance many miles.

Attachment and separation are two sides of the same coin. They constitute a declaration of love, though it may not look that way to Joyce who is rapidly becoming annoyed with Henry's clinging. As Joyce and the teacher, Diane, try to understand Henry's behavior, they realize that Diane had been ill for several days and a substitute had replaced her. Now they speculate that Henry is afraid that Diane might "disappear" again without warning — so he clings to Joyce for safety. Joyce reassures him that Diane will not be sick again today; she will be here all day to take good care of him. Joyce encourages Henry to make a painting that she can see when she comes back to pick him up. She hugs him, says goodbye, and leaves. He whimpers a moment, then goes off to the easel.

We can help children's transitions to new places and new people by acknowledging with them that while saying goodbye may be hard — we always come back.

Separations Can Become Moves to Independence

How you handle separations from your child can help him develop emotional strength. Here are some suggestions for turning partings into a growth experience.

• Visit the school or center before you decide to send your child. Make sure that you feel comfortable with the way children are treated and cared for. If you are not allowed to visit a classroom, consider another school.

• Meet your child's feelings about leaving head-on. Remember that most children are as worried about "leaving home" as they are about "starting school." When you acknowledge the scary, upset feelings, you are telling your child it's okay to feel that way and that you understand. "It's okay to feel angry, sad or afraid. Sometimes even I feel that way — lots of grownups do. It's hard to say goodbye."

• Tell your child in advance (but not too far ahead) that he or she will soon be going to school or day care. Paint a positive picture of the forthcoming experience and reassure your child that the school you have chosen is a good place for children.

• Examine your own feelings. Find out what the balance is between worry and excited anticipation. If worry predominates, talk this over with the director or teacher so that you can get some reassurance yourself. These sorts of feelings tend to filter down to children.

• Plan to spend some time in the classroom with your child so that the entry process is gradual. Don't choose a school that believes in "cold turkey" separations.

• When it's time for you to leave, allow your child to participate fully in saying goodbye — even if it means tears. *Never* sneak out — it makes children feel abandoned.

• Allow your son or daughter to bring a favorite toy or security object to school. It's like bringing a bit of home with them.

• If you are concerned about your child, arrange to talk to her on the phone from your office. You can reassure her that you will be back after work.

• Your photograph in his cubby or something of yours (like a hanky or scarf) often helps when the going gets rough.

Just remember that as an adult you have had experience with the separation feelings of anxiety and fear. You know that these unpleasant feelings will eventually go away. But children, because they have very limited experience, think the feelings will never end. That's why they need so much reassurance from you and from their teacher.

You may see children's reactions to separation in many other situations. It is common for children to protest parting when they return to school after an illness. You might see some clinginess if one, or both parents have been out of town, or if an important family member has been ill. A change in family routine, tension in the home, an impending move, the imminent birth of a sibling can all cause a young child to resist saying goodbye at nursery or day care.

Resistance to parting is seldom willful. Rather, it is behavior that aims to keep the loved person near, like lovers at an airport who cling together even though the boarding call has been made. Saying goodbye with confidence means that the child has learned that she will be safe and enjoyably engaged until her parent returns.

Paying attention to the needs of the young child who is missing home will surely bring rewards. It will breed self-confidence and build competence because children will learn that they can cope with these uncomfortable feelings through the support of their parents and teachers.

Chapter 29
Television:
Parents Make
the Difference

Susan E. Baker

*Only parents
can determine if TV
is being used wisely...*

When Angela returns from preschool each day, she heads straight for the TV. She doesn't sit down to watch right away and she probably doesn't even realize what program is on. She just likes the sounds of voices. After her snack, she keeps company with the TV and is not interested in playing with her friends.

Derrick is usually watching television with his mom. He has become interested in her soap operas and knows the names of the characters as well as she does.

Elizabeth and Jessica are sisters; they love cartoons and especially like the way the funny animals keep bopping each other in the mouth and head. After their favorite cartoons are over, mom is always getting after them for hitting each other or wrestling.

In the Marshalls' family, the parents regularly read the guide to television programs and review them to determine which are acceptable for their children. They then let their kids choose from among the shows that they have recommended.

The first three situations are more common than the last. While they may seem harmless, they are evidence of a society that is placing increasing importance on TV as a substitute for friends, family interaction, or other activities. Fortunately, more and more parents like the Marshalls are recognizing the need to keep a watchful eye on children's viewing habits.

Television can offer our children the opportunity to learn about a wide variety of places, people, occupations, ideas, life styles, and value systems. Television also can help children to think, question, to imagine, to create. It can empower them to act and make their world a better place. It *can* do all this, but parental guidance is needed if television is to accomplish these positive objectives.

Only parents can determine if TV is being used wisely and if it has a positive or negative affect on the way the family is living. It is the parents' responsibility to see if television is interfering with family talks, games, storytime, and other interactions which contribute to children's learning.

Television — The Main Course or Dessert?
By permitting TV to dominate the family's leisure time, we are allowing it to destroy qualities that make families unique: listening to music, reading together, participating in sports, socializing, etc. Television viewing has become a passive way of life for most of our young children. It is being used by our preschoolers as a baby-sitter, entertainer and the central learning tool. TV is being used as a "main course." Instead it should be a "dessert," something to look forward to, or as a special treat. This is not happening in many American homes.

Did You Know?
• Your children will attend elementary and high school for 12 years. If they watched television at the rate of just one hour each weekday during those 12 years — the 4,368 hours would be equal to two full years of school.
• Children three-to-five-years-old view TV an average of 54 hours each week.
• The average prekindergartner spends more than half his or her waking time before a television set.
• Murders occur twice as frequently on TV than they do in real life.
• Most U.S. children watch about 30,000 commercials a year on TV.

TV's Impact on Children
When children watch television, it can make a difference in their attitude. The more violence that occurs in shows they watch, the more accepting they are of aggressive behavior. Over the last decade, teachers, guidance counselors and school psychiatrists have reported greater tension, anxiety, restlessness, and suspicion among children in school. "Each year it gets worse," said a preschool teacher.

Studies have shown that looking at violent scenes for even a very brief time makes young children more willing to accept aggressive behavior of themselves and other children. Children tend to act out what they see, especially if it becomes an everyday occurrence. Other studies have shown that watching violence can reduce children's sensitivity to the pain and suffering of others. It also can make youngsters more fearful of the outside world and more likely to behave in aggressive and harmful ways. Even cartoons at times seem to promote violence, such as hitting, or an anvil falling on someone's head. Violent cartoons may be giving your child confusing messages, and may even be frightening. Young children don't understand what these programs really mean, because they are not yet able to distinguish fantasy from reality.

Negative effects of heavy TV viewing
What are the results of too much TV viewing by preschoolers? Below are a list of concerns of professionals and parents.
• Shorter attention span with non-TV activities. (After all, the screen constantly changes in color, story, and sound.)
• Thriving on noise, strife, confusion. (Children have become used to the deafening noise that invades their world day in and day out.)
• Confused by adult themes. (A four-year-old is not ready to deal with a bitter divorce feud on one of the soaps.)
• Lack of respect for parents' values. (They have seen too many shows where adults and peers encourage smart-aleck remarks.)
• More likely to settle disputes by violence. (Hardly surprising after they have seen thousands of violent acts used in place of negotiation.)

*Developing
Good TV Habits
for Your Family*

Quality Programs
A limited number of quality TV shows are designed for children, including such standards as *Sesame Street* and *Reading Rainbow.* Quality programs for children can be helpful and entertaining. Television is definitely a part of life, so watching and selecting educational programs is making the best of the situation. Parents should select programs that will benefit, help, and enhance the family and family values, not create more problems.

Suggestions to develop good TV habits for your family:
1. Play an active role in the use of television by your family. When used for baby-sitting, try to limit the time to one hour a day. Check the programs that you decide are appropriate for your child.
2. Schedule other family activities first, then fit television in.
3. Limit the number of hours and kinds of programs.
4. Monitor television watching by creating a family television log and reviewing it together. Write down all the shows that your family watches in a week's time. Use this list to decide which programs the whole family would enjoy watching together, which programs should be kept on tape, and which programs are inappropriate for your preschooler.
5. Watch TV together. This can be an enjoyable family time. Laugh together and communicate what is being seen in a relaxed family gathering.

6. Talk about the program. Children have questions about what they see on TV. This is also an opportunity to discuss family values — how the same situation might be handled differently in your family. Discuss what is real life and what is exaggerated for the sake of entertainment.

7. Build bridges between TV shows and books. For example, if *Sesame Street* has a section on sharing toys, get books from the library that tell stories on this subject.

Don't forget — a video or television doesn't smile and hug your children! It will not put its arm around them or say, "I love you!" It will not listen to them or make them feel significant. As parents, we need to ask: How important is the TV to our family? Are the programs making our children more thoughtful or caring? Are they helping preschoolers make appropriate decisions? Don't forget that the real question is: Are *we* making a difference in our children's lives or is television doing it for us?

Make the Difference
It is important that parents speak out for children's programming. The United Nations General Assembly December 1989 Convention on the Rights of the Child stated, in part, that mass media education should be directed to "the preparation of the child for responsible life in a free society, in the spirit of understanding, peace, tolerance, equality of sexes and friendship among all peoples, ethnic, national and religious groups..." That's a meaningful prescription for parents to use as a guide for their children's television.

Chapter 30
Working with
Medical Professionals
and Educators
in Your Child's Life

Toni Liebman

*...don't hesitate
to ask questions
until you are
fully satisfied.*

Susan's cough has persisted for days even after the use of a child's cough syrup. Her mother calls the pediatrician's office for a visit.

Although Ricky seemed to love his first week at preschool, he says that he doesn't want to go back. His mother decides to call his teacher for advice.

From the moment we become parents, we are responsible for our child's well-being. To help us, we seek the expertise of a variety of professionals. Delegating some of our child-raising responsibility to them is not always easy, and we must continually strike a balance between blindly accepting their every word and being too demanding; between showing a healthy concern for the child and becoming highly anxious and over-protective; between letting go and holding on too tightly.

Parents and professionals each contribute to the welfare of the child — professionals with their theoretical knowledge and experience, and parents with their intimate knowledge of their own children. The ability to work closely with the professionals in your child's life is an invaluable skill — one worth cultivating. Being a parent is not easy, and it helps to know how and where to get as much assistance as possible from knowledgeable professionals.

You and the Medical Professionals
Because it is important to understand the doctor's diagnosis or instructions, don't hesitate to ask questions until you are fully satisfied. (Sometimes professionals don't realize that parents do not understand medical terms such as *enuresis* instead of bed-wetting, *otitis* instead of earache, *pharyngitis* instead of sore throat.) Most doctors and nurses are more than willing to offer satisfactory explanations.

Using Medical Professionals as a Resource
Dan is four years old but he can't pedal a tricycle, catch a large ball, or hold a crayon to draw. Patti, at 26 months, has difficulty in putting two words together.

When there is concern about the physical, emotional or intellectual development of your child, the first person to consult is your pediatrician. If you still have anxiety after speaking with your doctor, a specialist or second opinion may be in order. You can get recommendations from: your doctor, hospital, medical association, or your local mental health, family service, or child guidance association.

Working with Childcare Professionals
As the director of a large nursery/kindergarten Parent Cooperative School, I always reminded my staff that unless they worked closely with the parents of their children, they were only doing half their job!

Early childhood caregivers are the first non-relative with whom your child will be spending a large proportion of his or her time away from home. It is extremely important that you feel you can trust them implicitly and that you develop a partnership with them.

Parent Interactions with Childcare Professionals

Interaction with a family day care provider is generally more informal than with a child care center. However, in both instances it is wise to have everything clearly spelled out and understood — from the daily schedule, meals, snacks, clothing, and fees to general attitudes about discipline and educational philosophy. The provider, childcare director, or teacher should be approachable and you should feel comfortable in enlisting her help whenever problems arise. Remember that most early childhood caregivers are trying to do their best for your child.

Establishing Good Communication with Teachers

It is important to let your child's teacher know that you respect her knowledge of child development and her experience with a variety of children. On the other hand, you certainly want her to respect your understanding of your own child. The way to accomplish this is to begin establishing an open, honest pattern of communication as soon as possible. Fostering good communication may take time, but the results are well worth the effort.

Parent/Teacher Conferences

Asking for a Conference

It is important to establish a relationship with your child's teacher from the beginning so that if you sense a problem at the preschool, you can contact the teacher and she won't be a stranger. It is best to deal with an issue when it arises, rather than wait and have it get out of hand. Ask for a conference so that you both can work on the problem together. Try not to get too deeply into the discussion during this preconference call, but use the time to state the reason for the conference and to make arrangements for a meeting.

The Conference

When teachers arrange a conference, they generally plan their presentation and have established goals. It is best for parents to follow this same procedure when *they* request a conference. Plan ahead and develop goals for the conference. Decide what you would like to accomplish by this meeting, and work out your questions and comments accordingly. Don't be afraid to bring written notes with you, so that you will be sure to cover all of the points that are on your mind.

Many preschools schedule parent/teacher conferences as a matter of course during the school year. When parents come to school at a teacher's request, they may feel anxious or nervous. Both parents and teachers need a positive attitude in order to share information and learn important facts about the child from one another. It is very important that both parties try to put themselves into the other person's shoes in order to develop the sensitivity needed for a successful conference.

Two-way Communication Is Essential

Messages must flow two ways in order to be better understood. That means, in addition to *talking* about any difficulties the child may be having, both parties need to *listen* to each other's words and observe nonverbal messages such as facial expression and tone of voice.   As parent and professional send and receive information, each needs to listen carefully to understand the other person's point of view. Each can then give feedback as to the other's ideas and suggestions, and discuss possible solutions. Solutions are usually more satisfactory when all parties have played a role in reaching them.

Your child will enjoy a better day care, preschool, or kindergarten experience when all the involved adults work together in a harmonious partnership.

Dos and Don'ts
When Working
with Professionals

Some Dos

• Do seek help when you have concerns about your child.

• Do enter into a working partnership with the professional right from the beginning.

• Do be your child's advocate.

• Do bring a written list of questions to discuss with the professional.

• Do ask for clarification if you don't understand something.

• Do be assertive: make sure the professional understands your viewpoint.

• Do respect the professional's experience with children in general.

• Do evaluate the professional's suggestions.

• Do respect the privacy of professionals; call them outside of normal work hours only for emergencies.

• Do read books to get more information about your child's growth and development (see Resources, page 211). Check with your librarian.

Some Don'ts

• Don't be afraid to seek out professional help when needed.

• Don't wait to get assistance once you suspect that there is a problem.

• Don't try to handle a difficult problem with a telephone call; instead arrange for a conference.

• Don't be intimidated by big words. Ask what they mean.

• Don't let your emotions keep you from trying to understand the professional's advice.

• Don't necessarily accept everything the professional tells you; if you still have doubts, a second opinion may be in order.

Resources for Section Five: Coping with Stress in Everyday Situations

FOR ADULTS

Starting School: from Separation to Independence — *a Guide for Early Childhood Teachers,* by Nancy Balaban. Teachers College Press, 1985. This paperback, by the author of a chapter in this book, offers many sensitive, practical suggestions to ease the separation process for a child first entering school or day care.

Toddlers and Parents, by T. Berry Brazelton, M.D. rev. ed. Dell, 1989. In addition to dealing with the developmental aspects of the first few years of life, the well-known physician/author gives parents insights into matters which involve their children and pediatricians.

Don't Sweat the Small Stuff...and it's all small stuff: *simple ways to keep the little things from taking over your life,* by Richard Carlson, Ph.D. Hyperion, 1997. A contributor of a chapter in this book, Dr. Carlson is a stress consultant, lecturer and best-selling author. In 100 brief, thoughtful chapters, he gently offers ways of being more peaceful, caring, and stress-free.

Helping Your Child Sleep Through the Night, by Joanne Cuthbertson and Susie Schevill. Doubleday, 1985. A step-by-step guide to establishing good sleeping habits in children from infancy to age five.

Solve Your Child's Sleep Problems, by Richard Ferber, M.D. Simon & Schuster, 1986. A practical approach to helping your child develop good sleep patterns by the director of the Center for Pediatric Sleep Disorders at Children's Hospital in Boston.

The Sleep Book for Tired Parents, by Rebecca Huntley. Parenting Press, 1991. Using illustrations, charts, and checklists as exercises, this paperback offers parents important information about sleep problems in an easy-to-read format.

Child Behavior, by Francis Ilg, M.D., et al. HarperCollins, 1992. An expert in child development gives specific advice on problems in child behavior.

The Dance of Anger: a woman's guide to changing the patterns of intimate relationships, by Harriet Goldhor Lerner. Harper & Row, 1985. This insightful book provides strategies for turning anger into a constructive force.

Vaccinate Your Infant Against the "Terrible Twos," by Michael K. Meyerhoff, Ed.D. A booklet providing a step-by-step behavior management plan for preventing temper tantrums and other serious discipline problems during toddlerhood and the preschool years. Written by a well-known child development expert who has contributed a chapter to this book, it may be obtained by sending $3.00 to: The Epicenter Inc., 452 Crooked Lake Lane, Lindenhurst IL 60046.

Love and Anger: The Parental Dilemma, by Nancy Samalin with Catherine Whitney. Viking, 1991. The author of a chapter in this book, Samalin writes in this important work about the issues that trigger anger between parents and their children. Using the actual experiences of individual parents, Samalin offers positive ways to redirect that anger.

Winning Bedtime Battles: How to Help Your Child Develop Good Sleep Habits, by Charles E. Schaefer, Ph.D., and Theresa Foy DiGeronimo, M.Ed. Citidel Press, 1992. Dr. Schaefer is Director of the Better Sleep Center and author of Teach Your Baby to Sleep Through the Night. The authors offer a practical, workable plan for eliminating bedtime problems and helping children develop long-lasting sleep habits.

Use TV to Your Child's Advantage, by Dorothy G. Singer, Jerome L. Singer & Diana M. Zuckerman. Acropolis Books, 1990. A readable and informative book filled with ideas and parent/child activities to "encourage parents to use television programs to stimulate their children's learning and creativity, and to help parents to influence their children to be more selective television consumers."

Teacher-Parent Communication:Working Toward Better Understanding, by Elizabeth J. Webster and Louise M. Ward. Preschool Publications (1-800-726-1708), 1992. The authors, specialists in the field of parent communication, explore issues such as: listening as the key to better understanding, defensiveness as a barrier to good communication, and appropriate use of description, inference and judgment.

Discipline Without Shouting or Spanking, by Jerry Wyckoff and Barbara Unell. Meadowbrook Press, 1984. The well-researched and throughly-tested ideas contained in this book provide practical solutions to the most common preschool behavior problems.

FOR CHILDREN

Ten, Nine, Eight, by Molly Bang. Mulberry, 1991. Warm and colorful illustrations show one small person's countdown to bedtime.

No Time for Me: Learning to Live with Busy Parents, by John M. Barrett. Human Sciences Press, 1985. A helpful book for a child whose parents are both working. It provides the opportunity for children and parents to discuss the important issue of separation and reunion.

Goodnight, Moon, by Margaret Wise Brown. HarperCollins, 1947. A bunny ritually says goodnight to many objects in the bedroom, making the separation a comfortable transition from the active daytime world into the dark, quiet sleeping world. Bit by bit, the room gets darker as the bunny settles down to sleep.

Ghost's Hour, Spook's Hour, by Eve Bunting. Clarion, 1987. Scary incidents at midnight frighten a little boy and his dog, but all turn out to have good explanations.

No Nap, by Eve Bunting. Clarion, 1989. Susie's daddy tries many exciting activities so that she will get tired enough to take her nap. But daddy is the one who zonks out.

The Best Teacher in the World, by Bernice Chardiet and Grace Maccarone. Scholastic, 1991. Bunny is thrilled to be chosen by her teacher, Ms. Darcy, to take a note to Mrs. Walker. But the little girl gets lost on the way to Mrs. Walker's room. She feels terrible, but Ms. Darcy, the best teacher in the world, teaches her that it's all right to ask questions when there's something you don't know.

Baby's Bedtime Book, by Kay Chorao. Dutton, 1984. Twenty-seven familiar and not-so-familiar illustrated verses create the mood for bedtime.

The New Teacher, by Miriam Cohen. Aladdin edition, 1989. Why did their teacher need a baby, when she had the whole first grade! But she left, and today there was going to be a new teacher. The children in the playground wonder what she'll be like. Then they meet her, and by the time the morning is over, they all know she is going to be just fine.

You Go Away, by Dorothy Corey. Albert Whitman, 1976. The simple text says, "You go away...and you come back" in a variety of separations involving children, men, and women of different ethnic groups. A mother hides behind a blanket and then reappears; two children lose sight of their mother in the supermarket; a little girl goes to kindergarten.

Lets talk about feelings series: All My Feelings at Preschool: Nathan's Day, by Susan Conlin and Susan L. Friedman. Parenting Press, 1991. As Nathan spends the day at his preschool, he experiences a variety of feelings: happiness, anger, concern, pride, and other emotions. Each page of this book focuses on a different feeling. Parents may want to use the book as a way to introduce a discussion of their children's own feelings.

Are You My Mother? by P. Eastman. Designer Books, Random House, 1960. A little bird falls from the nest and asks everyone, and everything, including a steam shovel, "Are you my mother?" In the end, the two are joyously reunited in a surprising way.

Bobby and the Brockles, by Adele Faber and Elaine Mazlish. Avon Books, 1994. Designed for parents and children to read together, this book teaches a gentle message about dealing with anger. The Brockles are two tiny visitors from another planet who explain to Bobby how problems can disappear when you talk them over instead of screaming and demanding your way. The authors wrote the bestselling book, *How to Talk So Kids Will Listen and Listen so Kids Will Talk.*

Fletcher and the Great Big Dog, by Jane Kopper Hilleary. Houghton Mifflin, 1992. Fletcher is riding his tricycle when a great big dog stands in his path. He is afraid and races away with the dog chasing him. Suddenly the little boy is lost, and it starts to rain. But when the dog licks his cheek in a friendly way, Fletcher is no longer afraid. It turns out to be a new neighbor's dog, and leads Fletcher home.

Bedtime for Frances, by Russell Hoban. HarperTrophy, 1996. When Mother and Father put her to bed, Frances uses every strategy she can think of to put off going to sleep. And then she imagines tigers and giants and spiders in her room. Will Frances ever fall asleep?

C is for Curious, by Woodleigh Hubbard. Chronicle Books, 1993. With bold, whimsical illustrations, the author/illustrator has created a unique alphabet book of feelings. *A is for angry* almost jumps out of the page, while *Q is for quiet* has a calm, peaceful feeling. Other emotions that are illustrated include shy, nervous, happy, and yucky.

Lizzie's Invitation, by Holly Keller. Greenwillow, 1987. Lizzie feels so disappointed that she didn't get an invitation to Kate's party, that, in school, she paints pictures of angry faces. On Saturday, the day of the party, she takes a sad walk in the rain and meets Amanda, a girl in her class who also didn't get an invitation. They have lunch at Lizzie's house, and have a good time playing together all afternoon.

When Sheep Cannot Sleep, by Satoshi Kitamura. Farrar, 1986. Woolly, a sheep with insomnia, counts sheep to fall asleep.

Pookins Gets Her Way, by Helen Lester. Houghton Mifflin, 1990. Pookins is a little girl who always gets her way, because if she doesn't, she makes faces, throws apples, and yells very loudly. One day she meets a gnome and threatens a temper tantrum unless her three wishes are granted. However, in the humorous ending to this story, she finds that getting your own way does not always lead to happiness.

Hello, Goodbye, by David Lloyd. Candlewick Press, 1995. As a tree stands in the sunshine, various creatures come over to say, "Hello!" Then it starts to rain and, "Goodbye!" say all the creatures. When they are gone, the tree says, "Hello," to the rain. A simple, humorous story about meeting and parting.

Nathaniel Willy, Scared Silly, by Judith Mathews and Fay Robinson. Bradbury Press, 1994. When Gramma kisses Nathaniel Willy goodnight and closes the door, Nathaniel Willy thinks he hears a ghost. Gramma tries to calm his fears by bringing him the farm animals, one by one, to keep him company. Young children will enjoy this funny book about overcoming fears.

Now Everybody Really Hates Me, by Jane Read Martin and Patricia Marx. HarperTrophy, 1996. Patty Jane is sent to her room, because she punched her little brother. (She only touched him — hard.) She is furious at her parents, and decides she will stay in her room forever. The little girl fantasizes about how her life will be when she never sleeps in her bed again, never cleans up, and never does chores. A funny and human story.

There's an Alligator under My Bed, by Mercer Mayer. Dial, 1987. A small boy has a big problem — there's an alligator under his bed and his parents can't see it. He coaxes it out with a trail of food that leads to the garage.

Peace at Last, by Jill Murphy. Dial, 1982. Mr. Bear spends the night searching for enough peace and quiet to go to sleep.

Tom and Pippo in the Snow, by Helen Oxenbury. Aladdin, 1989. In another book in the series about a boy named Tom, and Pippo, his toy monkey, Daddy takes Tom and Pippo sledding. Although Daddy says there's nothing to be afraid of, Tom thinks it only fair to let Pippo go down the hill on the sled first. After that Tom has his ride and finds that sledding is easy.

A Week of Lullabies, compiled and edited by Helen Plotz. Greenwillow, 1988. Two poems are offered for each day of the week, with charming illustrations by Marisabina Russo, each in a decorative frame.

The Spooky Eerie Night Noise, by Mona Raburn Reeves. Bradbury Press, 1989. Jenny hears a strange, scritchy noise outside at night. She imagines ghouls, beasts, and vampires. But with the help of her mom and dad, and a flashlight, she discovers the source of the noise under the backyard pear tree — two hungry skunks.

City Night, by Eve Rice. Greenwillow, 1987. An illustrated poem depicting the beauty and diversity of a city at night.

At the Beach, by Anne & Harlow Rockwell. Macmillan, 1987. With simple text and clear, bright pictures, this book describes a little girl's day enjoying the sand and the ocean. It could be a good introduction, for very young children, of what it is like to play at a beach and in the water.

Why Do Grown-Ups Have All the Fun? by Marisabina Russo. Greenwillow, 1987. Hannah wonders what her parents do after she is in bed, deciding that they probably eat ice cream with sprinkles and marshmallow, make play dough, and build with blocks.

Benjamin Bigfoot, by Mary Serfozo. McElderry Books, 1993. Benjamin feels big when he wears his father's shoes to play in. But when he wants to wear the shoes to kindergarten, his mother explains that there may be rules against wearing his big shoes there. At school, a wise and caring teacher helps Benjamin work out the problem himself.

I Was So Mad! by Norma Simon. Albert Whitman, 1974. A description of a variety of situations that make children feel angry or frustrated, with the message that it's okay to feel angry.

Naptime, Laptime, by Eileen Spinelli. Scholastic Cartwheel, 1995. A simple story that tells in rhyme about the places where animals like to sleep. It ends with a child cozily curling up in Grandma's lap at naptime.

Where We Sleep, by Nancy Tafuri. Greenwillow, 1987. In a book with cardboard pages for the youngest preschoolers, animals are pictured in their sleeping places, while the baby is shown in his crib.

Will You Come Back for Me? by Ann Tompert. Whitman, 1988. Suki feels worried when she is enrolled in a day care program for the first time. Will her mother come back for her? The little girl's mother reassures her in a unique and loving way.

Mommy Doesn't Know My Name, by Suzanne Williams. Houghton Mifflin, 1996. When Hannah's Mommy calls her loving pet names like pumpkin, funny monkey, and little devil, Hannah is angry and thinks — I'm not a little devil. I'm Hannah. Finally, when Mommy tells Hannah to be a quiet little mouse and go to sleep, Hannah sits up and tells her, "I'm not a mouse. I'm Hannah!" And Mommy says, "Yes, I know," hugs her and calls her Hannah.

The Napping House, by Audrey Wood. Harcourt, 1984. Humorous pastel illustrations and a simple text recount how everyone in a house tries to nap during a rainy day.

Let's Be Enemies, by Janice May Udry. HarperCollins, 1988. A story about two boys who irritate each other and decide to be enemies, only to become good friends again soon thereafter.

The Good-bye Book, by Judith Viorst. Aladdin, 1992. A little boy, whose parents are going out for the evening, thinks of a multitude of reasons for them not to go: he won't have fun with the baby sitter, his head hurts, and so does his knee, and he probably has 110 temperature. And he will never say goodbye. And then the pleasant young man who will be his baby sitter arrives, and they both wave goodbye from the window.

My Mama Says There Aren't Any Zombies, Ghosts, Vampires, Creatures, Demons, Monsters, Fiends, Goblins, or Things, by Judith Viorst. Aladdin Books edition, 1988. A little boy is not sure whether to trust his mama when she assures him that the creatures he's afraid of just don't exist. After all, sometimes even mamas make mistakes. But sometimes they don't.

Sleepy Book, by Charlotte Zolotow. HarperTrophy, 1990. In a beautifully written book first published in 1958, but newly illustrated, children learn how a variety of animals sleep, and how little girls and boys sleep in their cozy beds.

Section Six
Keeping
Your
Child
Healthy

Section Six
Keeping Your
Child Healthy

Introduction

I recently saw a documentary on television that illustrated the life of a different era: post-Revolutionary War America. It told the story of a brave, hard-working woman who was a midwife and a healer — yet her skills were not enough to save three of her children who died in an epidemic. How fortunate that we have so many more resources today to keep our children in good health.

Yet we still must be concerned about our family's health. Parents have to be aware of the necessity for immunizations from early infancy, the importance of adequate hearing in their child's development, and the need for youngsters to have regular checkups with their pediatrician.

Mothers and fathers can have fun teaching their preschoolers good health habits, as well as establishing a healthy, positive relationship while feeding their children nutritious foods.

All of these health topics are covered in the pages that follow, along with activities, strategies, and an immunization chart.

SECTION SIX

KEEPING YOUR CHILD HEALTHY

Chapter

Chapter 31
Does an Apple a Day Keep the Doctor Away?

Janet Dengel

*Parents have steps
they can follow to avoid
both colds and more serious
contagious illnesses.*

"An apple a day keeps the doctor away." But ensuring your preschooler's good health involves much more than following this old saying.

Prevention of Disease Through Immunization

The best prevention against serious childhood disease is immunization. Although these immunizations are started in early infancy, the preschool years are a good time to check with your doctor or local health agency to see what boosters are necessary. It is also a good time to update your records on your child's shots, since proof of immunization will be required when he enters school.

"Regularly scheduled immunizations will benefit your child, your family, and their school contacts," says Marie Buckey, R.N., B.S.N., longtime nurse in newborn care. "Not only do you help to prevent your child contracting anything [that is, "catching any diseases"], but you help to prevent epidemics. Your preschool child is beginning to go out into the world. If he or she is not immunized, you're taking chances with your child and every other child."

According to the American Academy of Pediatrics, immunization protects children against ten diseases: polio, measles, mumps, rubella (German measles), whooping cough (pertussis), diptheria, tetanus, hepatitis b, varicella, and Haemophilus influenzae type b (Hib) infections. (See chart on page 229.) These diseases can cripple, kill, or cause serious disabilities. All are preventable with immunization. If you do not have a family pediatrician, call your local health department, which will often provide immunization shots free, or charge a fee depending on income.

Preventing Serious Complications

As any parent knows, the majority of childhood illnesses so common in the preschool years, while not life-threatening, still cause a threat to the child's overall health and growth — the constant colds that settle into ear infections, the cough that becomes bronchitis, the sore throats that are diagnosed as strep.

Antibiotics now available have helped considerably in keeping the above complications under control. Prolonged low doses of antibiotics have succeeded in warding off these infections before they develop. However, colds and the flu, which are viruses, still have no cure. Children between the ages of two and six tend to get more colds than any other age group and have them longer. The average child under five may have as many as 8 to 10 colds per year, according to statistics of the American Academy of Pediatrics. As children attend preschool, play groups, or library story hours, they come in contact with more germs. These viruses do not respond to antibiotic treatments, and the only known cure is: rest, fluids, and time.

How to Avoid Colds and Serious Illnesses
Parents of preschoolers do have steps they can follow to avoid both colds and more serious contagious illnesses. The following are suggestions from health insurance companies, including Blue Cross and Metropolitan Life, doctors, nurses, and the American Academy of Pediatrics:

• *Keep your child away from people who have colds.* Although this is sometimes impossible, you can take the following steps: Avoid crowded malls during flu season. Ask friends and relatives if they are healthy before they visit, especially if your child is likely to have serious complications from a cold, such as ear infections. (One parent said she brings a towel to the supermarket to place around the handle of the shopping cart, since her three-year-old son has the bad habit of licking the bar when he gets bored.)

• *Teach your preschooler good health routines.* Have him wash his hands after using the bathroom and before eating. Use and properly dispose of tissues. Don't cough in the direction of others. The personal health skills that one learns during the preschool years can lead to a lifetime of better health. "The hand contact is the biggest transmitter of germs for children in school," explains Marie Buckey, R.N.

• *Take your child for periodic health exams.* Some guidelines recommend 3-4 physicals a year for children under two and once or twice a year from two to six. These physicals will ensure that your pediatrician has the opportunity to catch health problems before they develop. Don't be hesitant to phone when problems arise between check-ups.

• *Cooperate with local and state health agencies on community health measures.* Immunization schedules, vision and hearing tests, or lice checks in school are all conducted to guard your child against disease.

• *Help your preschooler to establish good nutrition, diet, and exercise habits.* Preschoolers can be finicky at the table, but by offering a wide variety of wholesome food and not overdoing snacks, your child will develop a taste for many nutritious foods. Exercise can increase appetite, improve general fitness and induce better sleeping patterns. Pediatricians will often recommend a vitamin supplement to your preschooler's diet to provide nutritional "insurance" for your child.

• *Fresh air is important.* Encourage your child to play outdoors and keep rooms in the house well-ventilated. Dress him properly according to the temperature, but don't overdress in the winter. Keep him away from drafts indoors. Insist on a hat, gloves, and warm boots in cold weather. "In excess of 70 % of body heat is lost through the head, hands, and feet," confirms Buckey. "When body temperature drops, children are susceptible."

What to Do When Illness Strikes

When your preschooler has even a simple cold, the most important concerns are to nurse him back to health, build his resistance back up, and prevent more serious complications from developing. Following these simple rules during most mild bouts of illness will ensure that your preschooler will soon be on his way back to good health:

• Encourage your preschooler to rest, but don't force him to stay in bed. Preferably, he should be kept away from the rest of the family members if the illness is contagious.

• Give him plenty of fluid — water, juices, soups — but do not force solid foods until he is ready. When he is feeling better, he will eat.

• If your pediatrician approves, administer acetaminophen — for example, Tylenol®—(not aspirin) to reduce your child's fever and relieve any discomfort. Consult your doctor as to how to treat other symptoms such as headaches, diarrhea, or coughing. Never give your child left-over medicines or a prescription belonging to another family member.

• Don't be overly concerned about your child's illness. A little extra attention is warranted, but guard against overprotection. The way you react to your preschooler's mild illnesses can often establish a life-long pattern. He may learn to accept minor symptoms, or, on the other hand, decide that a little ache or pain is reason to stay home from school.

When and how to call your doctor

Good pediatricians would rather be "bothered" by an unnecessary phone call than have a parent overlook a symptom which could indicate a more serious problem. Most ailments can be described over the phone and instructions can be given to ease your child's discomfort. A phone call allows your pediatrician to decide if, based on the symptoms you describe and your child's health history, an office visit is necessary. To get the greatest benefit from your call, follow these tips from the American Academy of Pediatrics:

• Call during office hours unless it is an emergency.

• Take your child's temperature before calling. Write down any other pertinent information or questions you may have, so you don't forget during the call.

• Have a pen and paper ready to write down any instructions from your doctor. Have the number of your pharmacy nearby, so your pediatrician can order any needed prescriptions.

Your child's pediatrician should always be called for these problems:

• Injury, poisoning, bleeding that cannot be stopped, unconsciousness, convulsions, sharp stomach pain, a black or bloody bowel movement, or severe diarrhea.

• Persistent crying or complaints of pain.

• An unusually high temperature or an above normal temperature that lasts for days.

• Any symptoms that are long lasting, such as a constant stomach-ache, headache, dizziness, blurred vision.

• Having difficulty in breathing.

• General poor health. A healthy child should be vigorous and energetic, have clear skin, bright eyes, shiny hair, and good muscles. If a child is continually listless, has a poor appetite or tires easily, he should go for a check-up.

• Sore throat, heavy coughing, and ear pain should always be reported. They may indicate that tests are needed to determine if strep, bronchitis, croup, or ear infections are present.

Preventing and handling emergencies

Although the health of your preschooler is threatened by common illnesses, a more life-threatening danger, and one that is preventable, is that of child-hood accidents.

According to Jay M. Arena, past President of the American Academy of Pediatrics, "Accidents are the largest single cause of death and disability in children under the age of fifteen. They account for one-third of all child mortality and kill more children than the six leading fatal diseases combined."

Poisoning and burns

"You have to think ahead to prevent accidents," advises Buckey. "Your house should be totally childproofed. If a young child sees something dangerous, he will think of a use for it." Preschool children are extremely curious and do not yet know what can be dangerous.

Keep medications in child-safe containers out of the reach of youngsters. Never refer to medicine as candy. Make sure all household cleansers are in their original, marked containers in a locked cabinet. Try to cook on the back burners of the stove, making sure that pot handles are turned away from the reach of young children.

Cuts
Keep knives, glassware, and easily breakable objects out of reach.

Falls and car safety
Falls within the home and out of doors also account for many injuries during the preschool years. The eyes and face are extremely vulnerable areas during these accidents. Besides automobile accidents, bicycles, stairs, steps, and sports are the main causes of childhood facial injuries, according to the Consumer Product Safety Commission.

To prevent these injuries, keep gates on stairways in the home and install railings on outdoor and cellar steps. Doors and windows in the home must be kept closed and locked when small children are present to prevent accidental falls. Check your preschooler's bicycle for loose handle bars or malfunctioning brakes. Lastly, when youngsters are involved in organized sports or even just backyard fun, make sure they wear proper equipment including a mouth guard, safety helmet, and facial mask. When in the car, your young child must sit in the back seat in an approved car seat, or, when older, must use a seat belt.

Eye Injuries
To prevent eye injuries, the American Optometric Association recommends that parents of preschoolers should check all toys and playground equipment for sharp edges. Do not allow the use of darts, bows and arrows, or BB guns. Teach your preschooler to put down pencils, scissors, or other pointed objects before getting up to walk or run. Also teach him not to throw sand or dirt while at the playground.

Street safety
Even though preschoolers do not yet walk to the store alone, now is the time to teach them road safety rules through example. Insist that they hold your hand and stop to look both ways for traffic. Teach them to cross at corners, stay in the crosswalk, wait for the green light or flashing "WALK" signal, and never to cross behind a parked car. Show them how to proceed cautiously at driveways and watch for cars backing up. Bicycles should only be ridden on the sidewalk or trails at this early age and helmets should be purchased along with the bike and worn from day one. Teach them never to run out in the street to catch a runaway ball.

Preschoolers are often testing their limits and striving for independence, but traffic safety is one area where there is no room for compromise. If your four-year-old insists on walking too close to the roadway after your warnings not to, take him inside immediately and revoke his privilege to play outside that day.

Choking

Many preschoolers still put small toys or found objects in their mouths, so keep them away from balloons, marbles, or toys with small pieces. Many toy stores stock an inexpensive device that tests a toy to see if it is dangerous because it is small enough to swallow.

Certain foods also present a choking danger, especially for children under four, who do not chew or grind their food well. Hot dogs, chunks of meat, grapes, and raw carrots should be avoided or chopped completely. Hard candy should not be given to a preschooler. Always insist that your preschooler sit down while eating. Do not allow him to have any food or candy in his mouth while playing or running. Teach him to chew foods thoroughly. Supervise what other people, especially older siblings and babysitters, give him.

Other Dangers

No list of precautions would be complete for preschool safety without a warning about accidental drownings. A preschooler should be taught to swim, but should never be allowed near water alone or even with slightly older children in charge. Do not rely on tubes or flotation devices and insist on Coast Guard approved life jackets when boating, even if you are watching or holding your preschooler. In the winter, do not ice skate on any pond that hasn't been deemed safe by local officials. Never leave a young child alone in a bath.

When Accidents Occur

Even with the huge array of safety products and widespread education on prevention, accidents still occur every day. When they do, keep calm in order to help your child. When there is serious injury or suspected poisoning, call your physician, local police or a community emergency number such as 911. Keep the numbers of your doctor, hospital, police, fire, poison control center, and other emergency numbers near your phone.

Basic First Aid for Common Problems

Many health officials believe that all parents should take a course in basic first aid and CPR. Contact your pediatrician or local Red Cross for more information, or consult the resources listed on page 255. While knowledge of first aid is helpful in an emergency, be sure to seek additional medical attention for your youngster, if needed.

Minor cuts: Wash with clean water and soap. Press firmly to stop bleeding. Apply sterile dressing. • *Bruises:* Rest the injured part and apply cold compresses. • *Nosebleeds:* Tilt the head back so the nose becomes the highest part of the body and pinch the nostrils. • *Insect stings:* If stinger is present, remove at the base. Apply cold compress. if any known allergies or reactions, transport child promptly to emergency center. • *Sprains*: Elevate injured part. Apply cold compresses. • *Foreign particle in eyes*: Pull the lid (by the lashes) away from the eye to let tears flush the object away. Irrigate thoroughly with water. <u>Do not use a moist swab</u> (like a Q-tip). *Keep in your medicine chest: Acetaminophen, a thermometer, absorbent cotton, calamine lotion, antibiotic ointment, bandages and gauze in several sizes, syrup of ipecac for poisonings.*

The information detailed in this chapter is based upon research into health-related materials, and interviews by the author with health professionals. It is, however, the responsibility of parents to check with their doctors as to any health questions they may have regarding their own children. The author and publisher cannot assume responsiblity for any consequences resulting from suggestions printed in this chapter.

Recommended Childhood Immunization Schedule, United States January-December 2000, courtesy of the American Academy of Pediatrics.

The following is a guide for ages only up through 6 years.
Your family physician is the authority on which vaccines
are to be administered to your child — and at ages that are appropriate.

(Vacines are listed under routinely recommended ages. │Bars│ indicate range of recommended ages for immunization. Any dose not given at the recommended age should be given as a "catch-up" immunization at any subsequent visit when indicated and feasible.

Vaccine \ Age	Birth	1 mo	2 mos	4 mos	6 mos	12 mos	15 mos	18 mos	24 mos	4-6 yrs
Hepatitis B		Hep B	Hep B		Hep B					
Diptheria, Tetanus Pertussis			DTaP	DTaP	DTaP		DTaP			DTaP
H. influenzae, type b			Hib	Hib	Hib	Hib				
Polio			IPV	IPV		IPV				IPV
Measles, Mumps Rubella						MMR				MMR
Varicella						Var				
Hepatitis A									Hepatitis A in selcted areas	

Chapter 32
Teaching Your Preschooler Good Health Habits

Janet Dengel

*...good hygiene, proper nutrition,
and regular exercise
learned at an early age
can lead to a lifetime of health...*

"Wash your hands!"

"Eat your vegetables!"

"Brush your teeth!"

As children we heard these lines hundreds of times. Now, as parents, we know that good hygiene, proper nutrition, and regular exercise learned at an early age can lead to a lifetime of health for our children.

Three cheers for handwashing!

It's a fact: children ages two to six get colds twice as often as nine-year-olds. As they enter daycare, school, or play situations, they not only meet new people but also come across new germs.

Holding hands with a partner, sharing toys that had been in children's mouths, and coughing are common ways germs can be spread. The Center For Disease Control reports that one-half of infectious diseases in daycare and the home could be prevented with proper handwashing by both adults and children.

By establishing handwashing routines at an early age, children can increase their odds for a healthy present and future. *The ABC's of Clean*, published by the Soap & Detergent Assn., states that hands should be washed at the following times:

- Before eating, drinking and snacking
- After using the toilet
- After playing outdoors
- After playing with pets
- After coughing or sneezing

Briefly, the four steps of correct handwashing are:

1) Wet hands under warm, running water.

2) Rub hands with soap to make a lather away from the running water. Wash the front and back of the hands, between fingers and under nails for 10 to 15 seconds.

3) Rinse well.

4) Dry thoroughly, preferably with a paper towel.

Other routines to promote good hygiene

Health experts suggest that young children be taught to cough into their sleeve, instead of covering their mouths with their hands. They should use tissues instead of handkerchiefs and then dispose of them properly.

Discourage your preschooler from putting toys and other objects in his mouth. Praise his efforts to drop his thumb-sucking habit. Let your preschooler know that sharing cups, food, and utensils with siblings or friends can spread germs.

A regular bathtime can easily be established for this age group with the emphasis on cleanliness and fun. Tub toys and special soaps make the bath more enjoyable. Because teachers and parents are role models for children, they can foster cleanliness in children by practicing good health habits themselves.

Exercise!

"It's just as important to grow up fit as to grow up smart," is the saying of the President's Council on Physical Fitness. And the good news is — the exercise habit can easily be acquired during the preschool age through these steps:

1) Keep it FUN! Avoid competition or comparison. Concentrate on what your child likes to do.

2) Build stamina through activities that require constant movement. Suggested activities: playing on jungle gyms, walking, running, jumping rope, and maneuvering through a backyard obstacle course.

3) Make it a family affair.

4) Get some fresh air at least one hour a day, three or more times a week.

5) Use fun activities, such as a family bike ride, as rewards.

6) Preschoolers are not ready for organized sports. They will have more fun hitting a ball and running bases in the backyard or park.

7) Have your child exercise with a friend. Exercising together is more fun.

8) Encourage your child to decrease the TV habit and increase the exercise habit.

9) Activities that can be enjoyed through life are: biking, skating, swimming, tennis, walking, and dancing.

10) Make safety a habit when exercising. Wear bike helmets, check playground equipment, and take your child for swimming lessons.

Exercise will build your preschoolers' muscles, improve coordination and stamina, control their weight, provide an outlet for their energy, and build self-esteem.

Nutrition

Good nutrition goes hand in hand with abundant exercise.

Experts agree that as long as the food choices your preschooler picks with your help are healthy, and junk food is kept to a minimum, children will balance their diet themselves over a short period of time. Check with your pediatrician for needed supplements such as vitamins and minerals.

Keeping an eye and ear on the future

Your child's eyes and ears are their most important senses for learning during the preschool years. Recognizing letters and numbers, hearing and interpreting language, listening to directions, and developing eye-hand coordination are necessary skills acquired and refined from ages three to five.

"Age three is when your child should start having regular eye checkups," advises optometrist, Dr. Diana Medlin. This is when the doctor can diagnose disorders such as: muscle imbalances, nearsightedness, and farsightedness. While many vision problems are inherited, your preschooler can develop good habits to protect his vision.

"Good posture equals good vision," says Dr. Medlin. "The most important thing a parent can do is encourage bilateral stimulation (the use of both eyes together.)" Teach your preschooler to sit up straight at a table when coloring, reading or writing (keeping the work at elbow length). Lying down while doing close work makes one eye work harder than the other and can cause eye strain.

Lighting is critical to good vision, with general room lighting the best option. Remind your child that light should be behind her as she does close work or watches TV. This diminishes the glare that front lighting creates which can cause eye strain. Television should be watched at a four foot distance.

Developing good safety habits can also protect your children's vision. Warn them to keep sharp objects away from their eyes. Since children spend so much time outdoors, parents can ask their eye doctor about UV (Ultra-violet light) protection from the sun's damaging rays with special sunglass lenses.

Fostering good ear care habits include both hygiene and protection against loud noises. Only the outside of the ear should be cleaned with soapy water. The inside of the ear should be washed with plain, lukewarm water on a cloth. Stress that your child should never stick cotton swabs or any object in their ears.

Loud noises are the major culprit in hearing loss. Preschoolers can be taught about the possible dangers. Preschoolers, who do not always adjust the volume correctly, should not be allowed to use headphones for music listening. If they do use them, ask the audio store about an attachment that can regulate the volume to a minimum level.

Keep 'em smiling

Somewhere between the ages of five and seven your preschooler will get his permanent teeth. Starting good dental care now can ensure a happy smile for life. Professionals advocate twice-yearly visits beginning at three years of age — earlier if the parents perceive a problem.

"At birth the permanent front teeth have already started forming," explains Dr. Virginia Tackney, D.M.D., F.A.G.D. "If baby teeth decay badly enough, it affects the permanent teeth." Baby teeth are important because they hold the space for the permanent teeth. If these first teeth become infected, decayed or lost prematurely, the permanent ones may be deformed, poorly spaced, or discolored.

The best prevention against tooth decay is brushing. Encourage your preschooler to brush after every meal and before bedtime. Make the process fun by using bubblegum-flavored or sparkling toothpaste. Toothbrushes with cartoon characters are a special treat for this age and some children get a thrill from an electric toothbrush. The toothbrush should be replaced every three months and also every time your child has an upper respiratory infection to avoid reinfection.

Urge your preschooler to take her time and be thorough when brushing. "A couple of minutes is an endless amount of time for this age," states Dr. Tackney. "Give them a three-minute egg timer and have them brush until the sand is out. We do suggest that parents monitor the brushing until the child is nine." Show your preschooler how to turn the brush to reach the front, back and top of the teeth. Compliment your children when they do a good job brushing. Say that you love their smile or "tell them their teeth sparkle like little pearls," concludes Dr. Tackney.

A healthy mind equals a healthy body

The effect of stress on physical health is well documented. It is never too early to help a child learn when to deal with stress and how to reduce it. Setting a schedule with dependable mealtimes, regular bedtimes, and planned fun times can let your child know what to expect.

Adequate sleep and rest is the key to beating stress. Preschoolers should average eleven hours of sleep a night. Nighttime rituals, such as a warm bath, a small cup of water, a relaxing story, and a goodnight kiss will trigger sleepiness. A nightlight, a stuffed animal, or a special blanket can provide a sense of security needed to lull a small child to sleep.

When a stressful situation occurs, practice relaxation together. Exercise to let off steam, spend time in the rocking chair, smell flowers outside, breathe deeply, or put your preschooler in a nice, warm tub while you sit nearby and sing his favorite songs. The best way to combat stress is a hug. By hugging and kissing their preschoolers often, parents can teach them the healthiest lifelong habit of all — how to give and share love.

NOTE: This chapter contains general suggestions for teaching your preschooler good health habits. It is not a substitute for regular doctor visits or an informed discussion with your child's physician.

Chapter 33
Helping Your Child
to Eat Well

Paulette Bochnig Sharkey

*A healthy, positive feeding
relationship with your child
grows out of trust.*

Zachary, age two, climbs eagerly into his high chair, folds his arms and announces, "I won't eat." His mother desperately replies, "But you have to eat. Have a spoonful. Look, here comes the airplane into the hangar. Mayday! Mayday!"

At the table his four-year-old sister, Emily, whines, "How many bites of broccoli before I get my cookie?" Sound familiar?

We all want our children to be "good eaters." We want eating times to be happy times. But sometimes they're not. What can we do? Here's advice from Ellyn Satter, author, lecturer, registered dietitian, and family therapist specializing in the treatment of eating disorders.

Trust is the key
"A healthy, positive feeding relationship with your child," says Satter, "grows out of trust — trust in her ability to eat in a way that's right for her and to develop the body that's right for her. Feeding is a cooperative process, not one of outsmarting your child."

How children eat
Preschoolers who are good eaters don't act like adults. They may eat a lot one day, and practically nothing the next. They may like a food today, but not tomorrow. Preschoolers typically don't eat everything at a meal—they stick to one or two foods. And they're very sensitive to their hunger and appetite. They will even stop in the middle of a bowl of ice cream if they get full.

Who's in charge?
The best parenting—including parenting with food—provides love and limits. Satter's golden role for feeding children is her *division of responsibility:* Parents are responsible for *what* food is offered, and (for children more than 12 months old) *when* and *where* it is offered. Children decide *how much*, and even *whether* to eat. Let's look at how this works.

Parents' Responsibilities
• *You are the gatekeeper on food selection.*
You decide what food comes into the house and goes on the table. After all, you know more about food, and about eating, than your preschooler. He wants and needs to learn from you. Put four or five foods on the table at mealtime: a meat or other protein source, milk, a fruit or vegetable or both, bread and another complex carbohydrate (potatoes, rice, spaghetti), and butter or margarine, and let your child pick and choose from what's available. Don't limit the menu to foods your preschooler accepts, but be sure to include one food that he usually likes. Always offer bread — he can eat that when all else fails.

• *You are the timekeeper on feeding time.*
You decide when to offer meals and snacks. Your child's stomach is small and his energy needs are high. So, he needs three meals a day with planned snacks in between to bring the feeding intervals down to about every two or three hours.

Don't let your preschooler have food or beverages at other times; that puts him in charge of the menu, as well as the timing. Offer water for thirst. If he grazes constantly—even on nutritious food or juice—he won't be hungry enough at mealtime to learn to eat a variety of foods.

• *You decide where.*
Feeding preschoolers only at the table teaches them to take eating seriously. It also keeps you from giving food handouts for skinned knees, hurt feelings, or general crankiness (this teaches him to eat when he gets upset).

• *It's up to you to make it friendly.*
 • Have family meals. Your preschooler needs to eat with you, even if it's more peaceful without her.
 • Make mealtimes pleasant: Don't scold or argue.
 • Let your preschooler eat in his own way—within reason. When "exploring" food becomes simply messing around to get you to react, let him get down from the table.
 • Modify food so your preschooler can eat it (for example: make food moist, cut meat finely).
 • Help your preschooler pay attention to his eating. To eat well, your child should be calm, rested, and hungry. Leave the television off—TV distracts him from eating and interferes with family social time.

Children's Responsibilities
For the division of responsibility to work, your child must also do her part. She decides:
• **How much she eats**
• **Whether she eats**
Children know how much they need to eat. Every child grows differently, and every child needs a different amount of food. Some days your child is hungry, some days not. Some days she is active, some days not. If you let your child follow her internal sense of hunger, appetite, and fullness, she'll eat the amount she needs to grow the way nature intended. If you get pushy with food, she can't eat well.

Your child's body

Some children are naturally tall and slender, others are more solid and muscular, still others are on the fat side. Your child's body type is determined mostly by heredity. Don't compare your child's growth with that of other children. If he follows predictably along one of the standard curves on his growth chart, he's doing fine. Your child shouldn't suddenly shift up or down from his usual curve. If he does, consult your doctor — something is disrupting his growth.

Supporting without managing

Children always do better when they are in control of their own eating. Forcing backfires — children eat less, not more. Let your preschooler turn down foods she doesn't want. Let her know she may taste a food and then not finish it. Let her decide when she's hungry and when she's full.

Trusting your child to eat frees you to enjoy her. If you stop worrying about getting food into her, you can pay attention, instead, to sharing her delight in learning to eat, to watching her growth unfold, and to doing a good job with parenting.

How to Feed Your Young Child

How to feed your toddler

Your toddler needs control over his own world. He also needs limits, to make his world the size he can handle. With eating, that means you choose the menu that's safe and nutritious; you choose the times for eating. Then let your child decide how much to eat, even when he eats very little.

• *Help him learn to like new foods*
Toddlers don't like new foods, but they learn to like them if they have time
and experience. Let your toddler see the new food on the table; let him see
you eat it. If you don't pressure him, eventually he will taste it. He'll take
it back out of his mouth, but don't despair! He's not rejecting the food, he's
getting used to it. He'll do this many times, until he knows the food well
enough to swallow it—and like it.

• *Choose your battles*
You can get your toddler to come to the table, but you can't make him eat.
Don't beg, bribe ("Eat your broccoli and you can have dessert"), threaten,
or play games ("Here comes the choo-choo"). Show your child that you
won't try to make him eat, and he will likely go ahead and do it on his
own. But you have to mean it—he'll know if you're trying to trick him.

• *Don't cater to food jags*
Your child may go through food jags when he wants to eat the same thing
all the time. Planning meals ahead makes food jags less of a problem. If
you ask your toddler what he wants to eat, he'll demand his favorite food.
So don't ask. Let him choose from what is offered at the table like the rest
of the family.

• *Don't short-order cook*
When your toddler says he doesn't like the meal, ignore it, or say "Oh,
okay." Don't jump up to short-order cook something else (that gives your
child control of the menu). Have his milk at his place and some bread on
the table, help him serve himself, and let him eat—or not eat.

How to feed your three-to-five-year-old
Your three to five year old wants to grow up with eating as much as she
wants to learn to ride a bike and write her name. She pays attention to
what you do. When she sees you eating green beans, she figures that she'll
someday eat green beans, too.

• *Don't pressure your child to eat*
Your child probably isn't as afraid to try new foods now as she was when
she was a toddler. And she'll no longer assume that if the taste is different,
it's bad. Still, don't force your child to eat, or even persuade her in a "nice"
way ("Come on, just one bite"). Children also like foods less when they're
given rewards for eating them. Perhaps they reason, "If my parents have
to give me something to make me eat this, it must not be so good."

Reassure your child that she doesn't have to eat anything she doesn't want
to. You can say, "When you get a little older, you'll probably like this." You
might tell her that trying a little bit, lots of times, can help her learn to like

foods. But don't insist. Take your child's word for it when she says she really doesn't want to eat something.

• *Accept some food waste*
Your food waste will go up with a child at your table. She won't be very good at estimating how much she'll eat. She'll take food on her plate and eat just a bit, or none at all. You can remind her, gently, not to take so much, but you shouldn't make her clean her plate.

• *Respect eating quirks*
Your child might love a sandwich cut in triangles, but refuse to eat the same sandwich cut in squares. She isn't trying to bug you—this is normal three-to-five-year-old behavior. Respecting her wishes won't spoil her or make her finicky.

Teach your child how to behave at the table
If you let your child misbehave at meals, she won't learn how to eat with others. Your three-to-five-year-old should be able to:
- Stay calm when she's hungry and must wait for food.
- Help herself when the serving dishes are passed.
- Say "Yes, please" or "No, thank you."
- Make do with less-favorite foods.
- Talk nicely while she eats.
- Sit at the table until she's finished eating.
- Eat in unfamiliar places with unfamiliar people.

If your child doesn't eat enough
• While it's natural to be concerned when a preschooler eats very little and grows slowly, it's likely your child is satisfied and comfortable with the small amounts he eats. If you try to get him to eat more than he's hungry for, he'll resist and may eat even less.

• Follow the division of responsibility. Schedule meals and snacks and let your preschooler decide how much to eat at those times. Don't give juice or a cookie whenever he comes around because you're so happy to have him eating something. You'll fill him up on bits and pieces and in the long run, he'll eat less.

• Be realistic about amounts. A preschooler's helping is about 1/4 to 1/2 the size of an adult's, or one tablespoon per year of age. There might be times when your child doesn't eat anything at all. Don't worry. He'll make up his nutritional needs at another meal or snack, later in the day or the week.

• If you're making special efforts to cook low-fat for your family, the food you serve may be too low in fat for your preschooler. If you think this could be happening, ask a registered dietitian about your child's diet.

If your child eats too much

• Some children eat a lot. It doesn't mean they'll get fat. If your preschooler is growing normally, it's safe to assume that she's eating the right amount for her. If you try to get her to eat less than she's hungry for, you'll frighten her. She'll worry that she won't get enough to eat, and she'll overeat when she gets the chance.

• Follow the division of responsibility for feeding. Offer structured meals and snacks. Let your preschooler eat as much as she wants at those times. Don't allow eating at other times.

• You can't — and shouldn't try to — control the size and shape of body your preschooler develops. Trying to make her thin could end up making her fatter than she might otherwise be. Let her grow in the way that nature intended. (It's normal for toddlers to be chubby; most start to lose that round baby look around the third year.)

• Your preschooler will grow up to eat the way you do. If you worry about food, or diet a lot, your child will, too. If you learn to listen to your body to know how much to eat, your child will grow up listening to her body, too.

(This chapter outlines ideas from Ellyn Satter's book, *How to Get Your Child to Eat... But Not too Much;* which is listed in Resources, page 255.)

Chapter 34
How Well
Does Your Child Hear?

Elizabeth J. Webster

*Hearing influences
language development
and socialization.*

I like to draw pictures. I drew a big fire engine for my little brother. My father, who was reading the paper, said, "Why don't you take it to bed?" I did, and my mother was terribly upset. She knew my father had said, "Why don't you make it red?" Anyhow, my mother and my father talked it over. They took me to see a doctor.

from *A Button in Her Ear* by Ada Litchfield
© 1976 Albert Whitman and Company.

Parents are right to recognize the importance of adequate hearing and to help their children learn listening skills. Parents also are right to seek professional help early for children suspected of having impaired hearing.

Hearing Influences Language Development and Socialization

Adequate hearing is essential in determining how quickly and easily a child learns language. Early in life, infants entertain themselves by babbling. They make all sorts of sounds, some of which are found in speech. The normally hearing infant quickly moves to the next stage of language development and imitates environmental sounds. She especially tries to imitate her parents' intonation and to say words she hears, such as "bye bye" and "up." Because such imitations are crucial building blocks of language, it is important that parents talk to children at this stage. The child who is hearing impaired cannot imitate a parent's words or intonation, but she may imitate facial expressions and gestures, also an important language skill.

Hearing also affects how easily children learn other skills acquired in the preschool years. The hearing child learns to follow instructions, although sometimes he may rebel. One who consistently ignores instructions because of a hearing problem may be considered stubborn or rebellious. A preschooler with adequate hearing learns routines such as waiting and taking turns, skills necessary to children's cooperative play. A hearing impaired preschooler may not understand such routines, so others may not choose to play with him.

Professionals Who Treat Hearing

Many preschoolers have temporary hearing problems that result from ear or throat infections. Such temporary losses clear up with prompt medical treatment. The child who frequently reports having an earache or misunderstands speech should be taken to a physician who specializes in such problems (otologist). In cases of an infection when the otologist decides that medication alone cannot take care of the fluid built up from the infection, he routinely does a minor surgical procedure in which a small tube is placed in the eardrum. Harmful fluid can then drain out, relieving discomfort and preventing continued hearing loss.

Otologists work closely with professionals trained to test hearing (audiologists). Audiologists can determine the loudness at which a child hears sounds, especially speech sounds. In the case of a hearing loss that cannot be treated medically, the audiologist can prescribe a hearing aid to help meet individual needs for additional loudness.

Learning to Use Available Hearing

Normally hearing preschoolers can hear sentences spoken at conversational loudness from more than 100 feet away in a quiet room. Speech must be louder, more distinct or spoken from a shorter distance in noisy conditions or when directed to the child with some degree of hearing loss. However, all children need to learn to listen and attend to conversation in both quiet and noise. The activities suggested on page 246 can be done at home or in the classroom to help preschoolers learn listening skills. The hearing impaired child will also need the following special attention if he is to follow conversation: he will need to sit where he can see the speaker, with his better ear toward her. Bright light should not be in his eyes, but rather on the speaker's face. If he does not know where the speaker is, he may have trouble locating the source of sound. He should be told specifically, "I'm in the kitchen," "I'm at the back of the room," etc. He will also find it easier to follow a speaker who is not moving from place to place.

Listening for Fun and Learning

Preschoolers will need to use all of their available hearing in order to develop conversational language skills. Parents can help them develop the ability to identify speech sounds. The goals of listening activities are:
1. to make listening enjoyable,
2. to help the child pay attention well enough to recognize differences between various sounds, and
3. to make listening to other people a pleasant way to relate to them.

The following activities can be used as games either in the preschool or at home. At home, older siblings can join in. Each listening period should be short enough to keep the attention of the listeners.

Repetitive Songs with Actions
Hokey Pokey and *If You're Happy* are examples of the kinds of games children as young as 3 1/2 seem to enjoy.

    Hokey Pokey
    Put your right hand in;
    Put your right hand out;
    Put your right hand in;
    And shake it all about.
    Do the hokey pokey and you turn yourself around.
    That's what it's all about.

If You're Happy
If you're happy and you know it, <u>clap</u> <u>your</u> <u>hands</u>.
(Repeat)
If you're happy and you know it, then you really ought to show it,
If you're happy and you know it, <u>clap</u> <u>your</u> <u>hands</u>.

In these games, children must listen carefully to see what action to take next. Be sure the child can see all participants and start by using gestures along with verbal cues.

For example, *Hokey Pokey* can be simplified to "Put your head in; put your head out; put your head in and shake it all about." Then, with the song's repetitions, use: *one arm, both arms, one leg,* and *whole self.*

You can use your imagination when singing *If You're Happy* and substitute for the underlined words in that song: *blink your eyes, pat your head, stamp your foot, give a smile,* or any other actions you can think of.

Children who have done such songs once or twice start remembering the routines of them. The leader can then omit the visual clues and have the children enact the songs from verbal directions alone.

Changing the routine also helps children rely on listening. For example, one version of *Hokey Pokey* may start with "put your arm in" and the next may start "put your leg in." Also, *If You're Happy* may begin with "stamp your foot" and end with "clap your hands."

A modification of *Simon Says* can also be an enjoyable listening game for preschoolers. *Gestures are not used by the leader.* Each instruction should start with *Simon Says.* This will encourage children to listen for the instruction rather than focusing whether or not Simon says to do the action. The following illustrates using what preschoolers know to create a *Simon Says* listening activity: "Simon says, 'stand up,' Simon says, 'shake your head for yes,' Simon says, 'wiggle your head for no,' Simon says, 'clap your hands,' Simon says, 'touch your nose,' Simon says, 'touch your ear,' Simon says, 'clap your hands again,' Simon says, 'that's all, sit down'."

Musical Instruments and Other Noisemakers
Simple musical instruments can be employed both to teach rhythm and also to teach skill in differentiating sounds. Various instruments, for example, two sticks, a triangle, a bell, and a drum, can be hidden from the child's view. The adult plays one of the instruments and asks the child to indicate which one she heard. The goal here is proper identification so pointing to the right instrument is as good as saying its name.

Using Everyday Activities

Everyday objects at home also can be used. A game can be played in the kitchen, for example, where the child identifies ordinary kitchen sounds. Make sure that the child cannot see the objects used as noisemakers. Then ask him to play the game of identifying what is making such everyday noises as the clank of a pot being put on the stove, the rattle of glasses or plates being taken from the cupboard, the sound of water running in the sink, or the squeak of a screen door.

There are so many sounds produced in a kitchen that it's tempting to use different sounds each time this game is played. However, it is wise to use the same noisemakers several times until he is very familiar with them, adding a new one each time.

Sounds accompany all sorts of activities: bath time, laundry time, indoor and outdoor play, etc. As children become more skilled at attending to various environmental sounds they are more ready to attend to speech sounds.

Chapter 35
Preparing Your Child
for
Medical Visits

Mary Margaret Dean

*Preschoolers need to be
prepared in order to minimize
their anxieties
about medical procedures.*

Whether visiting the doctor, clinic, dentist, or hospital, preschoolers need to be prepared for the visit in order to minimize their anxieties about medical procedures. Children's fears center on three issues: separation, bodily harm, and fantasies.

Fear of Separation

To the preschooler, doctors' and dentists' offices, clinics and hospitals are filled with unfamiliar equipment and strangers who seem to be intent on separating them from their mother. Young children do not have the experience necessary to cope with the overwhelming events taking place. They are not capable of understanding why adults tell them, "This is to help you." Your child, who may be outgoing and friendly in a more familiar environment, may cry and shriek when the nurse merely asks you to put her on the scale.

Fear of Bodily Harm

The anticipation of bodily harm can be very stressful for preschoolers. Young children have only recently learned to control their bodies. They feel very proud and protective of them. To have a stranger poke and prod at their bodies is very distressing.

Fantasies

Often we may laugh at children's harmless misconceptions. But their misconceptions about medical procedures can cause a great deal of stress to your child. Angela thought if the doctor drew blood, she wouldn't have enough and would die. Tommy believed if he opened his mouth for the dentist, the dentist would be able to see the cookie he wasn't supposed to have eaten. Jessica thought she had to go to the clinic because she was bad. These and other fantasies based on misunderstood words, strange equipment, and fears of bodily harm often cause stress to preschoolers.

Preparing Your Child

Today, we know that good health is more than going to the doctor once a year. We know that we have a responsibility to look after our health. We must act as a partner with our doctor. If preschoolers are encouraged to develop a comfortable relationship with their doctors, they will be more likely to consider their doctor as a partner in their future health care.

To guard against the fears and anxieties, you need to prepare your child for a medical visit. Be honest and as complete as possible when telling your child what will happen on the visit. Although you shouldn't overwhelm her with details, you should let your child know what to expect. "The doctor will look in your eyes and your ears. He will put a little metal circle on your chest to hear your heart beat." If something will hurt, let her know it will hurt and that it is okay to cry or say, "Ouch!"

Most procedures done by doctors or dentists hurt for a very short time. Reassure your child of this. After your explanations, listen to your child. Be aware of what her concerns are.

Before and after your visit, read to your child about health care. (See Resources, page 256.) A doctor kit or materials, such as cotton and band-aids, can help to encourage your child to play at being the doctor or patient before and after the visit. Play can be a learning and healing process. You can determine your child's areas of concern by observing or participating in the play.

If you can, hold onto your child while the doctor does most of the examination. Your presence is a support for the child. Allow your child to bring a favorite toy, security blanket, or doll to the office or clinic. If for some reason you can't be with your child, the toy will give him a sense of home and security.

When should you start preparing your child? It depends on his age and whether this is a first visit to the particular office or doctor. In general, older children and first visits need more preparation time. For the very youngest preschoolers, the morning before an afternoon appointment may be adequate. If you tell them too early, most preschoolers get anxious and confused. You know your youngster best and will be able to decide how much preparation time your child needs.

An Emergency Room Visit

An emergency room visit is not like a planned medical visit. Usually you do not have the time to prepare your child for the emergency room. You, yourself, may be upset and frightened. Before you go to the emergency room, call your child's physician or clinic. Often they can reassure you or provide you with an immediate appointment so that a visit to the emergency room will not be necessary. If the visit is necessary and you have time, try to remember to bring your health insurance and hospital card, a record of your child's immunizations, containers of any medicine your child is taking, and your child's favorite toy, blanket, or doll. If your child swallowed a toxic substance, bring a container of whatever he swallowed.

Tell your child where you are going and why. Remember your child is undergoing the same fears that a more routine medical visit entails, but which may be aggravated by immediate pain, a high fever, or discomfort.

Try to stay calm, as your child will know when you are afraid. If you can have someone accompany you to the emergency room, do so. You will need support in this difficult time also. Arrange for someone to watch your other children at home. You will want to give all your time to your sick child.

When you get to the emergency room, you may have to wait as the most serious cases are taken first. Try to distract your child with books or toys if they are provided. Explain the unusual sights and sounds to your child. Reassure your child people come to the emergency room for lots of different reasons and not everyone has the same treatment.

As in any medical visit, stay with your child as much as possible. Explain what is happening to your child and why. If a needle or something else painful is necessary, let your child know it will hurt. Let your child know it is all right to cry or say, "Ouch!." Distract your child if possible while procedures are taking place. Talk about the pictures on the wall, sing a song, recite nursery rhymes, count to ten together, read a book, talk about a recent family activity, something that happened in preschool, or play a simple game. Try having your child contract and relax muscles or breathe in and out slowly if tension is a problem.

After your visit to the emergency room, your child may be particularly clinging, show anger at you, demand a bottle which had been given up months ago, begin to wet the bed or have accidents, develop a sudden fear of ghosts or monsters, or have nightmares or disrupted sleep. All of these are normal patterns after a visit to the emergency room. Try to give your child a little extra time and attention. Play or talk with your child about the emergency. Read books to him about medical procedures. Let your child know it's all right now.

10 Suggestions to Keep Your Preschooler Happy When Sick in Bed

"When I was sick and lay a-bed,
I had two pillows at my head,
And all my toys beside me lay
To keep me happy all the day."

(from "The Land of Counterpane"
by Robert Louis Stevenson)

Having to stay in bed while recuperating will probably seem hard for your active preschooler. Here are some ideas that could help make the time pass more pleasantly.

1. Borrow a stack of books from the library. Read some to your child. Have her "read" some on her own.

2. Let your child hear some of the wonderful stories recorded on audio cassettes, records, or CDs.

3. Purchase activity books: (paper dolls, coloring books, sticker books, and stencil books). Send for Free Juvenile Catalog from Dover Publications, Inc., 31 E. 2nd Street, Mineola, NY 11501-3582, 516-294-7000.

4. Let older preschoolers work with a number of rubber stamps, a stamp pad, and some blank paper.

5. Do crayon rubbings. Place paper over a leaf, a comb, or a textured design. Remove paper covering from a crayon. Place the crayon flat (horizontally) on the paper and rub over the area where the leaf or other object is. The shape of the object will appear.

6. Make a paper bag mask. Cut two holes for eyes in a grocery bag. Let your child complete the mask with watercolor markers or crayons.

7. Make puppets out of paper sandwich bags or socks and act out familiar stories, such as *The Three Bears*.

8. Play an easy version of *Concentration* using only a portion of a regular deck of playing cards. For three-year-olds try using two kings, two aces, and two of the same numbered cards. Turn over the six cards and mix them up. You and your child take turns trying to turn over a matching pair. (Remember to turn them back over if they don't match.) As your youngster gets better at finding the pairs, you can add additional pairs to your game.

9. Play easy board games like Candyland or Chutes and Ladders. Also play with picture dominos, bingo, puzzles, and Legos® or other types of interlocking toys.

10. Your child may also be kept happily occupied with beads to string, sewing cards, dolls with clothing, and a doctor kit.

Resources for Section Six: *Keeping Your Child Healthy*

FOR ADULTS

Safe and Sound: How to Prevent and Treat the Most Common Childhood Emergencies, by Elena Bosque, R.N., M.S. and Sheila Watson, R.N. St. Martin's Press, 1988. This book focuses on the prevention of problems and assessment of your child's condition. It includes a tear-out, laminated, capsule description of infant and child CPR.

Hearing in Children, 4th edition, by Jerry L. Northern and Marion P. Downs. Williams and Wilkins, 1991. Sections on testing young children may alleviate some parental fears if they don't mind coping with the professional terms. This book also has suggestions for understanding what children with various losses hear.

Taking Care of Your Child: A Parent's Guide to Medical Care, 4th edition, by Richard H. Pantell, M.D., et al. Addison-Wesley, 1993 A comprehensive guide to your child's health and development from infancy to school age. Includes charts you can fill out detailing family records, growth, and immunization.

Pediatrics for Parents, Richard J. Sagall, M.D., editor. (747 S. 3rd St., Philadelphia, PA 19147-3324) This newsletter provides parents with recent, practical information about their children's health.

Child of Mine: Feeding with Love and Good Sense, by Ellyn Satter. Bull Publishing, 1986. A warm, supportive book for parents about basic nutrition for infants and young children. (Also available as a video.)

How to Get Your Kid to Eat ... But Not Too Much, by Ellyn Satter. Bull Publishing, 1987. Practical advice on building a healthy, positive feeding relationship between parent and child. Includes specific information for every stage from birth to adolescence, as well as special feeding problems: the sick child, eating disorders, poor growth.
(The resources by Satter, listed above, may be ordered from Ellyn Satter Associates, 4226 Mandan Crescent, Madison, WI 53711, 800-808-7976.)

For Parents of Deaf Children, by Jerome D. Schein and Doris Naiman. National Association of the Deaf, 814 Thayer Ave., Silver Spring, MD 20910, 1978. This book can be helpful to parents in acknowledging hearing impairment and explaining it to others.

The American Academy of Pediatrics: Caring for Your Baby and Young Child Birth to Age 5, Steven P. Shelov, Editor-in-Chief. Bantam, 1991. A comprehensive guide that addresses parents' concerns about young children's development, nutrition, safety, and health problems.

FOR CHILDREN

The Berenstain Bears Go to the Doctor, by Stan and Jan Berenstain. Random House, 1981. This book will help children understand what to expect at the doctor's office from the weigh-in to temperature, from eye charts to getting shots. Even Papa gets an examination.

Germs Make Me Sick! by Melvin Berger. HarperTrophy, 1995. With words simple enough for older preschoolers to understand, the author tells what germs look like, and how your body fights them.

Dinosaurs Alive and Well: A Guide to Good Health, by Laurie Krasny Brown and Marc Brown. Little, Brown, 1990. Providing information on nutrition, exercise, and stress, this appealing book entices the reader to live a more healthful life.

Arthur's Chicken Pox, by Marc Brown. Little, Brown, 1994. When Arthur gets chicken pox, Grandma Thora, who knows all about chicken pox, comes to take care of him. When he's all better, he gets to go to the circus.

Country Noisy Book, by Margaret Wise Brown. HarperCollins, 1976. When a little dog named Muffin goes to the country, he must be shipped there in a box. He can't see anything, but he can hear the sounds of the train and boat that transport him. Arriving in the country, there are more new sounds to hear, and the reader is encouraged to take part in discovering what the sounds could be.

Barney Is Best, by Nancy White Carlstrom. HarperCollins, 1994. A tender story about a little boy who needs to go to the hospital to have his tonsils taken out. He's a little scared, but it helps to take his stuffed elephant Barney, an old friend who has been with him through many different experiences.

Handtalk (Macmillan, 1984); *Handtalk Birthday* (Macmillan, 1987) by Remy Charlip & Mary B. Miller. Two books that introduce the reader to sign language, illustrated with bright color photographs.

An Edible Alphabet, by Bonnie Christensen. Dial, 1994. This is an ABC book with beautiful wood engravings of children enjoying the harvest. It transcends an ordinary alphabet book not only because of the artwork, but also by taking the reader to far off places. For example, the letter "U," is for Ulu, the Hawaiian name for breadfruit. Although many of the foods are familiar, some are not, so a glossary is included to describe each plant.

Spaghetti for Suzy, by Peta Coplans. Houghton Mifflin, 1993. This story begins realistically enough, with Suzy wanting to eat only spaghetti. Then it turns into a fantasy with three animals using spaghetti for fishing line, shoe string, and yarn. These animals are grateful for Suzy sharing her spaghetti with them and each gives her a gift of a piece of fruit in return. They help her change her attitude and her diet.

The Sleeping Bread, by Stefan Czernecki and Timothy Rhodes. Hyperion, 1993. In this charming South American folk tale, the beautiful, brightly colored illustrations transport the reader to Guatemala and village life. The story tells of a baker, a beggar, and a batch of bread dough that will not rise. This story shows the worth of each person in the community.

Eating the Alphabet: Fruits & Vegetables from A to Z, by Lois Ehlert, Harcourt Brace Jovanovich, 1996. Bright, colorful pictures introduce the preschooler to every good food imaginable, from Asparagus to Zucchini.

Feast for 10, by Cathryn Falwell. Clarion, 1993. Count to ten — twice — and see how members of a family shop and work together to prepare a meal.

Lunch, by Denise Fleming. Holt, 1996. Few words are needed to tell the story of a hungry mouse eating his way through a large — and colorful — lunch of fruits and vegetables.

Ms. Sneed's Guide to Hygiene, by Dale Gottlieb. Chronicle Books, 1997. Bright colors, lively language, and playful pop-ups help this book appeal to children who might not realize that hygiene can be fun.

Baby Duck and the Bad Eyeglasses, by Amy Hest. Candlewick Press, 1996. Baby Duck just got new eyeglasses and she doesn't like them. But Grandpa knows how to cheer her up and make her realize that her eyeglasses are not so bad after all.

Furry, by Holly Keller. Greenwillow, 1992. Laura's allergy to fur makes it difficult to find a pet that would not make her sneeze, have teary eyes, or break out in a rash. But her brother finds an interesting pet for her without fur.

When I See My Doctor..., by Susan Kuklin. Bradbury Press, 1988. Using colorful photographs, this book illustrates the experience of a young child going for a checkup. It includes factual information and gives preschoolers a reassuring look at a medical examination.

A Button in Her Ear, by Ada Litchfield. Albert Whitman and Co., 1976. Angela doesn't seem to hear very clearly when people talk to her. When her parents take her to the doctor, he tells her that she needs a hearing aid. The hearing aid helps her to hear nearly everything anyone says to her, and she decides that a button in your ear is a good thing, if you need one.

The Lion Who Had Asthma, by Jonathan London. Albert Whitman & Co., 1992. Sean pretends he is a lion, a hippo, or a giant. But when Sean the lion has a cough and can't breathe very well, his mom gives him a treatment with a machine that helps him. The book includes a note for parents of children who have asthma.

Outside & Inside You, by Sandra Markle. Atheneum, 1991. With vivid color photographs, this book takes the reader on a journey through the human body.

Bread Bread Bread, by Ann Morris. Lothrop, Mulberry, 1993. A photographic world tour exploring the many shapes, sizes, textures, and colors of bread and the diversity of people who eat it.

My Dentist, by Harlow Rockwell. Mulberry Edition, 1987. Simple text and clear illustrations describe a visit to the dentist, with explanations and pictures of the tools and machines that he uses.

Look At Me Books: Mealtime, with photographs by Stephen Shott. Dutton, 1991. In this book with heavy cardboard pages for the youngest preschoolers, there are colorful pictures of babies eating and drinking, and some of the foods they enjoy.

The Listening Walk, by Paul Showers. HarperTrophy, 1993. A little boy takes walks with his father and his dog. He doesn't talk but just listens to all the different sounds, from the sound of his dog's toenails scratching the sidewalk, to the whispering sound of the lawn sprinklers, to the eeeeee of the car brakes. He ends with the suggestion that readers take their own listening walks.

Glasses, Who Needs 'Em? by Lane Smith. Puffin, 1995. A young boy finds out how much he is missing out on by seeing a blurry world. Glasses clear things up for him.

Feel Better, Ernest! by Gabrielle Vincent. Greenwillow, 1988. In another story in the series about the warm friendship between Celestine the mouse and Ernest the bear, Ernest is sick and the doctor says he must stay in bed. Celestine nurses and entertains her friend until he is well again.

Section Seven
Exercise
and
Fitness
for
Young
Children

Section Seven
Exercise and Fitness
for Young Children

Introduction

During every season of the year, a parade passes by my window as I sit eating my breakfast. On the pleasant road near my house, I observe joggers, walkers, bicycle riders, and skaters — of all ages — enjoying outdoor fun and exercise.

The authors of this section applaud the many benefits of exercise and outdoor play. These can include increasing children's physical fitness and self-esteem, along with encouraging socialization and cooperation with others.

While we all need active times, we also need to find time for quiet moments. One writer describes the many calming and peaceful experiences that give children a chance to find the needed balance in their lives of both active and quiet activities.

SECTION SEVEN

EXERCISE AND FITNESS FOR YOUNG CHILDREN

Chapter 36
Promoting Physical Fitness

Ellen Javernick

*Older preschoolers
join their parents
as they jog, dance,
or exercise to music.*

It's such a hassle to bundle up the two-year-old twins, that they often don't get outside at all on cold days. Their doctor has mentioned that both boys are slightly overweight.

Johnny, three, is sifting sand in the sand box. The neighborhood children are climbing and swinging. When Johnny's mother encourages him to join them, he says he's too tired.

Since the new baby arrived, Maria and her mother have been doing their errands in the car. Test results indicate that Maria, at five, has a problem with elevated cholesterol.

Why should parents promote physical fitness?
Parents often believe that children need little encouragement to be physically active. Some children do spend lots of time running and climbing, but the children who need exercise the most are often the ones who don't get enough.

One study of the American Academy of Pediatrics (AAP) says that up to 50% of American children are not getting enough exercise to develop healthy hearts and lungs. Their studies show that many young children are at risk for heart disease because they are physically inactive. Pediatricians are concerned about childhood obesity because it is often associated with obesity in adulthood. Parents worry because they know that it can cause social and emotional problems. Because exercise patterns are established early in life, regular periods of vigorous physical activity are particularly important for preschoolers who have a tendency to be overweight.

When should parents begin to encourage exercise?
Because the level of physical fitness in the U.S. has been declining, the AAP is calling for greater family involvement in fitness at home. As parents we need to help our children develop strength, endurance, balance and coordination.

Even babies need exercise. Unconfined infants kick and reach as they explore their environment. They crawl for toys placed out of reach by their parents. They model adult behavior as they kick and splash in the bathtub. If provided with appropriate toys, toddlers push and pull and climb and jump. When encouraged by their parents, they walk daily to do errands, to visit the park, or to discover the wonders of their neighborhood. Older preschoolers join their parents as they jog, dance, or exercise to music.

(If you're concerned about how much exercise is good for your child, check with your doctor.)

What can parents do to encourage their children to be more active?
Parents should not discourage activities such as running jumping and climbing, but should set rules where safety is involved. While rules about jumping on beds or running in the house may be appropriate and necessary, it is important to find a time and a place in which you can encourage physical activity each day.

Researchers have discovered that young children are most often attracted to activities in which their parents participate. Although parents often play with their children, they rarely actively participate in gross motor activities (use of the large muscles) with them. If you want your children to be physically active, participate with them. Swim, dance, and hike with them. Kick a soccer ball together in the summer; go sledding in the winter. Mix family fun with family fitness.

Select a preschool/daycare program that includes physical development in their curriculum, as well as intellectual and social development. Visit the school or center to be sure that there is sufficient space and equipment for lots of active play. Ask whether the staff plans daily group exercise or creative movement activities.

What types of exercise programs are appropriate for preschoolers?
Public recreation departments or parks, YMCAs, etc. often advertise activity programs for preschoolers. Should you sign your child up for a session? Only after you have observed the program or talked with the instructor and you consider it appropriate for your child. Competition is inappropriate for preschoolers. Don't pick a program in which winning is an objective. Be sure that the emphasis of the program is on having fun, and that the expectations for the participants are not too high. Also look for programs that involve both the parent and the preschooler.

Exercise & Fitness Activities

Turn your home into a health club
Your home has the makings of a health club in which your preschoolers will exercise happily. Select activities that are appropriate for the space you have and the ages of your children.

Just like a real gym
If you have a spare room, you can equip it inexpensively to make it into a gym. Put an old bed mattress on the floor. Set up boxes for your child to climb through and step stools to climb over. Use a 4' long piece of masking tape to mark off a "balance beam" on the carpet or floor (the younger the child the wider the tape). Set empty waste baskets at opposite ends of the room as "basketball hoops" for foam balls.

Make your backyard exciting
Even if you cannot afford to invest in a playground structure for your backyard, you can make it an exciting place to play — a place that will encourage your child to be physically active. Cable spools (from the telephone company) or tree stumps (from your tree surgeon) make great climbing towers. Wooden barrels, or heavy cardboard tubes (from a paper company) make great tunnels for boys and girls to crawl through, and push around your "playground." Let your children help paint them to preserve

them. Wooden planks can be used for balance beams — the board should be 3 inches to 5 inches above the ground. The height of an inclined plane depends on the age and ability of each child (see picture on previous page). Boards need to be at least 1 3/4" thick to be safe for children to climb on. Tires of all sizes can be imbedded in the ground to climb on, or hung as swings.

Shaping-up in the city

City dwellers have to try a little harder to provide fitness activities for their preschoolers. You have to make an effort to go often to parks and playgrounds where your children can find running space. Most apartments don't have much room for equipment, but it doesn't take much space to do a daily workout. Music makes movement more fun in a small area. Turn on a tape, CD, or record and make movement a part of every morning.

Bikes on the blacktop

When your little bikers get bored, set up a bicycle course. Spread some pebbles as pretend "broken glass" for children to drive around, a stop sign to warn of danger, a picture of a dog for them to stop for. Use a carton from a large appliance on its side to drive through as a "car wash." Older children like to practice being paper carriers and throwing rolled-up newspapers to the steps of pretend houses.

Healthy helpers

Children love to help their parents work. You can promote physical fitness when you let your child help you rake leaves, sweep the driveway, shovel snow, wash the car, etc.

Music and movement

Play music while you and your children go on "adventurecises." Pretend to visit the zoo, fly through the sky like airplanes, zoom around the house like imaginary race cars. Encourage your child to join you as you do your jazzercise routine.

Wonderful walking

Physicians extol the value of walking daily. A walk for a child is always an adventure. You and your child can enjoy the wonders of nature as you walk your way to fitness.

The author and publisher cannot assume responsibility for any unforseen consequences resulting from any exercises and activities detailed in this chapter. They are only suggestions and it is the responsibility of each adult to develop and supervise a fitness program for children in their care.

Bounce board

Materials - 1" x 8" board about 4' long, 2" x 2" board 7 1/4" long, screws, a tuna can (check that edges are smooth). Screw the larger board to the 2" x 2" about 1/3 of the way from one end. Screw the tuna can about 2" from the other end. To use, put a foam ball in the tuna can. Jump on the opposite end of the long board. The ball will bounce up in the air. Try to catch it.

Body Builders

These inexpensive, easily built pieces of equipment will provide hours of fun and encourage exercise:

Stompers

Materials - 2 matching cans - begin with wide flat ones and as child's balance improves, progress to taller narrower ones.) Poke holes on either side of the bottom of the can. Thread with plastic clothesline rope, measured to be about as high as a child's hand.

Balance Board

Materials - 1" x 8" board about 3' long, heavy fiber tube (the kind newsprint comes in). Use the tube as a roller, balancing the board on the top by shifting weight from side to side.

Chapter 37
Active Time...
Quiet Time

Carol B. Hillman

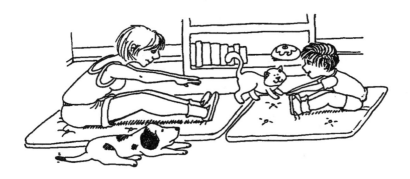

Each child should
have the opportunity
to enjoy both
active and quiet
moments.

At 7:02 A.M. Spencer is up and raring to go. His twelve hour sleep had refueled his engine. He is non-stop from dawn to dusk. Spencer is a doer. He likes to swing high, climb to the top of the jungle gym, and be the first of the car pool group to the nursery school door. He quickly gobbles down his chocolate chip cookie so that he can ask for more. Spencer travels in the fast lane. He never takes time to relax.

Nathaniel wakes up slowly in the morning. When outdoors, he likes to sit quietly, perhaps observing the progress of a ladybug crawling up a blade of grass. On his swing, he wonders why his shadow grows longer as the day progresses. Nathaniel likes to look at books and draw pictures; he is both a deep thinker and a slow mover.

Seeking a Daily Balance
As every parent knows, each child is an individual. He is born with certain characteristics that make up his temperament. Some children are full of energy and always on the go. Others are content with relatively little activity. As a parent, it is important to value both the active times and the quiet times for your child. You can help your child find the balance that will allow him the greatest fulfillment for each day. Each child should have the opportunity to enjoy both active and quiet moments.

Helping Your Child Enjoy Active Times
• *Participate with your child.* If your child always prefers quiet activities, he needs the encouragement, and whenever possible, parental participation in suitable physical activities. You could begin by starting to play catch with a large plush ball. Start gently, close together, and, as your child's skill increases, let him take a step backward. Make a chalk mark on the driveway or sidewalk where he stood on Saturday, so that on Sunday he can see the progress that he has made in one day. As your youngster's skill increases, you can also reduce the size of the ball.

• *Encourage your child to use playground equipment.* Most children love to swing. Learning how to do it by oneself can be an exhilarating new experience. Have your child start with the smallest slide and be there to catch him at the bottom. Applaud his climbing on the jungle gym, even if he only feels comfortable on the bottom rung. Just being there as a parent, encouraging your child's efforts, can bring forth positive results.

• *Exercise with your youngster.* Let him join you in doing morning exercises before breakfast. If you work out on a mat, provide a small one for your youngster. Having his own mat will foster a sense of personal pride. Let him enjoy the pleasures of taking a brisk walk—or a dip in a pool on a hot summer day. Let him see firsthand that exercise is an essential, joyful, and balancing element in life.

• *Let your child's athletic endeavors be short and enjoyable.* If he enjoys his tricycle, don't pressure him to graduate to a two-wheeler with training wheels. Let him gain confidence and skill at home before a "swim and gym" class is suggested. It is important to understand your child's desires as well as to look at his stage of development. Let him know it's okay if he never wants to join Little League and play competitive ball.

• *Try moving to music.* Play any kind of music that makes you and your child want to move: classical, jazz, or popular. Use scarves or yarn to wave as you both jump or turn. Or, with an empty cereal box as a drum, march around the room.

• *Participate in gardening projects with your child.* There are few activities that can bring greater satisfaction than tending growing things. Gardening can be a continual learning experience — it brings children and adults face-to-face with the cycle of life: birth, growth, deterioration, and death. With gardening there is anticipation, responsibility, joy, and a sense of accomplishment. Gardening involves getting your hands into the earth, and the knees of your jeans covered with dirt. Preschoolers often enjoy using child-sized hoes, rakes, and watering cans.

• *Take walks with your child.* There is so much to see and learn about the outdoors. If you live in the city, explore a park together. Run a short race to a nearby tree. Collect colored leaves, or bits and pieces of "found objects," and let him save them in his own "treasure box."

• *Let your preschooler participate in family chores.* A young child likes to be close to a parent and feel part of what is going on in the family. There are always chores to be accomplished: bringing in the newspaper, taking out the trash, helping to wash the car, carrying small packages home from the store. Let him participate at his own level.

Helping Your Child Enjoy Quiet Times
Just as the child who prefers quiet activities needs encouragement and support to be more active, the active child needs that same encouragement and support to become involved in more quiet endeavors.

• *Have arts and crafts projects available.* Take some clues from your child's preschool teacher or caregiver. Find out what his favorite quiet time activities are. If he enjoys arts and crafts, save pieces of fabric, paper, cardboard, old greeting cards, and magazines with colorful pictures. If at all possible, set aside a special corner where it doesn't matter if glue or paint gets spilled. If it can be arranged, move these activities out into the open air during pleasant weather; they can take on a whole new dimension when this occurs. (See Resources, page 286 for books about craft projects.)

• *Take time to read to your preschooler.* Perhaps one of the most appealing quiet activities to do with your preschool child is reading aloud. While many parents like to end a busy day with a story, reading aloud is also an activity which can be used at any time when you and your child need a few restful minutes together. Your child will be more likely to agree to this quiet activity if you let him choose both the story and the place to read.

• *Music can be a part of each day's activities.* Just as reading aloud can be a calming influence, so too can music. Music can be both the focus of a quiet time and as a background during a quiet activity, such as drawing or painting. Having music as an integral part of each day can add an element of beauty to your child's life. Sing a special song to him each night when you tuck him into his bed. These small moments are very important to children.

• *Provide dress-up clothes for dramatic play.* Young children love to imitate what they see around them. They learn by taking on the roles of family members. You can put together a variety of materials for pretend play: hats, ties, shoes, and jewelry or even part of a worn-out bedsheet to use as a cape.

• *Water and sand are relaxing and soothing mediums for young children.* Place a basin with water on a bench or low table so that your child can easily reach his hands inside. With the addition of Ivory Snow, an egg beater or a whisk, there is an endless amount of pretend "cooking" which can take place. Young children like to pretend they are making soup, pie or spaghetti with tomato sauce.

A simple wooden sandbox can provide hours of imaginative play for a young child. If you live in a house with a yard, position the sandbox so that it can be seen from your kitchen window. In that way household chores can be attended to while your preschooler is happily engaged, and being supervised as well. If you live in an apartment, you can provide a strong cardboard box half filled with sand or salt, with plastic cups to pour the sand back and forth.

• *Quiet times can take place outdoors as well as indoors.* You can have quiet moments walking around a garden, looking at the flowers, feeding ducks in a pond, or watching birds at the feeder. You can go to a beach, even in the cool weather, to watch the waves, and walk on the sand.

• *Let your child spend some time alone.* Whether a child is active or passive, or his energy level is high or low, he needs to be able to spend time alone. A child needs to learn to occupy himself, to follow his own pursuits, to enjoy his own company.

Part of growing up is to acquire an ever increasing self-awareness and self-assurance and reliance. Give your child the opportunity to be by himself a part of each day — to plan or play or just to dream.

Chapter 38
Fitness
and Fun

Rae Pica

For a preschooler,
success in any physical activity
is simply a matter of how much fun it is!

No pain, no gain. Target heart rate. Pumping up. These are all expressions we relate to fitness and exercise for adults. But when it comes to fitness for preschoolers, the only word we should associate with young children and exercise is *fun*.

Why consider exercise for young children at all? Don't preschoolers naturally get all the exercise they need just by being children? After all, how often do the words, "Why can't they just sit still?" or, "These kids are bouncing off the walls!" come to mind? Certainly, it seems as if preschoolers are active enough.

Currently there's much debate on just this topic. Some experts feel that up to age seven or eight, just being a kid provides exertion enough. However, others cite the fact that children two-to-five-years-old spend an average of 25 1/2 hours a week watching television as evidence that "being a kid" isn't what it used to be. And that statistic doesn't include any time spent playing video games or working with computers. Some studies show that up to 50 percent of American children are not getting enough exercise.

Here's what else the studies say:
• Forty percent of five-to-eight-year-olds show at least one heart disease risk factor, including elevated cholesterol, high blood pressure, and obesity. In the past, such risk factors were rarely seen in anyone under the age of 30.
• The first signs of arteriosclerosis are appearing at about age five.
• The number of overweight children has doubled in the past decade, with some studies indicating one in five school-age children are overweight. Obesity can lead to heart disease, diabetes, and high blood pressure. It increases stress on weight-bearing joints, lowers self-esteem, and affects relationships with peers. Obesity is greater among children and adolescents who watch TV, due not only to being sedentary, but also to consumption of high-calorie snacks.
• Obese children tend to become obese adults. Children with high blood pressure are likely to become adults with high blood pressure.
• Sedentary habits among adults are a major health problem in the United States, with an estimated 250,000 deaths a year due to low levels of activity and fitness!

Yes, the figures are frightening. But since scare tactics may not be the best means of motivation, here's the good news:
• Children who are physically active and experience success in movement activities show higher levels of self-esteem and a greater sense of accomplishment.
• Exercise helps children get through the day without fatigue and makes them more alert.

• Fit children are more likely to participate in sports, dance, games, and other physical activities (like rollerblading, swimming, and hiking) that improve muscular strength and endurance, flexibility, cardiorespiratory endurance, and body composition (the ratio of fat to muscle).

Although there's currently little research suggesting childhood physical activity significantly impacts childhood health, it's believed individuals who are physically active as children are likely to remain physically active in adulthood. So physical activity in childhood may indeed have an impact on adult health.

The key in early childhood is enjoyment. For an adult, success might be defined in terms of an extra lap run, an extra ten pounds lifted, or getting through an extra 15 minutes of aerobics. For a preschooler, success in any physical activity is simply a matter of how much fun it is!

The American Alliance for Health, Physical Fitness, Recreation, and Dance defines physical fitness as "a physical state of well-being that allows people to:
1) perform daily activities with vigor,
2) reduce their risk of health problems related to lack of exercise, and
3) establish a fitness base for participation in a variety of physical activities."

If this definition is to become a lifelong reality for your preschooler, establishing a pattern of daily physical activity should begin now. In fact, by the age of five, physical activity should be as much a daily habit as brushing teeth!

Suggestions for Parents

In a society that places less and less value on recreation, you may find it challenging to make physical activity a daily habit. But it's worth the effort because your regular physical activity will serve both you and your preschooler. The reason? One of the best ways to help your children become and remain physically fit is to act as a role model. If you exercise and take part in physical activities — and demonstrate a positive attitude about it — your children will likely follow suit.

Here are some other suggestions to keep in mind:

• Encourage, praise, and validate your child's physical activity at every opportunity. Young children learn to value what is valued by the people who matter to them.

• Competition is not developmentally appropriate for preschoolers, and an emphasis on competition and winning is often the reason children of all ages stop taking part in physical activities. Most experts agree the emphasis, before the age of six, should be on exploration and recreation rather than on organized sports and structured competition.

• If your preschooler has older siblings who participate in organized games, put the emphasis on involvement and doing one's personal best rather than winning. The message is an important one for children of all ages.

• Keep developmental, and not chronological, age in mind. Although most children acquire motor skills (use of large and small muscles) in generally the same order, they don't necessarily acquire them at the same time. So don't worry about the timing of your child's physical abilities; each child develops at his own rate. (If your child hears you worrying out loud that she may not be well coordinated or "athletic," she'll soon come to believe it herself.)

• Turn off the TV! The American Academy of Pediatrics recommends no more than two hours of viewing a day.   In a similar vein, you may want to monitor the number of hours your child spends playing video and computer games, which is just as sedentary as TV viewing.

• Select a preschool or child care center that includes movement as an integral part of its curriculum. Early childhood professionals know movement is the young child's most important mode of learning, yet often succumb to parents' wishes that the preschool or child care center be more oriented toward "academics." Let them know how important you consider movement to be!

• Be particular about the extracurricular programs in which you enroll your child. Look for the programs that emphasize exploration versus skills acquisition, and cooperation over competition.

• Make sure your children have plenty of space in which to play and to practice gross-motor (large muscle) skills. Maturation alone doesn't ensure motor skills will develop automatically; practice and instruction are needed. Your child will more likely take part in physical activities later if he's learned basic movement skills and feels confident and coordinated.

• When your children are outdoors, encourage them to run and climb and roll down hills. (It's more important than keeping clothes clean!) Provide toys and materials requiring manipulation and/or effort — like balls in a variety of shapes and sizes, swings, and wheeled (rather than motorized) toys.

• Provide opportunities for your preschooler to play with other children. Sometimes just adding one more child to the mix can make all the difference.

The importance of family activities.

Most important, plan family activities that involve movement. Go walking or bike riding after meals. Young children view such outings as adventures rather than exercise. If you have errands to do within walking distance, don't take the car! On a weekend afternoon, take a hike, or go to the park, or the local roller skating rink.

Sign up for swimming lessons or parent/child movement classes at the local "Y." Your efforts don't even have to be out of the ordinary. At home, put on a piece of music in a steady beat (Rock 'n Roll) and pretend to hold a track meet. Put on a recording of a march and hold a "parade" in the living room. Just put on a piece of music and dance. But don't let on that the real goal is fitness; rather, you're just looking to have some fun! (And music always makes moving more fun.)

You can also encourage your child to move with you while you do your own daily workout. The National Children and Youth Fitness Study II found a significant relationship between mothers who exercise and children who were physically active. But you have to demonstrate a positive attitude about exercising — try not to grumble as you go for that last sit-up!

In addition, you should ask for your child's help with physical chores like sweeping and mopping, raking leaves, shoveling snow, and dusting. And whistle while you work! Young children naturally love to move. So the most significant thing you can do is help ensure your child never loses that love. And you can do that most easily by making certain they experience lots of success in movement and physical activity. That means:
1) there's no right or wrong with how they move, and
2) it's fun.
If these ingredients are the biggest factors in your child's movement experiences, chances are he'll want to keep moving for the rest of his life.

Chapter 39
Back to the
Great Outdoors

Rae Pica

Share your childhood memories
of time spent outdoors.

Michael sits in front of the TV set, happy to be entertained by the characters on his favorite show. When the show ends, he promptly declares he's bored. But when his mother suggests he go outside to play, he feels dismissed and resists the idea. So, instead, he goes to his room to play — even though the sun is shining and the temperature is warm.

Scenes like this are occurring more and more frequently in young children's lives. If it's not lack of inspiration that keeps preschoolers inside, it's likely to be lack of time. Not only do parents have less time to supervise outdoor play or to take their children to the playground, but children also have busier schedules these days. It all adds up to a generation of young children who spend much less time outside than their parents did.

Why be concerned? Lots of reasons! Not only is the outdoors the best place for preschoolers to practice and master emerging physical skills, but it's also the place where children are likely to burn the most calories, which helps prevent obesity. Also, the outside light stimulates the pineal gland. This is the part of the brain that helps regulate our "biological clock." It is vital to the immune system, and makes us feel happier.

Preschoolers also learn through their senses. Outside there are different and wonderful things for them to see (animals and birds), to hear (the wind rustling through leaves), to smell (flowers and rain-soaked ground), to touch (a fuzzy caterpillar or the bark of a tree), and even to taste (newly fallen snow or a raindrop on the tongue). Children who spend a lot of time acquiring their experiences through television, computers, and even books are using only two senses (hearing and sight) which can seriously affect their perceptual abilities.

Outside, children are more likely to invent games. As they do, they're able to express themselves and learn about the world in their own way. They feel safe and in control, which promotes autonomy, decision-making, and organizational skills. Inventing rules for games (as preschoolers like to do) promotes an understanding of why rules are necessary. Later, sidewalk and sandlot games teach physical coordination, cooperation, and mastery.

Although the children are just playing to have fun, they learn:
• communication skills and vocabulary (as they invent, modify, and enforce rules)
• number relationships (as they keep score and count)
• social mores (as they learn to play together)

All of this helps advance physical, cognitive, social, and emotional development.

Then, too, there's the aesthetic value of the outdoors. Aesthetic awareness means a heightened sensitivity to the beauty around us. Because the natural world is filled with beautiful sights, sounds, and textures, it's the perfect resource for the development of aesthetics in young children.

And, of course, what better place than the outdoors for children to be loud and messy and boisterous? Outside they can run and jump and yell, and expend some of the energy that is usually inappropriate — and often annoying — indoors.

Think back to your own childhood. Chances are, some of your fondest memories are of outdoor activities and places. Perhaps you had a favorite climbing tree or a secret hiding place. Maybe you remember jumping rope or learning to turn cartwheels with your best friend, or playing *fetch* with the family dog. Do you recall the smell of lilacs, the feel of the sun on the first day warm enough to take off your jacket, or the taste of a peanut butter and jelly sandwich eaten on a blanket in the yard?

Think back, and then think of just how much you'd like your preschooler to someday have similar childhood memories.

Outdoor Ideas

Children usually have the same values as the important adults in their lives. When you show an appreciation for the great outdoors, your preschooler will follow your lead.

Share your childhood memories of time spent outdoors — and then take your child outside! She's less likely to feel dismissed or punished by the words,"Go out and play" if you go out with her. Teach her the games you used to play. Bring a blanket outside and have a picnic lunch. Lie in the grass and find the "creatures" in the clouds.

A nature walk is a great way to enhance your child's appreciation of the natural environment. Point out the sights and sounds and smells. Encourage him to touch — to discover the smoothness of a rock, the roughness of bark, and the fragility of a dried leaf. For a young child, these are science experiments.

A "listening" walk makes for a wonderful sound discrimination activity. As you walk with your child, point out the sounds of the birds, passing cars, whistling wind, even your footsteps on the sidewalk. What sounds can your preschooler identify on her own? Which are loud and which are soft? Which are high and which are low? What are her favorite sounds? (You might even want to take a tape recorder along so she can try to identify the sounds at a later time.)

Is the library or park within walking distance? Then don't take the car! And if your preschooler absolutely can't miss his favorite TV show, tape it and schedule viewing for a rainy day.

Plan play dates, perhaps taking turns with other parents, so your child has lots of opportunity to play with other children. Not only is the social interaction important, but playing in groups offers a chance to do things one child can't do alone. For example, they can take part in circle games and parachute play (where children gather around a large, circular piece of fabric — an old sheet will do — shaking it, circling it, making waves with it, and such (see Resources, page 286).

This helps to foster cooperation and develop large muscle skills. Playing with others also means your preschooler will have a chance to practice emerging manipulative skills, like throwing and catching. But try to avoid any temptation to impose adult rules on the games children play; they're happiest — and learning the most — when they make up their own.

For those times when your preschooler will be playing alone, make sure she has a range of materials available. Balls in a variety of shapes and sizes ensure practice with throwing and kicking, and a sheet tacked to the side of the house makes a "can't-miss" target. Large, empty plastic soda bottles are also great targets and enhance a preschooler's burgeoning knowledge of cause and effect.

Let your child play with sand and water. Water painting ("painting" the side of the house with a brush and a bucket of water) exercises arms and upper torso while teaching about wet and dry, light and dark, and evaporation. Chasing bubbles gives children a chance to run and enjoy watching the bubble burst.

An obstacle course made with old tires, large appliance boxes, and tree stumps teaches important concepts, like *over, under, through,* and *around*. Pumping a swing helps develop one of the body's midlines and promotes understanding of the concepts of *high* and *low, forward* and *backward*. Of course, you can't forget the tried and true tools of childhood: the jump rope and the tricycle. By five, preschoolers have generally acquired the skill of skipping rope. And from the time they're two, children love riding small-wheeled toys, which gives them a chance to move across space under their own power.

A balance beam offers new and exciting challenges for preschoolers. A low balance beam can be purchased, or a plank or two-by-four placed on the ground. Encourage your child to move along the beam in forward, backward, and sideward directions, at high and low levels. Present open-ended challenges that foster divergent thinking and creativity. For example, ask him to find at least two different ways to move along the beam at a low level (like creeping on hands and knees and scooting on his bottom).

Challenge her to find three different ways to get over the beam (she might respond by slithering over it on her tummy, stepping over it, and jumping over it). And remember, it is the process more than the product that matters most in a young child's explorations and education.

Constant practice and continual mastery of skills in all areas of motor development are critical at the preschool stage, and there's no better place for both to occur than the outdoors. So discourage "couch potatoism!" Shut off the TV, save the housework and chores for another time, take your preschooler by the hand, and go out to play!

Resources for Section Seven: Exercise and Fitness for Young Children

FOR ADULTS

Facets Non-Violent, Non-Sexist Children's Video Guide, compiled by Virginia A. Boyle. Facets Multimedia, Inc. (1-800-331-6197), 1996. This guide was created to help parents use video as a positive force in children's lives. It includes lists of videos indexed by title, age recommendation, and subject. For example: look under *Dance and Creative Movement* for video titles that relate to the topic of physical fitness.

Creative Movement for the Developing Child, by Clare Cherry. Fearon, 1971. This book is chock full of ideas for spur-of-the-moment activities and poems that inspire movement.

I Saw a Purple Cow and 100 Other Recipes for Learning, by Ann Cole, Carolyn Haas, Faith Bushnell and Betty Weinberger. Little, Brown, 1972. Celebrating 25 years since it was first published, this classic book of creative projects will give teachers and parents many ideas for active time and quiet time with young children.

Sharing the Joy of Nature: Activities for all Ages, by Joseph Bharat Cornell. Dawn CA, 1989. The emphasis in this book is on developing a love and respect for nature, and it also includes examples of nature games to play with children.

The Outrageous Outdoor Games Book, by Bob Gregson. Fearon 1984, This book offers 133 games for groups of 10 to 30 children. Promoting both group interaction and individual self-expression, the games are designed for sunny, snowy, and windy days, and for tight spots as well as wide open spaces.

Look at Me, by Carolyn Buhai Haas. Chicago Review Press, 1987. Focusing on babies and toddlers, the author suggests creative activies for: *indoor/ outdoor fun, imaginative play, arts and crafts, cooking,* and many other useful ideas.

Movement Activities for Early Childhood, by Carol Hammett. Human Kinetics, 1992. This paperback includes a collection of classroom-tested activities for preschoolers that makes learning new skills fun. The author divides the book into four areas of movement, targeting a child's ability rather than age in the areas of 1) locomotor skills; 2) ball-handling skills; 3) gymnastic skill; and 4) rhythmic activities.

The Outside Play and Learning Book, by Karen Miller. Gryphon House, 1989. A thick book filled with ideas for outdoor activities, including dramatic play, creative art, games, and things to do with sand, mud, and water, among others. Suggested ages are listed, along with materials needed, and learning objectives.

Things to Do with Toddlers and Twos, by Karen Miller. Telshare Publishing Co., 1984. With suggestions about active times, such as in the chapter *Different Ways of Moving* and quiet times as in *Playing with Water,* this book describes activities appropriate to children who are approximately 12 months to three years of age.

Experiences in Movement, by Rae Pica. Delmar, 1995. Written by the author of two chapters in this book. this text explores the role of movement in the child's physical, social, emotional, and cognitive development — in both indoor and outdoor settings.

Preschoolers Moving & Learning, by Rae Pica, with music by Richard Gardzina. Human Kinetics, 1990. This resource is a complete movement program featuring 200 movement activities within 40 developmentally appropriate lessons. The program includes five audiocassettes of original music to inspire movement.

Let's Move & Learn, by Rae Pica and Richard Gardzina. Human Kinetics, 1990. This is a two-tape set of 32 movement-motivating songs geared toward toddlers, preschoolers, and kindergartners through third graders. Parents may follow the easy movement suggestions in the accompanying booklet or let the song lyrics and music guide and inspire the children.

More Music for Moving & Learning, by Rae Pica and Richard Gardzina. Human Kinetics, 1990 . This package comes with an instructional booklet and six cassettes featuring 62 songs and five favorite themes, including animals, holidays, relaxation (quiet times), exploring different cultures, and pretending.

Hug a Tree and Other Things to Do Outdoors with Young Children, by Robert Rockwell, Robert Williams, and Elizabeth Sherwood. Gryphon House, 1983. Guide children on a magical discovery tour of the outdoors. Activities indicate appropriate age, include a list of vocabulary words, and develop skills like observation, counting, classifying, recording, and measurement.

Parachute Play, by Liz and Dick Wilmes. Building Blocks Publications, 1985. Lots and lots of parachute games geared to preschool children. It also includes information on how to introduce the parachute to children.

Bubbles, by Bernie Zubrowski. Little, Brown and Company, 1979. This book was developed at the Boston Children's Museum and offers many ideas for blowing bubbles and having fun with them.

FOR CHILDREN

Those Summers, by Aliki. HarperCollins, 1996. Oh, the delicious memories of summers gone by when you and your family collected shells on the beach, plunged into the waves, built sandcastles, and ate sandy sandwiches. Those carefree days outdoors are reborn in this happy trip to the seaside.

Voices on the Wind Poems for All Seasons, selected by David Booth. Morrow, 1990. Beatrix Potter, William Blake, and Robert Louis Stevenson are among the poets represented in this collection of seasonal poems, ideal for reading during quiet times.

Caps, Hats, Socks, and Mittens, by Louise Borden. Scholastic, 1992. Activities for each season of the year are described in this lively book, with illustrations by Lillian Hoban.

D.W. Flips! by Marc Brown. Little, Brown, 1987. At first, D.W. can't even do a forward roll in gymnastics class. But with persistence and much practice, she finally learns to do flips. Preschoolers will enjoy her success.

Hide and Seek In the Sand, by Kate Burns. Little, Brown, 1996. This Pull-the-Tab and Lift-the-Flap book is full of delightful surprises for young children, as they participate in the adventures of two young children playing at the beach. The brightly colored illustrations are by Dawn Apperley.

Grandpa's Garden Lunch, by Judith Caseley. Greenwillow, 1990. Sarah helps Grandpa work in his garden, planting, watering, and waiting—until one day she and Grandma and Grandpa sit down for a special lunch with foods that they grew in the garden.

One Hot Summer Day, by Nina Crews. Greenwillow, 1995. With collage illustrations made from color photographs taken by the author, this lively and beautiful book shows a little African-American girl running, eating, and dancing in the city streets on a hot summer day.

Gilberto and the Wind, by Marie Hall Ets. Viking, 1978. The story of a small boy discovering a new companion—the wind—and learning the "tricks" it can play.

Play with Me, by Marie Hall Ets. Viking, 1955. The story of a little girl who finds a different way of playing in the meadow.

Rain Song, by Lezlie Evans. Houghton Mifflin, 1995. In this sprightly story in rhyme, two little girls watch the rainstorm from indoors, and then go out wearing their galoshes and yellow slickers, and splash happily in the puddles.

On the Move, by Deborah Heiligman. HarperCollins, 1996 (Let's-Read-and-Find-Out Science® Stage 1). In this celebration of all the ways our bodies can move, a young child takes you through his active day of outdoor play.

Snow Day! by Barbara M. Joosse. Clarion, 1995. The school bus can't get through, so the whole family stays home and enjoys the fun of playing in the snow.

The Snowy Day, by Ezra Jack Keats. Viking, 1969. A Caldecott Medal award winning book about a young boy discovering the joys of the snowfall.

Going to My Gymnastics Class, by Susan Kuklin. Bradbury Press, 1991. A little boy describes the fun and excitement of being in a gymnastics class — including the kinds of exercises they do and the types of equipment they use. Illustrated with color photographs.

Alison's Zinnia, by Anita Lobel. Morrow, 1996. With gorgeous floral illustrations, this is an alphabet book to treasure as you rest after your gardening work is done.

Things I Can Make, by Sabine Lohf. Chronicle Books, 1994. This is a unique craft book because of the clear, colorful illustrations that show children how to make creative projects on their own, with a minimum of written instruction.

Let's Go, Froggy! by Jonathan London. Viking, 1994. Spring is here and Froggy and his father plan a bike trip and picnic together. But before they can leave, Froggy must find his helmet, butterfly net, and other items to pack on their trip. When will he finally be ready? Just in time, in this humorous story.

Let's Go Riding in Our Strollers, by Fran Manushkin. Hyperion Paperbacks, 1993. The world is abuzz with sights and sounds as two toddlers are wheeled in their strollers through the city streets to the park.

Sam Saves the Day; Summer Business, by Charles E. Martin. Greenwillow, 1984. These two books describe the very active lives of Sam and the rest of the island children. In the first book, Sam has a busy summer: taking a vacation trip out west, coming home to help with the lobster traps, and finally joining his friends in the big baseball game. In the second story, Sam and his friends want summer jobs, but are told they are too young. So they start their own business—running a flea market, walking dogs, and selling lemondade.

Toddlerobics, by Zita Newcome. Candlewick Press, 1996. It's time to jump and roll and bend down low in the toddler gym! Energetic toddlers invite readers to join them as they practice all their amazing moves.

Play Ball, Amelia Bedelia, by Peggy Parish. An I Can Read Book®) HarperTrophy, 1995. Amelia Bedelia knows nothing about baseball, but she is willing to help out the neighborhood team and substitute for a sick player — with hilarious results.

Where Is Ben? by Marisabina Russo. Greenwillow, 1990. Mama is baking a pie, and Ben is busy too—finding hiding places all over the house, and calling for mama to find him. Finally he hides in his bed, just in time to take a nap.

Freddie Works Out, by Ruth Tilden. Hyperion, 1995. Freddie is an active little frog, doing stretches, push-ups, and jumping jacks. The reader helps by pulling the tabs on each page so that Freddie can go through his fitness program in this delightful interactive book.

If You're Happy and You Know It, by Nicki Weiss. Greenwillow, 1987. These eighteen story songs with music are fun to act out, or just to sing. They include: *Hush, Little Baby, There's a Hole in the Bucket,* and *Five Little Ducks.*

Section Eight
Young Children's Safety

Section Eight
Young Children's Safety

Introduction

Of all the gifts that parents can give to their children, one of the most important is the gift of a safe and secure environment.

At each stage of your child's life, there are safety rules to follow, from keeping chemicals in a locked closet, to practicing how to cross the street safely, to teaching young children not to go anywhere with a stranger.

Incidents of child abuse have been widely reported in the media over the last several years, and parents and teachers have been concerned about how to protect youngsters from those who would prey upon them.

The authors provide specific strategies to help children to remain safe and secure while, at the same time, allowing them the independence that is appropriate to their stage of development.

Chapter 40
Keeping
Your Preschooler Safe

Paulette Bochnig Sharkey

*Parents have the difficult task
of providing safe environments
while allowing children to explore
the world around them.*

Parents have the difficult task of providing safe environments while allowing children to explore the world around them.

One-year-old Patrick plays happily on the kitchen floor while his mother prepares dinner. She has ensured his safety by keeping cleansers and other chemicals in a locked cabinet, placing pot handles so that they can't be pulled off the range, and limiting his ability to leave the area by use of safety gates.

At two years, Amanda can not only walk, but can turn doorknobs. Her parents make sure that doors to the outside are kept locked. Although she loves water, she is never left alone in her bath or backyard pool, even though there may be only a few inches of water. (This is good advice with regard to all preschool children.)

Three-year-old Katy is permitted to ride her tricycle on the sidewalk near her house, as long as she stays within the chalk boundaries her parents have drawn. She knows that she must not ride in the street, driveway, or garage. She also knows that she needs to hold an adult's hand when crossing the street.

At four years, Steven is allowed to walk alone to pay a visit to his friend Mark who lives two houses away. His mother watches him as he safely reaches his destination and is greeted by Mark and his mother. When Steven plays ball with his friend, they have been told that if a ball rolls into the street, they are not to go after it. Instead, they must ask an adult to get the ball for them.

Five-year-old Lisa is looking forward to starting school soon, and her parents have been carefully preparing her for the big day. Lisa's father is teaching her to stand in a safe place while waiting for the school bus. She is learning how to cross the street, looking both ways and crossing only when it is safe. (Parents should practice with their child to make certain that they are capable of following the safety rules.) Lisa knows that if a stranger should approach her in the street or schoolyard, offering candy or toys, or suggesting that she accompany him, she should refuse and tell a trusted adult about it right away.

Basic rules for child safety are:
1. *Define* the boundaries of safe behavior for the many potentially dangerous situations your child will encounter. Prevention is the single most important element in child safety. Remember that hazards change according to your child's age and stage of development. Try to pass along to your child as much responsibility for his own safety as you feel is appropriate.

2. *Teach* these limits patiently until your child understands and accepts them. If your instructions are specific and your safety rules simple, your child will be more likely to remember and abide by them.

3. *Reinforce* these limits whenever your child forgets them. Continual review, consistency in applying safety rules, and your good example are all important reinforcement tools.

Parents can help insure safe environments for children in two ways: by safety-proofing their environments, and by teaching children how to protect themselves.

Safety Suggestions

From the moment a child is born his safety is in an adult's hands.

Creating Safe Environments
At Home
• Post phone numbers for police, fire department, poison control center, ambulance, and pediatrician by every phone.
• Purchase "Mr. Yuck" stickers to discourage your child from sampling foreign substances. These have proven more effective in controlling accidental poisoning than the traditional skull-and-crossbones symbol.
• Plan a fire escape route for your family and practice it frequently. Include a meeting place outside the home where everyone can assemble and be counted.

• Use gates at the top and bottom of stairs to protect your toddlers from falling.

• Keep medicines in child-proof containers, stored out of your child's reach.

• Cover unused electrical outlets with safety plugs so that preschoolers will not probe into them.

• Never leave a bulb out of a plugged-in lamp.

• Because a recliner's mechanism can be accidentally closed on a child, the recliner should never be left unoccupied in an open position.

• In order to be able to hear your preschooler when he is in his room, install an intercom.

• Always give the babysitter a telephone number where you and your pediatrician can be reached.

In the Car

• Use seat belts and buckle your child into a car safety seat <u>on the rear seat of the car</u>. (Research shows that there is a significant reduction of fatalities and nonfatal injuries to children under five years when seat restraints are used.)

• Never leave children in a car without an adult, even on your driveway.

• Caution children to keep their hands and heads inside the car.

• Provide games, books and soft toys for your preschooler. Ask him to play quietly during the drive so as not to distract the driver.

Outdoors

• You are your child's role model. Cross the street at the corner, and with the green light. Teach your child to recognize traffic signs and Walk/Don't Walk signs. Also, where there are no sidewalks, walk facing traffic.

• Wading pools should be supervised. Swimming pools should be fenced in, with a locked gate. Teach your child how to swim. (The bathtub can be used when beginning water safety lessons.)

• Avoid falls by keeping toys off steps and driveways.

Playing"What would you do if...?

Safety is a topic that relates to almost every aspect of life. It cannot be taught all at once. As with most lessons, safety lessons are learned best when they can be related directly to an experience. One way to teach your child about safe ways to respond to a wide variety of potential dangers would be by playing the "What would you do if..." game. The idea is to ask a question and to discuss the possible answers. Then you may act out the experience, with you and your child taking different roles. The following are examples of "What if...?" questions. Suggestions for discussion are in brackets after each question.

1."*What if* we were in a shopping mall and you got lost?" [Talk about how to recognize security guards and police officers. Teach your child her first and last name, address, and phone number.]

2."*What if* you found an animal that was hurt?" [Discuss the dangers of touching or feeding an unknown animal. Explain that he should tell you or his caregiver who will call for help for the animal.]

3."*What if* you found something on the ground that looked good to eat?" [Talk about the dangers of eating something that may be unhealthy. Tell your child to ask for permission before eating anything.]

4."*What if* you see a wire hanging from a pole?" [Discuss the fact that a live wire can hurt so he should not touch it. Explain that he should tell you so that you can report it.]

5."*What if* a stranger tells you that he knows your mother and she said it was all right to go home with him?" [Teach your child that she should say "No" to an adult who makes such a request, and report the incident to a trusted adult. She must always check directly with you before going anywhere, even to a friend's home.]

6. "*What if* you saw a friend having trouble in the water?"[Explain that the best way to help a friend would be to tell an adult about it right away.]

Discuss your child's responses gently, in a positive manner, so that she never feels ridiculed or worries that her feelings or fears are wrong. Talk out different solutions. Let your child know that you believe in her ability to stay safe and that you are there to help.

Be realistic without being scary. You are teaching your child about possible hazards not to frighten him, but to keep him safe. Emphasize the things that children can do to protect themselves, not the bad things that can happen.

Chapter 41
Protecting Young Children from Abuse

Toni H. Liebman

*While our aim is to instruct
our preschoolers about child abusers
who can harm them, we must guard
against terrifying them
with tales of an "evil world."*

Creating a Safe Environment
Young children have an overwhelming need to feel safe and secure in their environment, and we, the adults, have the responsibility to make certain this happens.

The Problem of Child Abuse
In the past few years, incidents of child abuse have been widely reported in the media, raising concerns as to how to protect our children against being victimized. (Child abuse includes any type of physical, mental, or emotional injury inflicted deliberately on children. When the injury involves exploitation of a child for sexual gratification, it is considered sexual abuse.) We need to face the issues squarely, but we must proceed with caution.

Finding a Balance
While our aim is to instruct our preschoolers about child abusers who can harm them, we must guard against terrifying them with tales of an "evil world." Children need warm, caring people to hug and cuddle them, and we don't want to alarm them with the idea that every loving person is a potential sexual abuser.

What Parents Can Do To Help Prevent Abuse:
Supervise your preschooler as he plays. Get to know his friends and their parents.

Be particular in your choice of an early childhood program. Spend a few mornings at the center yourself before enrolling him. Make sure there is good communication between staff and parents, and that parents are welcome to visit at any time.

Check references of babysitters and other caregivers carefully. Talk to parents who have used their services.

Build Your Child's Self Esteem
Give your children loving affection. Children at risk for sexual abuse are those who exhibit low self-esteem, and crave affection. Encourage your preschooler's desire for autonomy — doing things for herself, such as dressing and feeding. This helps your child to feel good about herself, and builds self-esteem.

Parent-Child Communication
Foster open communication with your youngster. Children who are treated with respect, and who know that their problems and ideas will always be heard, are less likely to be victimized by molesters.

Teach your youngsters that they can always tell you about any unusual situations; that they will be listened to, and not ridiculed, no matter how strange a tale is told. Abusers sometimes try to swear a child to secrecy. Tell your child that it is wrong for adults to ask them to keep secrets.

It's My Body
Teach your children to develop pride in their own bodies. Give them the accurate anatomical names of all their body parts in a matter-of-fact manner.

They should be helped to understand that they "own their bodies," with the right to refuse physical advances of any kind (yes, even an unwanted kiss from a doting grandparent). It is critical that they feel no obligation to submit unquestioningly to all adult authority. Though we want them to be respectful, they certainly have the right to say "NO" if anyone is touching them in a manner that makes them feel uncomfortable.

Apply the "What if?" Game
One valuable technique for teaching children to protect themselves is to play the "What if?" game. Begin with simple scenarios, and work toward those that are more complicated: "What if you and I were separated in the supermarket?" "What if the neighbor asks you into his house to see new baby kittens?" "What if the baby-sitter promises to let you stay up later if you let him tickle you?" Talk out possible solutions with your child.

Children need to feel safe and have a fundamental belief in the goodness of humanity. They also need to build a healthy, age-appropriate sense of independence at every stage in their growth. In addition, we can help them learn to protect themselves from those *few* who would seek to hurt or exploit them. It is not an easy task, but a healthy balance can be achieved by thoughtful, well-informed parents.

A parent's reaction...

Elizabeth Kulman

When Peter and Susan went out on Saturday night, they used a baby sitting service. The young man who showed up to take care of four-year-old Mara had not worked for them before, but the service had an excellent reputation and the young man appeared to be very pleasant.

However, on Sunday morning Mara seemed exceptionally quiet. When Susan asked her how she had liked the new babysitter, Mara said that she did not want him to come back. Susan asked if something had happened that bothered her. Mara told her mother that when the babysitter put her to bed, he touched her bottom in a way that she didn't like. Susan asked her what she meant. Mara said that he had patted her vagina.

"Oh dear," said Susan. "That must have been upsetting to you. Did he hurt you?" Mara said he did not.

"What did you do?" Susan asked.

"I told him to go downstairs and leave me alone," replied Mara.

Susan asked, "Did he go?"

Mara answered, "Yes."

Susan said, "Good for you, Mara. He shouldn't have done that. You were right to tell him to go away. I'm really glad you told me. We'll make sure he doesn't come back."

Susan gave Mara a hug, and Mara went off happily to play. When Mara had left the room, Susan phoned the agency and reported the incident to them.

Distressing as this story may seem, it is really a success story. There is no way, despite our best efforts, that we can absolutely guarantee that our children will never come into contact with an adult who will try to exploit them sexually. There are several things we can do, however, to arm our children against the harmful intentions of sexually predatory adults.

Susan takes Mara's account at face value without pressing for details. She praises Mara for telling the babysitter to leave her alone. She is reassuring and calm. Mara takes her cues from her mother. The problem was serious, but mommy is pleased with the way Mara Handled it. Mommy will make sure that the babysitter will not come back again.

Mara is a self-confident child who trusts her instincts when the situation with a strange babysitter takes an alarming turn. Despite the fact that he is an adult and has been put in charge of her, she does not hesitate to tell him to leave her alone. She also trusts her mother. Naturally curious about her body, Mara has asked her mother questions about sex. Susan has answered these questions in the same simple, matter-of-fact manner with which she has responded to questions about digestion, breathing and circulation. Mara knows it is safe to tell her mother about the incident, even though she also knows it is upsetting. She knows that she will not be punished for confiding in her mother or blamed for a situation she did nothing to create.

Research on sexual abuse of children shows that, if a child tells a sexually intrusive adult to leave her alone, if she does it with confidence and decisiveness, in most cases the adult will comply. Research also shows that one isolated incident like Mara's story will not have long lasting negative consequences when it is well-handled by the child's parents.

Mara can put the incident behind her and go off happily to play. Susan, having reported the offender to the agency which employs him, can have an easy mind.

Resources for Section Eight: Young Children's Safety

<u>FOR</u> <u>ADULTS</u>

Child Safety is No Accident, by Jay M. Arean and Miriam B. Settle. Berkeley Books, 1987. This book offers guidance on developing a safe family lifestyle, preventing accidents by taking sensible precautions, and giving emergency first aid.

The Cordes/LaFontaine Pocket Guide to Safe Babysitting, by Betty Cordes, CRNA. Troutbeck/Greycliff, (PO Box 1273, Helena MT 59624, 406-443-1888) 1995. This little book with wipe-clean pages has space for emergency information and parent location and describes specific safety concerns for children, danger zones to avoid, and common first aid techniques.

Don't Get Burned: A Family Fire-Safety Guide, by Gary A. Glenn and Peggy Glenn. Aames-Allen, 1982. A compilation of vital fire safety information, including the correct way to report a fire, how to conduct fire drills at home, and how to design a fire escape plan.

A Better Safe Than Sorry Book: A Family Guide to Sexual Assault Prevention, by Sol Gordon. Prometheus Books, 1992. This book is designed for children aged three to nine years, as well as for concerned parents and professionals.

A Sigh of Relief: The first aid handbook for childhood emergencies, 2nd revised edition, by Martin I. Green. Bantam Books, 1994. A fully illustrated guide on how to prevent and handle any childhood mishap. Includes first aid procedures and information on accident prevention and home safety.

Safety Zone: A Book Teaching Child Abduction Prevention Skills, by Linda D. Meyer. Warner, 1985. A read-together book to help parents teach their children how to recognize and avoid dangerous situations involving strangers.

Follow the footsteps to fire Safety: A Prevention Program for Young Children. Saint Paul Department of Fire and Safety Services, 100 East 11th Street, Saint Paul, MN 55101. Phone (612) 228 6203. This fire-safety and burn-prevention program is designed to assist adults in teaching important fire-safety skills to preschool and kindergarten children. *Footsteps* curriculum was awarded the 1996 Award of Honor from the National Safety Council. A 12-minute video, appropriate for ages 3-6, is also available to accompany the curriculum.

FOR CHILDREN

The Berenstain Bears Learn About Strangers, by Stan and Jan Berenstain. Random House Books for Young Readers, 1985. The Berenstain Bear cubs learn not to be overly friendly with strangers. They offer their six basic rules which are musts for every child. (Can also be obtained as a book and cassette package.)

Dinosaurs, Beware! A Safety Guide, by Marc Brown and Stephen Krensky. Joy Street/Little, Brown, 1984. Dinosaurs give safety tips for situations at home, in the car, at the playground, at the beach, and in other familiar places. Colorful, sometimes hilarious illustrations reinforce each message.

It's My Body, by Lory Freeman, Parenting Press, 1983. This paperback teaches young children how to resist uncomfortable touch, whether it is tickling or a more serious assault. (It is also available in the Spanish language version, *Mi Cuerpo es Mio.*)

Three Ducks Went Wandering, by Paul Galdone. Clarion, 1987. When they wander away from the nest, three little ducks are blithely ignorant of the dangers they encounter and return tired and safe.

Hansel and Gretel, by Jacob and Wilhelm Grimm. Retold by Rika Lesser. Putnam, 1985. Beautifully illustrated by Paul O. Zelinsky, this is a well-known folktale about an evil witch and the brother and sister who outwit her. It could be a basis for discussion with children about child abuse and other dangers.

Alfie Gets in First, by Shirley Hughes. Mulberry Books, 1987. Alfie accidently locks his mother and baby sister outside the house and can't reach the latch to let them in. All ends happily as the whole neighborhood gets involved in getting the door opened.

Section Nine
Finding
the
Positives

Section Nine
Finding
the Positives

Introduction

Throughout this book, you'll find the thread of positive thinking woven through its pages. Whether the topic is, *Alternatives to Saying, "Don't,"* *Constructive Communication with Your Preschooler,* or *Teaching Young Children Good Health Habits,* the emphasis has been on "accentuating the positive."

Why is it so important to focus on the positives? Can't you also warn children against bad behavior? One author in this section explains that pessimistic words become a powerful instruction, forming a negative picture in the child's mind. The youngster may then follow that inner picture, acting out the the negative scenario rather than the positive behavior that the parent desires.

Parents and teachers sometimes find it impossible to say anything positive about a child's behavior when he or she is going through a difficult time. One contributor points out ways that parents can find the positives, no matter how small, and acknowledge to their children that they are considerate, cooperative, and lovable.

Chapter 42
Finding and Promoting the Positives in Your Preschooler's Behavior

Carol B. Hillman

Acknowledge your child's good qualities.

There was a little girl
Who had a little curl
Right in the middle
of her forehead;
When she was good,
she was very very good,
And when she was bad she was horrid.

All parents have experienced times when this Mother Goose rhyme seemed to describe their preschooler's behavior. Samantha's mother had a week in which she really tried to find the moments when her little girl was "good." Each day Samantha awakened her younger sister, Sally, by talking at the top of her voice. Within minutes after she got out of bed, her room looked as if a cyclone had struck. She raced around the house and fought her mother's attempts to get her dressed for preschool. Then, after school, when Joey, her friend from next door came to play, she would refuse to share her toys and Joey usually went home crying.

A parent is hard pressed to say anything positive about her preschooler when faced with actions such as those described above.

Finding the Positives
As difficult as these times may be, the reassuring news is that all children go through stages as they grow. These are usually temporary phases in which their behavior is often called "naughty" or "difficult." Parents can take some comfort in the fact that child development experts say that when the child is most unsettled or "out of bounds," he is going through a growing stage where he is learning new abilities. And they state that this phase is followed by another where he is relatively calm and settled.

How Parents Can Survive
What can Samantha's mother do to get through these difficult times? No matter how many bad moments there were during the week, she can try to remember other incidents that had occurred, no matter how small they were, that showed that Samantha was considerate, cooperative, or lovable. It is important for her mother to think about these positives and then share them with Samantha:
  • How, on Tuesday, Samantha really tried to talk in a quiet voice in the morning.
  • How she helped Sally put on her sweater when they were in a hurry to go to the store.
  • How she picked a bouquet of dandelions for the dinner table.

• **Acknowledge your child's good qualities.** As a parent, your own positive attitude about your child has the greatest influence in creating your child's healthy self-image. Therefore, it is particularly important to 1) "step back" each day for a few moments to reflect upon your youngster's behavior; and 2) "step forward" to communicate the positive things that took place.

• **Talk to your child about specific positives.** If you say, "That was so thoughtful of you to share your favorite blocks with Joey this afternoon," it has far greater meaning to your child than telling her that she is a "good girl." Other meaningful statements are: "What a big help you were to me when you helped set the table," or "Thank you for finding Sally's slippers for her this morning." It is important for a child to know that her contributions to the family are significant.

• **Listen to others for clues about your child's positive behavior.** Often your child's teacher can tell you something noteworthy that has happened in school or day care. "Samantha is so interested in the stories that we read; she has become such a good listener." This is information which you can share with Samantha, to let her know how pleased both you and her teacher are with her new growth. You can reinforce your child's interest in books by reading to her every day.

• **Be your child's role model.** As a parent, you are your child's first teacher. She will imitate your behavior, even to the point of using your favorite words and phrases. As often happens, most parents are shocked when they hear their children repeat things they've heard from adults. Being a parent is a big responsibility!

• **Take the time to be alone with your child.** When you spend time alone with your child, let your child lead the conversation and you will learn more about his ideas, feelings, and needs. Particularly if your youngster is one of several children, he will welcome the chance of being "an only child" for the moments when he has you all to himself.

Strategies to promote positive behavior are outlined above. The important factor is making sure that, in one way or another, you communicate to your youngster what a terrific person he is!

Encouraging Positive Behavior in Your Preschooler

Although your preschooler may be going through a "difficult" phase of his development, you, as a parent, can provide guidance to promote his positive behavior.

√ Set Clear Limits

Perhaps one of the most important things that you, as parents, can do to encourage positive behavior in your preschool child is to provide a set of realistic, age-appropriate expectations for him to live by. There are excellent books that describe children's behavior at various ages, so that you can understand more about how young children grow and develop. (For a selection of books, see Resources on page 321, or ask your librarian.)

Of equal importance, as mothers and fathers, you need to clarify your ideas about limit setting, so that you may come to some agreement. You then can provide your child with a clear set of guidelines for him to follow.

√ Be Consistent

Let the message that you've agreed upon be the same message day after day. Just as a young child paints a set of blue and red stripes over and over again to reinforce her knowledge, so, that same young child will reinforce her knowledge of what is acceptable behavior by being told or shown the same thing over and over again. Knowing what is acceptable can be the first step in the learning process.

√ Give Clear Messages

The words you use with your preschoolers are important. Your words, and the manner in which they are spoken, can give your child a clear message as to what you really mean. For example, when you say, "Stay near the house when you play outside," the words "near the house" are too vague. Instead, define the limits so that there is no misunderstanding. You might say instead, "You may play only in our own front yard."

√ Recognize the Limits of Your Child's Capabilities

Books may give you general guidelines as to how children develop, but, as every parent knows, each child is unique. Your preschooler may be loud and exuberant, while another child tends to be quieter; your youngster may love to meet new people while another child needs time to "warm up"; your child may be always on the go, while another child may not like to be very active. Understanding your child's individual personality helps you to accept her limitations.

√ Share the Notion That Adults Aren't Always Perfect

Neither adults nor children can always to do what is expected of them. A child needs to know that his parent was young once, and didn't always put his toys away when asked to do so. A child also needs to know that even when you are a grown-up, it is sometimes hard to remember to take the library books back on time. A child needs to know that an adult is not perfect, and that an adult, just like a child, is always trying to do a better job. Sometimes you and your child can work on accomplishing the same task together, such as keeping track of the books to be returned to the library. It is always reassuring for your child to have a support system very close at hand.

√ Record Your Child's Positive Actions

You can find the positives in your child as you observe him throughout the day. Try to write down all the positive things your child does and says. Well-trained teachers often do this, observing and recording each child's behavior. Keeping a record of your child's positive behavior in a special notebook, and sharing this record with him, is one way of reinforcing the behaviors you would like to promote in your child.

Chapter 43
The Importance of Sending Positive Messages to Your Children

Richard Carlson

*It's possible to give a child
a negative message
even when you have
the best of intentions.*

Four-year-old Laura is about to carry a glass of milk to the dining room table. Her mother wants to prevent her from spilling the milk on their new carpet. She calls out a warning, "Whatever you do, DON'T SPILL THAT MILK!" You can imagine what happens next: Laura's hand becomes unsteady and the milk splashes down on the new carpet.

Why do you think Laura spilled the milk after hearing her mother's warning? Upon hearing her mother's words, Laura formed a picture in her mind of the milk pouring from the glass on to the carpet. She didn't want to anger her mother, but the negative image of spilling the milk actually became a powerful instruction. In the next moment, she followed that inner picture, and acted out her mother's scenario.

If Laura's mother had changed her wording to, "I'm glad you're always so careful when you carry your milk to the table," the words would have formed a positive image in her mind, and would have encouraged a more careful action.

As parents, it's important to become very aware of the choice of words we use with our children. It's possible to give a child a negative message even when you have the best of intentions.

As mothers and fathers, we are concerned about many different aspects of our preschooler's growth and development. Whether the concern is our child's self-esteem, getting along with others, achievements in school, etc., the words we use play a key role in the end result. Our children look to us to tell them who they are and what their capacities are. They listen to our specific words — they don't stop to interpret "what we really meant."

Affirmations
An affirmation can be either positive or negative. It is a word or series of words that we can repeat to ourselves — a verbal "instruction" to remind ourselves of what we want our life to be like.

Some examples of positive affirmations are: "Life is fun to me," and, "I have nice friends." Some examples of negative affirmations are: "I never say the right thing," and, "I'm never on time."

Our words contain a tremendous amount of power and influence over how we feel, and how we see ourselves. Just about everything we say to ourselves (or hear from our parents when we are little) will be stored in our memory and will come back to either help or hurt us. The more we hear or repeat affirmations (positive or negative), and the more conviction we put into them, the more influence they will have over us.

Many of the affirmations we use are unconscious, meaning we repeat them out of habit, rather than by conscious choice. Without even knowing it, we might be delivering to ourselves and to our children many negative messages every single day. These very messages are the ones forming our view of ourselves and helping our children to form theirs. Comments such as "You're so hyper," or "You're such a klutz," or "You always overeat," may seem innocent, but they are forming the way your child views herself. This view will become her self-concept.

Using positive affirmations can help your children gravitate toward greater happiness and self-esteem. It can also help to eliminate inconsistencies you have between what you really want for your children and the hidden messages you might currently be offering to them through your words. If your interactions with your children conflict with what you are hoping to teach them about themselves, you will be working against yourself, and against the goals you have for your children.

Suppose, for example, that one of your goals for your preschooler is to help him to be able to play by himself. If, when your child starts complaining about having nothing to do, you say to him, "Can't you play by yourself like other children do — what's wrong with you?" you will have reinforced the idea that he is not capable of being creative and finding something interesting to do.

The negative affirmation that he can't play independently becomes a self-fulfilling prophesy. The repetition of those words in his mind can encourage him to view himself as not being as good as other children who can play by themselves.

Instead, you might have phrased your affirmation in a more positive way. "I know that you have lots of good ideas. I'm sure you'll think of something fun to do."

When you use a positive affirmation, you're not denying any real issue your child is facing. For example, you're not saying, "Be happy," to an unhappy child. When you tell your child that he can think of new ways to have fun, you are trying to start a new train of thought by helping him see himself in a more positive way.

If you happen to forget and use negative words or conversation around your children, don't be concerned. Everyone slips at times. Work toward the goal of sending messages that will boost your child's feelings of self worth. Gently guide your child to speak and think of himself in ways that encourage positive growth.

Helping Your Preschooler to Develop a More Positive Self Image

Ultimately, children respond to life according to how they view themselves. Children who think of themselves as confident will act confidently. Children who think of themselves as attractive will feel good about their appearance.

Positive affirmations can help us get into the habit of speaking to ourselves and our children more positively. If your child learns to speak well of himself in this way, he will be more likely to love himself and the world he lives in.

Positive Affirmations as a Tool
In addition to becoming more aware of what you say to your children, you can practice positive affirmations as a fun and useful exercise. If your children are old enough, you can teach them to repeat affirmations to themselves. If not, you can recite the affirmations to them. The spirit of the affirmations is what's important. You are attempting to instill into your child an attitude of celebration and happiness.

Affirmations to Share With Your Children

- I'm such a happy person
- I'm so lucky to be alive
- I make the best of everything
- I have a great imagination
- I can do anything
- People love me
- I love my life
- I'm so smart
- Life is easy and fun

Tips to Make Affirmations Useful
- Affirmations are meant to be light, easy, and fun. Don't turn them into something your child "must do."

- The shorter and simpler, the better. Affirmations should be clear, direct statements that convey a strong and positive feeling.

- Affirm what you want, not what you don't want. Positive affirmations, like negative statements, will form a picture in your child's mind. The negative statement "I won't fall down," will likely promote a vision of a person falling down, whereas the positive affirmation "I am so athletic," brings up the visual image of a coordinated person.

- Phrase affirmations in the present tense as if what you are affirming already exists. For example, "I am happy" works better than "I will be happy."

- Enthusiasm is an important element. Kids love enthusiasm! Encourage your children to say their affirmations as if they really mean them.

- Use repetition to reinforce the notion. The more the better!

Creating a Self-Talk Audiotape
Helping your children create a self-talk tape will encourage them to use affirmations efficiently and effectively. A tape of your voice (or their own, if they are old enough) can be a powerful tool for change. By listening to this tape, children hear over again the positive messages you want them to hear about themselves.

Some guidelines
- Make a specific list of affirmations that you want your child to hear. Arrange them in an order that makes sense to you.

• Use your child's name in the statements. If your daughter's name is Megan, say, "I, Megan, have a great imagination."
• Use present tense. Say, "I have nice friends," rather than, "I will have nice friends someday."
• Use only positive words and phrases.
• Believe that what you are saying is the truth. Your belief in your children will come across on the tape.
• Avoid seriousness. This exercise is meant to be fun for your children.

Resources for Section Nine: Finding the Positives

FOR ADULTS

What Do They Mean I'm Difficult? by Louise Bates Ames. Programs for Education (Box 167, Rosemont, NJ 08556), 1986. Written from the point of view of the child, this little book discusses children's behaviors from the age of 18 months through six years, in a lively conversational style.

Celebrate Your Child: The Art of Happy Parenting, by Richard Carlson, Ph.D. New World Library, 1992. This helpful guide, by the author of a chapter in this book, shows parents a way of passing on to their children an attitude of celebration and happiness. In such chapters as, *Self-Esteem: The Foundation of Happiness, Looking for the Good,* and *Cultivating a Grateful Attitude,* the author discusses how parents can become a mirror for their children, reflecting the positive, life-affirming messages children need for happy lives and healthy self-esteem.

Teaching Four-Year-Olds: A Personal Journey, by Carol B. Hillman. Phi Delta Kappa Educational Foundation (PO Box 789, Bloomington, IN 47402-0789),1989. The author is a master teacher who writes about her personal joys and discoveries during her many years of teaching young children. She also offers practical suggestions for preschool teachers, including ideas on *Setting Up the Classroom, Science for All Seasons, Parent Conferences,* and *Finding the Positives in Children.*

"I Think I Can, I Know I Can!" Using Self-Talk to Help Raise confident, Secure Kids, by Susan Isaacs and Wendy Ritchey, Ph.D. St. Martin's Press, 1989. "Although we may not be aware of it, we all talk to ourselves — sometimes out loud and sometimes internally..." This self-talk, whether negative or positive, exercises power over our lives. The authors discuss how we can help children develop positive inner voices.

FOR CHILDREN

Rainy Day Kate, by Lenore Blegvad. Margaret K. McElderry Books, 1988. A little boy is excited that his friend Kate is coming to his house. He thinks about all the fun things they will do. But it's raining so hard that Kate can't come to play. So the little boy finds a way to *make* a Kate out of pillows, old clothes and string, and then he and his toys have a party with this pretend Kate.

Preschool Power! Jacket Flips & Other Tips, by Concept Video, (4809 Morgan Drive, Chevy Chase, MD 20815, 1-800-333-8252), 1990. Accompanied by lively music, and acted out by children ages two-to-six, this 30 minute video shows preschoolers mastering such skills as buttoning, zippering, pouring from a pitcher, putting on a jacket, and spreading peanut butter. It encourages young viewers to have the idea that, "I can do it too!" helping them to feel good about being self-reliant. (There are a total of 8 videos in the series for this age group.)

Will There Be a Lap for Me? by Dorothy Corey. Albert Whitman, 1992. It's difficult to find a place to sit on mother's lap while she is pregnant. Kyle is happy to find that after the baby is born, his mother's lap is again "just right for resting, and talking, and listening to stories..."

You Can Do It, Rabbit, by Paul Dowling. Hyperion, 1992. Rabbit learns to ride a bicycle, with the help and encouragement of her friends.

It's My Birthday, by Heidi Goennel. Tambourine Books, 1992. Using just a few words on each page, and bright, colorful illustrations, this book tells how a little girl experiences the joy of a birthday celebration.

The Friendship Book, by Woodleigh Hubbard. Chronicle Books, 1993. With thoughtful words and colorful, imaginative illustrations, the author/illustrator celebrates the joys of friendship.

Good Morning Baby; Good Night Baby, by Cheryl Willis Hudson. Scholastic Cartwheel Books, 1992. The illustrations in these two appealing books show African-American babies enjoying their daily activities. The heavy cardboard pages make them ideal for the youngest preschoolers.

The Story of Ferdinand, by Munro Leaf. Viking Press, 1936. This well-loved classic tells the story of the unusual bull who prefers to sit under the cork tree and smell the flowers, rather than battling it out at the bull fight in Madrid.

Frederick, by Leo Lionni. Pantheon, 1976. An endearing tale of a young mouse who lifts the spirits of his family with his unique artistry.

Jess Was The Brave One, by Jean Little. Viking, 1992. Of the two sisters, Jess and Claire, Jess was the brave one. Claire was afraid at the doctor's, afraid of the dark, and afraid of climbing trees, among other things. "Claire suffers from an overactive imagination," says her Dad. But when some bullies try to run off with Jess' favorite toy, it is Claire with her imagination who saves the day.

Something Special, by David McPhail. Joy Street/Little, Brown, 1992. Everyone in Sam's family can do something special. One sister plays piano, another is a whiz at baseball; his father cooks, and his mother carves wooden birds. Then Sam discovers that he has a real talent too, and that makes him feel special.

Am I Beautiful? by Else Holmelund Minarik. Greenwillow, 1992. Young hippo, out walking, sees different creatures admiring their children. "Am I beautiful?" he asks each parent. Finally, the loving answer he is looking for comes from his own mother.

Sometimes I Feel Like a Mouse: A Book About Feelings, by Jeanne Modesitt. Scholastic, 1992. A little boy compares his emotions to animals. He feels brave — like a horse galloping, warm— like a cat snuggling, and so on. It ends with the positive affirmation, "I have lots of feelings. It's wonderful to be me!"

Abuelita's Paradise, by Carmen Santiago Nodar. Albert Whitman, 1992. Although her grandmother has died, Marita still feels her love, as she sits in Abuelita's rocking chair and remembers the stories she had told about her life as a little girl in Puerto Rico. (Available in Spanish as *El Paraíso de Abuelita*.)

What We Like, by Anne Rockwell. Macmillan, 1992. In this lively and cheerful book, children can hear about what most children like to eat, like to wear, like to do, etc. and can add some favorites of their own.

On Mother's Lap, by Ann Herbert Scott. Clarion, 1992. A little Eskimo boy discovers that there is room on mother's lap for him, along with toys, puppy, and baby sister.

Mufaro's Beautiful Daughters An African Tale by John Steptoe. Lothrop, 1987. This memorable story is visually stunning, illustrated with lush, colorful paintings. It tells of Mufaro's beautiful daughters, one kind and gentle, responding to all creatures with consideration, and the other of opposite temperament, selfish and inconsiderate—and what happens when the king is looking for a worthy and beautiful wife.

Through Moon and Stars and Night Skies, by Ann Turner. Harper Trophy edition, 1992. A little boy who came from far away remembers how frightened he was when he flew on a plane through moon and stars and night skies to be adopted by a couple in the United States. He remembers how he came to know his new poppa's face and his new momma's smile, and to feel at home with his new loving family.

Crow Boy, by Taro Yashima. Viking Press, 1955. A young country boy in China has a difficult adjustment in school, until his classmates learn of his marvelous talent.

This Quiet Lady, by Charlotte Zolotow. Greenwillow, 1992. In a touching and joyful book, a little girl traces her mother's life, while looking at photographs taken from her mother's birth to the present. At last she finds a baby picture of herself with her mother, saying, "And here is where I begin," affirming the continuity of life. The lovely illustrations are by Anita Lobel.

About
the
Contributors

Susan E. Baker, M.S., a former elementary school principal, is the Parent Resource Coordinator for the Horace Mann School at Northwest Missouri State University in Maryville. She is the mother of two girls.

Nancy Balaban, Ed.D., is Co-director, Infant and Parent Development and Early Intervention program at Bank Street Graduate School of Education. Her book, *Starting School: from Separation to Independence — a Guide for Early Childhood Teachers,* was published by Teachers College Press in 1985. She authored revisions for the 4th edition of *Observing and Recording the Behavior of Young Children* (Teachers College Press) by Dorothy Cohen, Virginia Stern & Nancy Balaban.

Cynthia Burns is an award-winning writer whose work on family issues including education, child development, and emotional growth has appeared in *The Record* and *KIDS Magazine.* Both are publications in Bergen County, New Jersey.

Richard Carlson, Ph.D., is a nationally known lecturer and stress consult-ant in private practice. He is the author of many books, including the best-seller, *Don't Sweat the Small Stuff...and it's all small stuff* (Hyperion, 1997).

Elizabeth Crary is a parent educator, speaker, and author of over twenty - six books, among them: *Without Spanking or Spoiling, Love and Limits,* and *Pick Up Your Socks.*

Judy David, Ed.D. Her doctorate is from the Harvard School of Education and she taught at Bank Street College in New York and Wheelock College in Boston. She is coauthor of *The Preschool Years* (Times Books, 1988).

Mary Margaret Dean, M.A., is a member of the New York City Affiliate of the Association for the Care of Children's Health.

Janet Dengel is the mother of three children, Linda, John, and Paul. She is a free-lance writer and editor of *KIDS Magazine* in Westwood NJ.

Pegine Echevarria, M.S.W., lectures and consults on parent issues. She conducts Minority Motivational Seminars, and has written a book, *For All Our Daughters: How Mentoring Helps Young Women and Girls Master the Art of Growing Up,* published by Chandler House Press, 1998

Betty Farber, M.Ed., is President of Preschool Publications, Inc. She was the Editor and Publisher of *Parent and preschooler Newsletter* for 11 years, and edited *The Parents' & Teachers' Guide to Helping Young Children Learn,* (Preschool Publications, Inc., 1997). She directed early childhood programs in St. Louis and Memphis and was Instructor and Early Childhood Coor-dinator at LaGuardia Community College of the City University of NY.

Susan Eaddy (illusstrations) has worked as an art director in book publishing for 8 years and is currently the art director for RCA Records in Nashville. Her portfolio includes illustrations for more than 80 books as well as magazines, CD covers, greeting cards, and newsletters. She has won international awards for her cut paper design and works in a variety of media. She is especially proud to have been the illustrator for the *Parent and preschooler Newsletter* since its inception in 1985.

Lester Feldman (cover design) has spent his professional life as an Art Director for a NYC/international advertising agency where he created many ad campaigns during his almost 40 years there. A dozen of his TV commercials are in the Museum of Modern Art collection of "classics," and he's won the gold and the silver medals from the Ad Club of New York.

Ellen Galinsky is a past president of the National Association for the Education of Young Children, and is one of the founders of the Families and Work Institute. She is coauthor of *The Preschool Years* (Times Books, 1988).

Fredric C. Hartman, Ph.D., is in full-time private practice specializing in treating people across the lifespan who are having difficulty coping with dying, death or other kinds of loss.

Harriet Heath, Ph.D., Director of the Parent Center, Thorne School•Child Study Institute, Bryn Mawr College, PA, is a licensed developmental psychologist, educator and researcher. She is the author of a parents' manual, *Parents Planning*, a decision-making approach to parenting, and a curriculum for school aged children, *Learning How to Care: Education for Parenting*. Her newest book will be on implementing values into family life.

Carol B. Hillman, M.S.Ed., M.Ed, is Adjunct Professor, Early Childhood Education, Westchester Community College, Valhalla, NY and Adjunct Lecturer in Education, Manhattanville College, Purchase, NY. She is a former member of the Board of Trustees, Bank Street College of Education, New York. Hillman is the author of *Before the School Bell Rings*, and *Teaching Four-Year-Olds: A Personal Journey*, both published by Phi Delta Kappa Educational Foundation.

Bruce V. Hillowe, J.D., Ph.D., is an attorney and psychologist in full-time private practice in Mineola, NY. He is affiliated with Long Island Jewish Medical Center, New Hyde Park, NY, as teaching attending psychologist.

Ellen Javernick, M.A., is a former preschool director, who now teaches first grade in Loveland, CO. She writes for numerous periodicals and has written ten books, including, *What if Everybody Did That*, and *Ms. Pollywogs Problem Solving Service*.

Katrina Katsarelis is a writer and mother of two young children. She writes a column for *Bay Area Parent* and *Valley Parent Magazines* in Northern California.

Elizabeth Kuhlman, M.A., M.S., is an Early Childhood Special Education Consultant.

Toni H. Liebman is an Early Childhood Consultant to nursery schools and child care centers. She conducts workshops and seminars for professionals as well as for parents at schools and corporations in the New York metropolitan area. Liebman is the former director of a large parent cooperative early childhood program.

Michael K. Meyerhoff, Ed.D., a former researcher with the Harvard Preschool Project, is executive director of The Epicenter Inc., "The Education for Parenthood Information Center," a family advisory and advocacy agency located in Lindenhurst, Illinois.

Rae Pica is a movement consultant and author of 11 books and numerous articles. She conducts movement and music workshops for parent and early childhood groups throughout North America.

Nancy Samalin has been a parent educator for over two decades and is founder and director of *Parent Guidance Workshops* in New York City. She is the author of *Loving Your Child Is Not Enough; Love and Anger: The Parental Dilemma;* and *Loving Each One Best*, about sibling relationships.

Neala S. Schwartzberg has a Ph.D. in Developmental Psychology and has written extensively on children and parenting. Her articles have appeared nationwide and have been reprinted in many anthologies. She is a regular contributor to several publications on health related topics. Dr. Schwartzberg has been the editor of *Parent and preschooler Newsletter* since January, 1997.

Paulette Bochnig Sharkey, M.L.S., has been a freelance writer and librarian, and is currently the Developmental Editor for Ellyn Satter Associates.

Bette Simons, M.S., writes about preschool children and the adults that care for them based on her experience as a training teacher in the Preschool Laboratory of California State University, Northridge, as well as in her own child care center, First Step Nursery School in Woodland Hills, CA.

Aletha Solter, Ph.D., is a developmental psychologist, international speaker, and author of *The Aware Baby; Helping Young Children Flourish;* and *Tears and Tantrums*. She lives in Goleta, CA, and is the founder of The Aware Parenting Institute, a world-wide movement promoting attachment-style parenting, non-punitive discipline, and acceptance of emotional release.

Elizabeth J. Webster holds a Ph.D. in Developmental Psychology and is Professor Emeritus, University of Memphis. Dr. Webster is the author of many books and articles on counseling parents. She retired to Deerfield Beach, Florida, where she is an active member of The Writer's Workshop. Dr. Webster is the coauthor of *Teacher/Parent Communication: Working Toward Better Understanding,* Preschool Publications, 1992.

James Windell is a psychotherapist who has specialized in working with children and their parents for 30 years. For the past 10 years he has taught parent training classes and has written the "Coping With Kids" column for The Oakland Press in Pontiac, MI. He is the author of journal articles and books, including, *Children Who Say No When You Want Them to Say Yes; Discipline: A Sourcebook of 50 Failsafe Techniques for Parents;* and *8 Weeks to a Well-Behaved Child.*